Reclaiming Beauty
for the Good of the World:
Muslim & Christian
Creativity as Moral Power

Reclaiming Beauty for the Good of the World: Muslim & Christian Creativity as Moral Power

by George Dardess, PhD
and Peggy Rosenthal, PhD

FONS VITAE

First published in 2010 by
Fons Vitae
49 Mockingbird Valley Drive
Louisville, KY 40207
http://www.fonsvitae.com
Email: fonsvitaeky@aol.com

Copyright Fons Vitae 2010

Library of Congress Control Number: 2010935422
ISBN 9781891785610

Printed in Canada

Act beautifully, as God has acted beautifully towards you
Qur'an *Sura al-Qasas* 28:77

She has done a beautiful thing for me.
Gospel of Mark 14:6

Contents

Preface: A Personal Experience of Two Faiths ix

Introduction xiii

A Note on Dual Authorship, Gratitudes, and Scriptural Quotations: xv

Opening Dialogue: A Christian and a Muslim first meet, in good faith xvi

PART I: WHAT IS OUR BEAUTY? 1

CHAPTER ONE: MUSLIM BEAUTY 3

Chapter 1a. The Source of Beauty: "God is the Light of heaven and earth" 3

Chapter 1b. The Beauty of God: "God's beautiful names" 11

Chapter 1c. The Beauty of Humankind: "Beautiful patience" 16

Chapter 1d. The Ugliness of Humankind: Yielding to "the soul inclined to evil" 22

CHAPTER TWO: CHRISTIAN BEAUTY 26

Chapter 2a. Christ's Beauty: "He is the image of the invisible God" 26

Chapter 2b. The Transfiguration: "And his clothes became dazzling white" 32

Chapter 2c. The Beauty of the Cross: "Jesu, thy blood and righteousness/ My beauty are, my glorious dress" 37

Chapter 2d. The Ugliness of Humankind: "Doing evil deeds" 42

Dialogue: A Muslim and a Christian compare their beauties 47

Moving On: And what does this have to do with the life of the arts and the art of life? 55

PART II. ART IN ISLAM AND CHRISTIANITY 61

CHAPTER 3: ART INFORMED BY MUSLIM FAITH 63

Chapter 3a. The Beauty of Voice: The Qur'an as God's Art 63

Chapter 3b. The Beauty of Voice: The Adhan (Call to Prayer) as Epitome of Muslim Art 68

Chapter 3c. Generosity and Wonder: Muslim Architecture and More 75

Chapter 3d. Islamic Calligraphy as Invitation to Worship: "Music for the eyes" 91

Chapter 3e. Playfulness and Immediacy: "And now, God, you're scratching my head!" 102

Chapter 3f. Longing for Transcendence: "The fountain in my midst is like the soul of the believer" 112

CHAPTER 4: ART INFORMED BY CHRISTIAN FAITH ... 123

Chapter 4a. "Beauty is always ready to give more." ... 123

Chapter 4b. Playfulness and Surprise: "Defamiliarizing the familiar" ... 129

Chapter 4c. "Life pulsing with mystery" ... 141

Chapter 4d. "Broken Beauty" ... 150

Chapter 4e. Longing for Transcendence: "Beauty enchants and this enchantment comes from God." ... 159

Dialogue: A Muslim and a Christian compare their arts ... 172

Moving On: And what does the life of the arts have to do with the art of life? ... 185

PART III: BEAUTIFUL PEOPLE, BEAUTIFUL COMMUNITIES ... 191

CHAPTER 5: CREATIVE MUSLIM LIVES ... 193

Chapter 5a. Imitating the Prophet: The Sunnah as "truly sacred art of Muslim culture" ... 193

Chapter 5b. The Beauty of the Shari'ah: Source and Goal of the "Greater Jihad" ... 201

Chapter 5c. Rebuilding Córdoba: "A time of transformation" ... 209

CHAPTER 6: CREATIVE CHRISTIAN LIVES ... 220

Chapter 6a. Standing with Jesus: "The art of daily life" ... 220

Chapter 6b. Beauty as Justice, Justice as Beauty: "Imagining how to live an alternative life" ... 228

Chapter 6c. The Beauty of Christian Witness and Sacrifice: Giving our Life out of "love for enemies" ... 236

Closing Dialogue: A Muslim and a Christian, walking together in God's light, reach toward the Good of the world ... 247

Conclusion: The Beauty of Interfaith Action ... 254

Glossary of Christian Terms ... 258

Glossary of Muslim Terms ... 265

Permissions Acknowledgements ... 270

Preface: A Personal Experience
of Two Faiths

In 1983, when we were in our thirties, we were baptized into the Roman Catholic Church. We had both been raised in loving households where religious faith was not practiced and God not spoken of. Early in our marriage, soon after receiving our Doctorates in Literature, we began to sense that something was profoundly missing from our lives. Why it was that Christianity and the Catholic Church were what God drew us to is a mystery. But we do know that our lives as Catholic Christians have been joyously fulfilled in ways we couldn't have imagined: by the rich tradition of Christian spirituality, by the Bible's prophetic call to social justice, and by the beautiful lives of Christians we have met.

Initially these fulfillments led us along separate paths. Peggy was moved to apply her literature background and her college teaching experience to help people use the arts, especially poetry, to deepen their spirituality. She has published several books on the subject, and co-founded a nationwide ministry called Poetry Retreats.

George has found himself moving in a different, and wholly unexpected, direction. The 1991 Gulf War shocked him into chagrin at his ignorance of Islam and of the place of Islamic culture in the Middle East; he responded by making friends at the Islamic Center of our hometown, Rochester, New York, and from them learning to read the Qur'an in Arabic. Who ever knows what God has in store for us from the seemingly small steps we take? George's immersion in Islam and his ever-increasing love for its beauty — as manifested in the Holy Qur'an and in the lives of the Muslims he came to know —developed into a passion to share his love for Islam with other Christians.

This passion received a new stimulus after the tragic events of September 11, 2001. Horrified by the demonization of Islam and of Muslims that followed those events, George determined to devote himself to helping Christians understand Islam's marvelous richness and it depths of beauty. Out of his former Doctorate in Literature and now additional studies that led to a Masters degree in Divinity and to ordination as a deacon in the Catholic Church, he wrote *Meeting Islam: A Guide for Christians* (Paraclete Press, 2005), which recounts his personal journey into Islam and the way his understanding of Islam enriched his own Christian faith. This book was followed by one comparing passages from the Bible and the Qur'an, addressed to Muslims and Christians alike: *Do We Worship the Same God: Comparing the Bible and the Qur'an* (St. Anthony Messenger Press, 2006).

George's attempt in this book was to bring Muslims and Christians together around discussion of scriptural passages on themes common to both religions. These two books have been welcomed by readers both Muslim and Christian, all who are eager for a deeper personal and spiritual connection to the "other."

And yet God had still more plans for George's bridging of these two faiths. Because of the popularity of his two books, George was invited to give talks and workshops on Muslim-Christian relations around the country. This interfaith dialogue has become a key part of his ministry.

Then a few years ago, at 30,000 feet altitude on a flight home from a vacation, we said to each other, Why don't we combine our passions — Peggy's for spirituality and the arts, George's for Muslim-Christian dialogue — into a book? We thought we could do this by emphasizing a concept we felt was too little discussed or appreciated among Christians, and certainly not discussed at all when Christians spoke about Islam. This was the concept of Beauty. Beauty seemed to us to offer both Muslims and Christians an escape from their usually tense, dry, and often hopelessly stalemated interchanges on theology and politics. Beauty elicits joy, an ingredient usually missing from such interchanges. And beauty is central to both religions. All the more is beauty central — and necessary — to their dialogue with each other.

But how were we to bring beauty into the center of the dialogue between the faiths? We felt we could do it both by what we said about beauty and by how we said it. Beauty could inform content and style. As for content: We felt that we could develop a structure showing three things: how beauty is core to both faiths, how the arts of both religions stimulate a love for that beauty, and how, filled with that love, Christians and Muslims could be inspired to live truly beautiful lives—lives dedicated to service to God and neighbor. As for style: We felt that our own writing should model the joy that is beauty's surest sign. Our book, while everywhere based on facts, would have to be personal, not academic. We had to speak from our hearts. Beauty demands no less.

We ask readers to keep in mind our aims as they read this book, the down-to-earth result of our conversation at 30,000 feet. While we have done all in our power to make sure we are speaking accurately about each religion's focus on beauty, we have also decided to speak openly and joyfully about how our own lives have been transformed by beauty: the beauty of our own religion and the beauty of the religion of the Other. We have tried to extend that joy into our dialogues between imagined representatives of the two religions. Our personal focus means, however, that we express ourselves in ways that are special to ourselves and not necessarily in ways that other believers, whether Christian or Muslim, would express their own feelings about God's beauty.

Take Peggy's expression of her grateful joy in the Risen Christ in Chapter 4c. (Peggy is the primary author and the "I" of the chapters on Christianity.) She expresses there the depth of her gratitude as she genuinely feels it. Other Christians reading her account might very well not feel exactly her joy; their understanding of Christ as Son of God might very well be different from hers. Such Christian readers shouldn't assume, however, that Peggy's expression is the "right" one or the "only" one. We hope they will instead do what Peggy has done: reflect on the way they would express their own relation to God's beauty. For that is what Peggy is trying to do: to bring God's beauty into readers' direct focus so that all can feel free to express their response to that beauty in their own way.

Similarly for Muslims reading that same chapter or any other Peggy has written: They are not at all meant to accept the content of Peggy's account of her love for the Risen Christ. Muslims couldn't possibly embrace as truth what she is saying there, since Muslim understanding of Jesus' identity is radically different from Christian understanding. We hope instead that Muslim readers will appreciate Peggy's openness in expressing what her feelings really are, and why she feels them. We hope Muslims will be stimulated by that openness to express their response to God's beauty in their own way.

As for George's sections (he is the primary author of our book's chapters on Islam, and the "I" of those chapters is he), readers are asked to remind themselves that George speaks of Islam not only from his personal experience, as Peggy does about Christianity, but also as an outsider, a Christian. We admit that this is a potentially risky stance to take. Certainly untold mischief has been committed by Christians attempting to speak about Islam. Yet we believe there is great value in people of one faith immersing themselves in another faith — the "passing over" that Notre Dame theologian John S. Dunne speaks of in his classic work on the subject, *The Way of All the Earth.* To help ensure our book's accurate representation of Islam, we've asked many Muslims to read and critique parts or all of the manuscript. While we've heard the objection that no Christian, however well-informed or well-meaning, is able to offer Islam's beauty as if from "inside" the faith, most of our Muslim readers have expressed gratitude for our book's celebration of Islam and of the beautiful art and beautiful lives that Islam inspires.

We believe, though, that the most fruitful response to our book would be an outpouring of other books on Muslim and Christian beauty from readers eager to bring to bear on the subject their own different responses and perspectives. How happy we would be if a Muslim couple, whether flying at 30,000 feet or standing firmly on the earth, undertook the same project as we have! They would necessarily write a very different book, in many respects. But it would be a book written in joy, and in that sense it would point in the same direction as ours or as anyone else's on this subject: towards (as a hadith puts it) the "God who is beautiful and loves Beauty."

May that book be written, and written soon. We are eager to read it and to be swept up in delighted new understanding of God's beauty because of it.

Introduction

The year we had to miss the family Thanksgiving gathering because we both had pneumonia, our granddaughters — then ages five and six — mailed us "get well" pictures that they'd drawn and colored themselves. The six year old had drawn a big multi-colored butterfly; the five year old's picture was a girl with a bright cheery flower. We phoned them to say "thank you, what beautiful gifts for us, they make us feel better already." Were we thanking them for the beauty of their art or of their act?

We're standing at the end of the Menemsha pier on Martha's Vineyard with a crowd of twenty or so other vacationers. We all face west in silence to watch the famed sunset, red-oranges and golds spread across the sky in a continuously changing light show as the sun descends. When the sun slips below the horizon and the glorious colors suddenly bleach out, everyone spontaneously applauds, faces beaming joy and gratitude. Turning to stroll back down the pier, we hear murmurs of "beautiful... beautiful."

A Sunday afternoon in our favorite chamber music hall. We are tingly with anticipation as a piece we always delight in begins: Schubert's Quintet in C. The luscious melding of sounds emerges from the musicians' very beings to enter our own; we are transported especially by the first movement's ravishing melodic motif, as it interweaves its way among the various voices. During the pause at the movement's close, we smile happily to each other and silently mouth "beautiful."

Our neighbor's elderly father dies. She has attended to him lovingly for years. In our condolence note to her, we write: "You took beautiful care of him; we hope that consoles you."

What *is* beauty? When we say of someone "she lived a beautiful life" or when we thank someone for an act of kindness with "you were beautiful to have done that," what do we mean? And when we praise the beauty of a cathedral or a mosque, a painting or a poem or dance performance, do we mean the same thing by "beauty" as when we use the word for a gesture or lifetime of goodness?

These are questions we will explore in this book in the specific context of Muslim and Christian faith. Both faiths affirm the beauty and goodness of God's creation: sunsets and seacoasts and — yes — human nature as well. But both Islam and Christianity also teach that God has endowed humankind with freedom of will. That is, unlike the natural world (which has no choice but to obey God's will), we humans are given the choice of how to orient our lives. To choose to praise God and serve God's creation is to bathe in the light of beauty. To reject this praise and service is to fall into the dark of ugliness. How people manifest such moral choices is our book's motif; hence we leave sunsets and the rest of the natural world aside. Our purpose is to explore how these two major faiths call us to beauty, to creativity that has the power to transform the ugliness caused by our bad choices — the ugliness of hatred and violence, of economic oppression, of desecration of the environment, and (alas) of so much more.

But don't all religious faiths do this; don't all call us to transformative healing for the good of the world? Why limit our subject to Christianity and Islam? The limitation is both practical (these are the faiths we know well, the faiths we are comfortable speaking about) and politic: there is an urgency now to Muslim-Christian dialogue, and we hope by this book to contribute to this crucial enterprise. Dialogue must begin with a genuine desire for understanding. Unfortunately, much of what passes for "dialogue" between Christianity and Islam is instead diatribe: ignorant attempts to demonize the other. And even among people of good faith of both religions, there is an astounding ignorance of the other, an ignorance born simply of unfamiliarity.

But ignorance must no longer hide from Christians and Muslims the fact that their God, *our* God, creates us to create: to take as our model God's own creation of a beautiful world. Yes, there are intriguing differences between the ways that Islam and Christianity conceive of God's own beauty and our participation in it, so Part I of the book will lay out what beauty means to each of the faiths. Then Part II will explore how this beauty may manifest itself in the artistic creations of each faith, as we understand it. Specific art works will be the focus, since art *is* always specific; art takes the stuff of our sensual world (color, line, sound, word, stone, bodily movement, ink, thread...) and shapes it in a unique way that draws us beyond the work to a culturally shared meaning. So we will look, for instance, at the Dome of the Rock and at Rumi's poetry, at Michelangelo's *Pieta* and at Rouault's paintings of Christ, but also at works by contemporary Muslim and Christian artists — who speak to us directly about how faith informs creativity in our own day. From the life of the arts, we move in Part III to the art of life. Again, we will draw on concrete cases: people and communities living out their faith's beauty for the common good. Through such examples, we will seek an overarching understanding of the qualities of beautiful lives: self-sacrifice, solidarity, stewardship, generosity and justice. We will explore how the life of the arts and the art of life enrich and inspire one another, and how both are creative manifestations of the power which is God's goodness infusing our world. Each of the three Parts will offer the Muslim and then the Christian perspective, followed by an invented *Dialogue* in which imagined representatives of the two faiths, reflect on the topic at hand. These *Dialogues* are deliberately light-hearted and even playful. By their spirit they proclaim their shared faith in a God who calls all creatures to creative joy.

Evil and ugliness are real and dreadful forces, but as Psalm 119 says, they "lie in wait only to destroy" (verse 95). With so much of our world apparently in their destructive grip, we desperately need to be recalled to creativity's transformative power. Our bodies, our beings, are crying out for goodness, for beauty. We need these living models of creativity as moral power, so that we all can share in the crucial work of reclaiming beauty for the good of the world.

A Note on Dual Authorship, Gratitudes, and Scriptural Quotations:

As we mentioned in the Preface, George is the primary author of our book's sections on Islam, and the "I" of those sections is he; Peggy is the primary author and the "I" of the sections on Christianity.

Throughout the process of writing this book, we have run ideas and drafts by many colleagues and friends, Christians as well as Muslims. For their generous encouragement of the project, we thank Mohammed Ali, David B. Burrell, CSC, Ginger Geyer, Mark Jarman, Daisy Khan, Jamal Rahman, Imam Feisal Rauf, Peter Sanders, Dr. Muhammad Shafiq, Luci Shaw, Asma Shikoh, Soraya Syed, Fatima Talib, Jeanne Murray Walker, Sister Anne Wambach, OSB, and Mohamed Zakariya.

Unless otherwise noted, all English versions of Qur'anic passages are those of George Dardess, and all biblical quotations are from the New Revised Standard Version (NRSV).

Opening Dialogue: A Muslim and a Christian first meet, in good faith

Christian: Let's begin in the name of the Father, the Son, and the Holy Spirit.

Muslim: Oh dear. I can't begin that way.

Christian: Why not? That's how I always begin.

Muslim: I don't call God "Father" and I don't believe God could have a Son.

Christian: Amazing. What *do* you call God?

Muslim: Always Allah. But He has 99 names.

Christian: And not one of them is Father?

Muslim: No, I'm afraid not. But here's how *I* begin: In the name of Allah, the Beneficent, the Merciful.

Christian: Is Allah the same as God?

Muslim: Sure. It's just the Arabic word for God.

Christian: Well then, I could begin that way too. I like the "beneficent and merciful." But I can't leave out the Son.

Muslim: Why not?

Christian: Because that's what Christianity *is*: the faith that in Jesus Christ, God gave Himself to humankind by taking on human life, suffering a dreadful death at human hands, and rising to eternal life so that all humankind could rise with Him.

Muslim: I don't believe that. But I love and honor Jesus as a prophet, peace be upon him.

Christian: I thought your prophet was Muhammad.

Muslim: He is! But the Qur'an calls him the "seal of the prophets," the last of the line of prophets beginning with Adam and then ending with the greatest of all: Abraham, Moses, Jesus, and finally Muhammad, blessings and peace be upon them all.

Christian: I'm pleased to know that Jesus is dear to you. But what I don't get is why there had to be a prophet *after* Jesus. Are you saying that Muhammad had something new to say?

Muslim: No, not at all. What I believe is that God has given only one message to humankind: that you should love God and God alone and that you should do good for your neighbors, especially those who are poor and vulnerable. The problem is that this message that the prophets gave to people kept getting corrupted and forgotten. So God sent the Qur'an to humankind through Muhammad in God's own exact words as one more chance for humankind not to spoil or neglect the message again.

Christian: I think I see now where you're coming from. Let's try to begin again. You start this time.

Muslim: With pleasure. Here's how the Qur'an actually starts. I recite this every time I pray. It's the first sura in the Qur'an, and it's called *al-Fatihah*, or in English "The Opening":

> *In the name of God, the most beneficent, the most merciful.*
> *Praise belongs to God, the Cherisher and Sustainer of all the worlds,*
> *The most beneficent, the most merciful,*
> *The master of the Day of Judgment.*
> *It is you we worship, it is you we ask for help.*
> *Guide us on the straight path,*
> *The path of those to whom you have given your favor,*
> *Not those upon whom there is wrath or who have gone astray.*

Christian: Hmm, I don't see why I can't pray that with you. I've got a core prayer, too, which I include in all worship. It's called the Lord's Prayer, because Jesus (who is Lord for me, remember?) says in the Bible that "this is how you are to pray."

Muslim: How does it go?

Christian: "Our Father…" Oops. No, you can't say "our Father." I understand that.

Muslim: How about after that?

> *Hallowed be Thy name.*
> *Thy kingdom come, Thy will be done*
> *On earth as it is in heaven.*
> *Give us this day our daily bread*
> *And forgive us our trespasses*
> *As we forgive those who trespass against us*
> *And lead us not into temptation*
> *But deliver us from evil.*

Muslim: That all sounds fine to me. I can pray that with you.

Christian: So we're ready to go?

Muslim: Go where?

Christian: Into the book. Into the concepts of beauty for both our faiths.

Muslim: I'm not quite ready. I need to clarify one more thing first. What are you basing your concept of beauty — or of anything else— *on*? For me the source of all my beliefs is clear: the Qur'an is God's word. It is truth. But your Bible is so chaotic: four different accounts of Jesus' life that don't even agree with each other. How can you be sure *what* you believe?

Christian: I believe in God's Word, too. Truly. And I believe the Bible —

my Holy Scripture, I call it — is divinely inspired. But God's Word is most fully present for me in Jesus Christ himself — the Word made Flesh.

Muslim: One could say that Moses, peace be upon him, received God's Word revealed as two tablets, that the Blessed Virgin received God's Word as a child, and that the Prophet Muhammad, an illiterate, peace be upon him, received God's Word as a book.

Christian: So in all three instances, God's Word is revealed.

Muslim: Yes. So we both are confident that God does speak to humankind. The Qur'an for me, Jesus Christ for you: they are God's communication to humankind.

Christian: Communication of what, would you say?

Muslim: Of God's love. Of God's mercy. Of God's beauty.

Christian: God's love I know in my heart. God's mercy I melt before in gratitude. But God's beauty: how shall I picture *that*?

(Together): Let's see…

PART I: WHAT IS OUR BEAUTY?

CHAPTER ONE: MUSLIM BEAUTY

Chapter 1a. The Source of Beauty: "God is the Light of heaven and earth"

The Light Verse: from *Sura an-Nur* 24:34

> God is the light of heaven and earth.
> The parable of his light is like a niche
> in which there is a lamp,
> and the lamp is in a glass,
> and the glass is like a radiant star
> lit by the oil of a blessed olive tree
> neither of the west nor of the east;
> yet it is as if this oil itself would shine
> though no fire touch it.
> Light upon light!
> God guides to God's light
> the one God wills to guide,
> and the one who wills to be guided.
> God speaks to humankind in symbols,
> for God is beyond all measure
> in God's knowledge of created things.

The beauty of the Light Verse now seems obvious to me. But at first I was puzzled by this verse — or perhaps just by the form in which I was introduced to it, printed in English translation in fancy lettering on a glossy card with a photo of a blazing sun at the top. It wasn't a verse I was familiar with at the time. This was in 1994, when I had been studying the Qur'an in Arabic with some members of the Islamic Center of Rochester for about a year. That particular afternoon, I was sitting cross-legged at the back of the mosque's prayer area, a copy of the Qur'an carefully balanced on my knees, when the Center's Imam, Dr. Muhammad Shafiq, brought this card over to me.

"Do you know the Light Verse?" he asked, handing me the card.

"No," I said, puzzling over the picture and quickly scanning the words below. "I'm still working through *al-Imran*"— Sura three of the Qur'an, I meant. "This verse on the card is from Sura twenty-four. I'll be a hundred years old before I get to it!"

"But you should know of it now," Dr. Shafiq said. "It is so beautiful. And it is one of the most loved verses in the whole Qur'an." He paused, smiling. "Take the card, it's yours— we have lots of others."

I wanted to ask Dr. Shafiq some questions. Why was the verse so loved? Because it is beautiful? Or is it beautiful because it is loved? I know how fussy, overly philosophical that way of putting it sounds. But I was surprised by Dr Shafiq's use of the words beauty and love with relation to the Qur'an. The sheer grind of learning enough Arabic to decipher its words had occupied my attention almost completely during the past year. I hadn't gotten in a position as yet to appreciate the language aesthetically. But I had had moments during my laborious study when a repeated phrase would jump out at me, seize my attention, and then seem to place me in a state of holy quiet. The sensation of slogging would quickly return, however, as I struggled to figure out a complex verb form or to decide from various commentaries how to fill in the sense of the Qur'an's many ellipses. Still, love and beauty…— yes, these words used by Dr. Shafiq did resonate with some intimation I'd already had of the powerful attractiveness of the Qur'an.

I didn't get a chance to ask my questions right then, though, because, as so often happens at the Center, Dr. Shafiq was called away to handle a multitude of pastoral emergencies.

So I was left to mull over the Light Verse as best I could by myself.

Was it beautiful? And if so, what was meant by "beautiful"?

I sat with the glossy card in front of me, on top of the open Qur'an.

Discounting the Kodak-inspired sun and the greeting card lettering of the verse beneath, I began to ask myself, What is there about this verse, even in English, that would inspire most or maybe all Muslims to call it beautiful?

No ready-made answers leapt out at me. But then, after staring at the card a little longer, I found myself pushing it to the side so that I could find that very verse in the Arabic Qur'an underneath it, on my lap.

Perhaps I felt a little guilty in doing so — jumping over twenty-one intervening suras like that. But I knew the Qur'an well enough by then to know that its power does not consist in a dramatic building-up of effect, of narrative plotting. Yes, it does contain dramatic moments or movements, where the connection and development of words, thoughts, and images push the reader forward with gale-like force. But these forward or horizontal thrusts are continually fractured and flattened by what I can only describe as a vertical downward energy, like lightning seeking its ground. It is as if God — who is the only speaker in the Qur'an — seeks both to honor our dependence on time, on things following each other in sequence, and also to limit time's hold over us by continually intervening in it, shattering it. The result, in plainer terms, is that the Qur'an does not require to be read in any particular sequence. The very arrangement of the suras shows this. After the first short sura (called *al-Fatihah*, the Opening), the Qur'an moves in order from the longest of the suras to the shortest. Suras from the early, Meccan period of the Revelations tend to be found towards the end of the sequence, and suras from the later, Medinan period come at the beginning.

Unkind critics of the Qur'an find the arrangement of big before little and of last before first simply bewildering, or even worse: confusing, incoherent. I knew what the critics were talking about, but I had begun to pass beyond that initial frustration. I had at least begun to allow myself to believe that what might seem bewildering to me was simply a reflex of my own ignorance and that if I opened myself to the possibility of a different ordering of divine speech than I was used to in the Bible, I might well be enriched and rewarded. And after all, the ordering of Saint Paul's letters in my own New Testament — from the longest (the Letter to the Romans) to the shortest (the Letter to Philemon) — was actually not that different.

At any rate, thoughts like these enabled me to get over my qualms about leaping over those twenty-one suras and thirty-four verses to land upon verse thirty-five of *Sura an-Nur* (Light), upon the Light Verse itself.

It did not at first make much sense to me in Arabic because much of the vocabulary of the first few lines was new to me. "Niche," "lamp," "glass"— I had to guess which Arabic words they corresponded to. But gradually a kind of shapeliness began to emerge. Words repeated themselves within the verse and acted like hinges: the repeated word "lamp" reflecting and repositioning "lamp," "glass" reflecting and repositioning "glass" within the unfolding of the image. The words for "olive tree" and "oil" were different forms of the same root. But the greatest shapeliness was provided by the repetition of the word for "light," of course— a word similar in sound to the word for "fire"— which frames the image first projected by "niche."

These are details which you might not notice in your native tongue. But in a language you're struggling with, every word stands out in naked relief, like green growth on a desert floor.

Sound and rhythm next — because the Qur'an literally means a "reciting," that is, an "audition" in the sense of the human voice being directly subjected to the divine Word and stretched to utter it. This understanding goes back to the very first revelation that came down to Muhammad in the cave on Mt. Hira' where he had gone on a retreat to meditate. "Recite!" is the very first word Muhammad was given on that occasion. The words that immediately followed, "In the Name of Thy Lord," (now found in *Sura al-'Iqra*) and that then continued for the next twenty-two years till the Prophet's death in 632 CE constitute the totality of the recitations which we know as *the* Qur'an.

So even for a Christian student of the Qur'an like myself it was imperative to hear the Light Verse before visualizing it.

But how to give the reader a feeling for how beautiful the Light Verse sounds in Arabic? The translation above is a pale echo of the original, as all translations of the Qur'an inevitably are. The special sonorities of Arabic cannot be mimicked in English. And while the Qur'an continually insists that its language is not "poetic"— to distinguish its utterance from that of mere bards under the influence of who knows what source of inspiration—, still, its properties of rhythm, rhyme, metaphor, and compression of meaning are those of all true poetry. And like any other true poetry, the Qur'an is realized adequately only in its original idiom.

So the beauty of the Light Verse as apprehended by Arabic speakers and even by outsiders like myself with only a basic knowledge of Arabic is impossible to convey to those without the minimum background.

Alas and alack! Does answering my original question about what makes the Light Verse both beautiful and beloved run hopelessly aground on the reef of competence in Arabic?

I think not. Pale though the echo of any translation may be, the greater truth is that God, as the Qur'an says again and again, is *ar-Raheem*, the Merciful One. God does not want us to be ignorant of God's message for us. Yet God never forces the message upon us and if necessary will employ humble means of conveying it.

Here, perhaps, is a clue to the question I raised at the beginning, as to what it is that makes the Light Verse beautiful. Above and beyond the formal poetic properties that might make the Light Verse beautiful to the ear of Arabic speakers, there is the beauty of the intention that motivates it: God's mercy. The beauty of God's mercy fills with love and desire those with ears to hear its voice. For mercy by its nature does not impose itself but invites. Even modest things can transmit such beauty. In fact, modest things might have an advantage over great things in transmitting beauty because modest things cannot by their nature overwhelm. Even a translation of the Light Verse that is a pale copy may convey beauty.

For ultimately, after all of its words have been understood and its poetic qualities appreciated and absorbed, it is the Light Verse as parable of God's mercy that resonates in and expands the heart.

The Light Verse is a parable of divine descent and ascent expressed through recognizable images. That we are invited to become part of the descending and ascending movement from the unimaginably grand to the lowly and back again is a key to its beauty.

The Light Verse begins in a realm far above our vision and grasp and comprehension. For to say that "God is the light of heaven and earth" is not to describe God. It is not even to create an image for God, properly understood. We are not talking of a light *in* heaven and earth, but of what gives light *to* them: what the source of all light everywhere in heaven and earth is. And it is clear from what follows that the light pointed at in that first line is primarily spiritual in nature. That is, it illuminates the totality of the human being and invites the human being towards Itself.

Enter a parable, to rescue us from a splendor beyond our senses.

If parables are symbols in story form, then the parable of the Light Verse begins on the plastered wall of a simple home such as Dr. Shafiq grew up in — as he much later told me — in the mountains of northern Pakistan.

There was a niche high on that wall in which his parents placed an oil lamp surrounded by a clear protective glass. The lamp's light, reflected off the shining wall surface, illuminated the whole room and made possible all the activities occurring within it. The oil fueling that lamp was not, in that particular place, made from olives. But it would have been in the Arabia of Muhammad's day. The olive tree from which the oil came would have stood in the family grove. Only the best oil would be used. That would have come from an olive tree in the center of the grove, protected from the west and east winds — "lit by the oil of a blessed olive tree neither of the west nor of the east." A blessed tree, yes, but a humble one, really. Not prepossessing to look at: low, gnarly, but tough, resilient, enduring.

There's nothing ornate about any element of the unfolding picture of the lamp's light as that picture is built for us step by step, from niche to lamp, from lamp to glass, from glass to oil, from oil to light to tree to oil back to light… except that each time we witness this light it seems to grow more brilliant ("like a radiant star") and then to dissolve into pure transparency ("it is as if this oil itself would shine/though no fire touch it") and finally to become invisibly *the* light once again, "light upon light!"

Nothing ornate, maybe, but also nothing that impedes — and everything that encourages— our ascent from that simple home in Pakistan or anywhere else to the way God's own reflected light spreads out from the purity of its source to illuminate and guide what surrounds it. All along we have been observing the construction of a parable — the Light Verse has already announced that fact. A challenge is set for human interpretive power. Orthodox Muslim interpretation sees the niche as the heart of the ideal believer, the lamp as God's revelation of the Qur'an, the light as its core truth, and the believer's personal character — the believer's personal character at its best — as the clearest glass through which the divine light of revelation passes to others.

A picture of the true Muslim flows from such interpretation, a person who, because wholly obedient to the Qur'an's voice, becomes a pure conduit of revelation to others. For Sunni Muslims, this ideal person can be no other than the Prophet Muhammad himself, whose life and sayings provide the pattern for righteous living for all Muslims everywhere and so allowing the best of them to become conduits of light themselves.

But symbols being what they are, meanings tend to expand. And there has been a division of interpretation of the Light Verse along sectarian lines, between Sunnis and Shi'as. For Ja'far as-Sadiq, the sixth Shi'a Imam and the greatest of Shi'a Qur'an commentators, the Light Verse is God's special communication to the Shi'a. Ja'far claimed that while God's light is Muhammad himself, the glass is a reference to the prophetic knowledge that he passed on to Imam Ali, Muhammad's son-in-law, the first and greatest of the Shi'a Imams. That the "oil in the lamp would shine though no fire touch it" refers to the divine knowledge that comes from each Imam's mouth, though Muhammad himself had not spoken it.

Sufis, who are Muslim mystics, take it farther. The "blessed olive tree neither of the west nor of the east" means that God's word cannot be contained even within Islam. And indeed the Qur'an itself claims that it has not been sent to institute a new religion but to reconfirm the original one given to humankind at the dawn of humankind's creation. The ideal believer illuminated by God's light would be anyone who seeks God and God alone and who serves others as equally beloved by God.

But while it is important to know about these interpretations, too much focus on them risks diverting attention from the kind of power and indeed beauty that has inspired such commentaries. What is there about the Light Verse that warrants such depth and variety of response — a response not exhausted even by the interpretations listed here? Why would the simple image of the lamp in a niche evoke such a passionate burst of insight?

Context holds the clue. For the Light Verse is not, as its publication in that glossy greeting card format first suggested to me, an isolated event, a show piece, a kind of divine performance that can itself be placed apart in that niche and be particularly revered. Yes, it is often so revered, inscribed in fine calligraphic hand on the walls of mosques, but those who revere it in this way know full well how it fits into the broader movement of the Qur'an's voice.

Situated where it is, almost in the middle of *Sura* 24, the Light Verse is not a set piece at all. It is a sudden surge of illumination within a swirl of human murk.

For the verses of *Sura an-Nur* leading up the Light Verse, as well as the majority of those that follow it, are not metaphorical. Nor do they point us to heavenly realms. Nor do they paint a flattering picture of a willingly guided or illuminated humankind, whether Sunni or Shi'a or Sufi or anything else.

The verses preceding the Light Verse are painfully concrete in their efforts to rescue the young Muslim community from its pettiness: from its love of gossip, even of slander, from its disrespect for each other's privacy, from its disdain for its less well-off members. The pettiness has threatened even Muhammad and his family. Backbiters assail the honor of his wife

Aisha; grumblers balk at his requests; hypocrites say yes to his face then do the opposite; intruders give him no peace.

More positively, the Qur'an in these pre-Light Verse passages lays out the broad outline of a household code of good conduct. Take the two verses immediately preceding the Light Verse. "Do not force your slave-girls into prostitution, when they themselves wish to remain honorable, in your quest for the short-term gains of this world, although, if they are forced, God will be forgiving and merciful to them" (verse 33). Then, summing up in the manner of a wise, patient elder (the manner of its address thus far), the Qur'an states: "We have sent these verses down to you people clarifying the right path, examples of those who passed away before you, and advice for those who are mindful of God" (verse 34).

Now, like the thunderbolt I mentioned earlier, the Light Verse descends upon the ear and the heart. Its beauty is part and parcel with the surprise of its appearance, its way of abruptly setting aside the discussion of what we should *do* in favor of what we should *be*. The Qur'an speaks now to quicken and illuminate our hearts, to animate our good behavior as a simple reflex of gratitude and joy, rather than as dutiful obedience — or, better, as obedience enlivened by joy.

Joy and wonder: "God is the light of heaven and earth." God is all: "Light upon light!" And equally wondrous is God's care to bring us, poor petty humankind, to this light: "God guides to God's light the one God wills to guide, and the one who wills to be guided." Two wills are engaged here — God's and ours. A grammatical ambiguity in the Arabic leaves open which is prior: does God choose the one to be guided, or does guidance to the light depend on human choice? In fact, both readings must be held in the mind at the same time. God's choice of us and ours of God are held in the balance.

Of course, though, priority is always given to God, because it is through God's mercy that human volition comes into play at all, that it even exists. For human volition is itself of God, as is everything else. Our free will is the sign of God's *ruh*, God's spirit, given to humankind uniquely among the creatures God has made. Strange gift, that allows for the rejection of the giver! Who can fathom such generosity? And such mercy for us as we are allowed to ponder our response to what has been given? God does indeed "speak to humankind in symbols."

Symbols leave open an interpretative space, and this is certainly true of the Light Verse's core symbol of light itself. The light produced by the lamp (or the human heart transparent to God) is a result of the purity of its substance, of its fuel, of its oil — not directly of an external flame or the light of heaven itself. Muslim interpretation of all stripes notes this fact and attributes it to a characteristic reluctance on the part of the Qur'an to bring God directly into the material world. Yes, God may be "closer than your jugular vein," as the Qur'an states in a famous verse (*Sura Qaf* 50:16). But God always keeps a significant space between God and us. God does this because of God's very "otherness." But God does it for our sakes too, to protect and preserve our freedom. We might also say that this space is the space of metaphor, and of the possibility of the divine beauty which attracts us without overwhelming us.

We are never permitted to grasp it fully. Reference to that boundary is found in the Light Verse's last line — "for God is beyond all measure/ in God's knowledge of created things." Many Qur'anic verses end this way, with God's naming of the Divine Essence that puts God out of our reach, again because this is who God is — the Other — and because God protects us from a closeness that would consume us, as flames consume moths.

So to say, as Dr Shafiq said to me, that the Light Verse is beautiful and that it is one of the most-loved verses in the Qur'an means that for Muslims it arouses a yearning for God in a most sublime way. Its appeal is not primarily to the intellect but to the heart. Light is its sign, light that warms and illuminates what is cold and dark. We turn towards this light as flowers to the sun.

But what is beautiful is not beauty itself. "God speaks to humankind in symbols." A symbol of that beauty is the Light Verse. Beauty's source is God alone.

Chapter 1b. The Beauty of God: "God's beautiful names"

To God belong the Beautiful Names. So call upon Him by means of them, and leave to their own devices those who profane and put to improper use the Beautiful Names — they will receive a just reward for their deeds. (*Sura al-A'raf* 7:180)

Say: 'Call upon Allah, or call him the Most Beneficent (*ar-rahman*) — however you call on Him you do well, for to him belong the beautiful names. Do not say your prayer in a loud voice, nor in a soft one, but seek a path between those extremes. (*Sura Isra'* 17:110)

Allah — there is no god but He — to Him belong the Beautiful Names. (*Sura Ta'ha'* 20:8)

He is Allah, the Creator (*al-khalaq*), the Originator (*al-bara'*), the Fashioner (*al-musawwil*). To Him belong the Beautiful Names. All things in the heavens and on earth give him praise, for he is the Exalted in Might (*al-aziz*), the Most Wise (*al-hakim*). (*Sura al-Hashr* 59:24)

Our friend Yasmin and her family had recently come back from the Hajj, the pilgrimage to Mecca all Muslims are obliged to make at least once in their lifetimes if they are able. Peggy and I had invited Yasmin, her husband, and her two teen-agers to dinner because we wanted to share in their experience of the Hajj. Mecca is off-limits to non-Muslims, so it is a place Peggy and I will never visit, and the Hajj a celebration we will never take part in, except vicariously.

I've never met a Muslim who does not return a gesture of hospitality with an outpouring of gifts. This evening was no different. Yasmin brought a delicious main course, as well as many presents purchased in Mecca for both of us.

Chief among my own presents was a black velvet case that opened up to display in gold leaf on red plush background the *asma Allah ul-husna*, the Beautiful Names of God, all ninety-nine of them, in Arabic calligraphy, arranged grid-fashion within an ornate frame. Just above the grid appears line 7:180 from the Qur'an as given above: "To God belong the Beautiful Names. So call upon Him by means of them..." And then the list begins: God ("Allah" in Arabic), then The Beneficent, then The Merciful, then The Sovereign Lord, then The Holy One, then The Source of Peace, then The Guardian of Faith, then The Protector...

If I hadn't known better, I'd have thought, when I saw that grid, that I was looking at a table of the chemical elements. But the Names aren't merely a compilation of abstract religious data about God. The Names originate in the Qur'an. When a Muslim sees any of the Names, what immediately jumps out at him or her are the verses in the Qur'an where the particular

Name appears. And then there gathers around that Name the context in which it is used. So in a sense the listing of the Names is a digest of the whole Qur'an, a window into it, a jog to memory, and an aid to delighted re-recognition.

The first forty-two names in the display Yasmin gave me are arranged with a slight but significant asymmetry that doesn't reveal itself till the end. The arrangement starts out evenly enough. The first forty-two Names are arranged seven across in six rows. Then come four rows across with two names on either side of a space sufficient for twelve names. In this space appears instead, in much larger calligraphy, the great Qur'anic statement of monotheism, "He is God... there is no god but He." The four rows of two names on either side of this statement make sixteen in all. Add them to the previous forty-two and you get fifty-eight. That leaves forty-one spaces to go to make ninety-nine. Six rows of seven across follow beneath the space in the middle. But wait! Six times seven would make not forty-one but forty-two more names, adding up to one hundred in all!... ah no. The final square on the left-hand side bottom of the grid (Arabic reads from right to left) is empty. Ninety-nine.

That last empty space on the grid has become for many Muslims the most potent of all. It has acquired, especially for Sufis — who are Muslim mystics — a mysterious otherness symbolic of the unnamable essence of divinity into which Sufis long to lose themselves. For other Muslims, devout but perhaps less self-abnegating in their love of God, the one-hundredth name — or the space left for it — represents the incapacity of human speech fully to name God. The space is a necessary check or brake on human ambition and even on an otherwise commendable enthusiasm for absorbing the names and for making them one's own through constant repetition and contemplation. One must never suppose that even in one's most pious moments one could in any comprehensive way "know" God, even through the Beautiful Names.

Such intellectual recognition of human limits correlates with Muslim behavior. Muslims' very love of the Names — of, say, The Mighty, The Compeller, The Majestic, The Creator, The Evolver, The Fashioner — makes Muslims joyfully cautious. Not through diffidence but through modesty, itself enjoined upon them by Qur'anic verses like 17:110 above: "...Do not say your prayer in a loud voice, nor in a soft one, but seek a path between those extremes." So yes, if you mention any of the Beautiful Names to a Muslim — if you say The Great Forgiver, The Subduer, The Bestower of Good, The Provider, The One who Begins —, his or her face will light up instantly, in just the same way as many Catholic faces do at mention of Mary or other favorite saints, or as all Christians' faces light up at the mention of Jesus himself. These ninety-nine names aren't simply items in a list as in a telephone book. They are terms of address and endearment. To mention any of these divine qualities — like The All-knowing, The Restrainer, The Expander, The Exalter, The Honorer, The One who Humbles — brings God in all God's dimensions to consciousness, and into one's heart. But all the more reason to carry the ballast of humility lest one's spiritual boat capsize in the gale of emotion, and the lover be lost.

It is always a joy and an inspiration to observe this phenomenon of mixed enthusiasm and reserve whenever the Names are mentioned among Muslims.

So I rejoiced when Yasmin gave me the case with the Beautiful Names as much for her manner of giving as for the gift itself. Her smile was as broad as my own must have been when I opened the case and saw what was within it. But there was a reticence about her too. She didn't have to explain to me why such a gift is precious, nor did she try. A few months before the dinner party, she'd burned a CD for me of a recorded reflection on the Names, a CD she loves to listen to on her way to Rochester's Islamic Center where she runs an Islamic parochial school. On this CD the speaker works through each name, lovingly pausing over each one to explain its meaning — over The All-Hearing, say, or The All-Seeing, or The Judge, or The Just, or The Subtle One, or The Aware. I'm sure Yasmin remembered that she'd already expressed herself ardently to me on the subject of the Names when she'd presented me with this earlier gift. She wasn't going to lay it on thick again.

Recalling that CD and now admiring the display Yasmin had given me brought back to mind the many forms in which I'd seen the Beautiful Names presented, a multiplicity always aimed at the one goal of attracting and holding the attention: in wall framings in mosques, in colorful, beauti-fully-designed books, in songs for children, in booklets for ease in chanting during meditative prayer.

The Names lend themselves to chanting and song because, as I said above, they are terms of address and endearment as well as awe and rever-ence even when they seem to point to a God whose distance above human-kind, even in God's mercy, is infinite. The Forbearing, The Highest, The Always-Forgiving, The Grateful One, The Sublime, The Grand — these are not frightening Names. Part of what mitigates the sheer Otherness of God is the fact that the Names are not so much titles — as if they designated the particular medals and ribbons of royalty — as they are descriptive. And descriptive not of what God is, but of what God does. The Protector refers not to a titanic figure, even a benign one, looming over the worshipper. It refers to the way God is supremely active at each instance in keeping guard over God's creation. And similarly with the Maintainer, The Reckoner, The Glorious, The Generous, The Watchful.

Or take two Names we've already met in the Light Verse. First *an-nur*, "the Light," that is, "that which illuminates." We've already touched on the challenge of trying to say what this word might mean when used of God, who is not "light," exactly, but the One who brings light, especially the light of spiritual insight and personal transparency. Then at the very end of the Light Verse, as the very last word in the verse (the syntactical position where the great majority of the Beautiful Names appear in the Qur'an), we find another Beautiful Name, *al-alim*, literally "the one knowing," but perhaps best translated as the one "beyond all measure/in God's knowing of created things."

By using these or any of the other ninety-seven Names of God — like The Responsive, The All-Embracing, The Wise, The Loving, The Powerful, The Resurrector, The Witness, The Truth—, we're not, then, appealing to or addressing a fixed attribute of God. What we're doing instead is calling upon an activity of God powerfully operative not only in the past but in the present as well, in our own present. We call upon that divine activity in wonder and praise because in its origin and true dimensions it escapes entirely our capacity to comprehend it. But we also call upon that activity — or, better said, to God who manifests that activity — that we might ourselves be strengthened in that activity according to our own capacities and limitations. And so by calling upon God as "the Light," we are both praising God's illuminative might as well as seeking for ourselves a spiritual transparency that will enable us to be a light to others. Or when we call upon The Trustworthy, we ask to be trustworthy ourselves, according to our own human strengths and limitations. Or when we call on The Resolute, we ask to share in that characteristic using the strength God has given us.

The beauty of the Names consists, then, in their double capacity to evoke our praise for God as well as to welcome within ourselves a call to act in God's image. Not that there is always an easy or obvious correlation between God's activity and our own. The Unique One, The One, The Independent — Beautiful Names of this sort refer to the key assertion of Islam, that there is no God but He. Humankind cannot in any way participate in the divine unity. But we can praise it. And we can direct our own understanding and regulate our own behavior according to the firm belief that Oneness (*tauhid* — a key Muslim concept) lies behind all multiplicity. This belief enables us to overcome our tendency for violent separation— for destructive, rivalrous divisions between "us" and "them" in our dealings with each other and for a selfishly instrumentalist treatment of our environment.

Names pointing to God's Oneness are traditionally called Names of Perfection. There are two other traditional categories. One of these, and the most frequently-occurring type, is Majesty. Among those would be The Dominant, The First, The Last, The Hidden, The Manifest. Their frequency indicates Islam's emphasis on God's Transcendence.

But there is a third type, and its name is Beauty. It gathers the Names pointing to God's Immanence and Mercy. The fact that Beauty is a less populous category than Majesty doesn't mean, however, that the Names it gathers are less important than the others. Let's recall 17:110 above: "Say: 'Call upon Allah, or call him The Beneficent (*ar-rahman*) — however you call on Him you do well, for to Him belong the Beautiful Names." There cannot be a division among Names any more than there can be division within God. Divisions or, better, differences among the Names are concessions to our dependence upon making distinctions. Intellectually we need to sort a thing into categories before we can see it as a whole.

But ultimately it is to enable us to see God as a whole that the Names have been given us. They exist not for God's use, but for our own. That is why they are all of them Beautiful, even if they belong in the category of Perfection or Transcendence. They are all beautiful because God's very Self is beautiful — beautiful for us.

And yet — what does this mean, to say that God is beautiful for us? Does putting it that way mean that God is not beautiful in Himself?

No, clearly it doesn't mean that, if for no other reason than it isn't given us to know God in that way, in God's essence. But we created beings have been given access to our Creator, not simply by our Creator's providing a path for us toward Him, but by our Creator's attracting us along that path. Beauty has been given us to engage us, lighten our way, and draw us to Him.

Yet the possibility of rejecting beauty has been given us as well. God the Merciful opens the door and invites us towards the light on the other side. To become beautiful ourselves we must choose to walk through this door.

Chapter 1c. The Beauty of Humankind: "Beautiful patience"

One person who walked through that door was Joseph, or Yusuf, as he is known in the Qur'an. The account of what happened once Joseph emerged into the light on the other side is told in what the Qur'an calls the "the most beautiful of stories" (*ahsan-al qasisi*) — so beautiful, in fact, that the Qur'an refuses to interrupt it. *Sura Yusuf* — the "sura on Joseph" — is the only sura in the Qur'an where the narrative line is unbroken from beginning to end.

So is its unbrokenness what makes the story beautiful? That is, does the unbrokenness encourage the artful building of suspense? Is the beauty of this story a function of its difference from the rest of the Qur'an, where narratives are either only alluded to or given only in separated pieces — like the story of Moses, which is told in over forty different segments throughout the Qur'an?

Not at all! What *Sura Yusuf* teaches, and teaches by Joseph's example, is the very reverse of a beauty that hinges on suspensefulness — on action, drama, exaggerated emotion. It teaches "beautiful patience" instead, and uses the dramatic circumstances of the well-known Joseph story to make its point clear.

The source of the story in Judaism and Christianity is Genesis 37-50. In that account we *do* get suspense, through the way the character of Joseph develops over the course of the story. From the gifted but perhaps arrogant young man who brags to his brothers about his dreams of future glory to the wise administrator who chooses reconciliation with his brothers over vengeance is a wide gap indeed. And in addition, the narrative style of the Genesis version is marked by hints and ambiguities — the very stuff of what is usually considered effective story-telling.

Sura Yusuf as revealed in the Qur'an is subject to a different aesthetic. For one thing, the character of Joseph, and of his father Jacob as well, is fixed from the start. We meet Joseph only after he has emerged into God's light — not before. The story focuses not on the transformation of character but on character transformed. We see that character, Joseph's but his father's too, tested by what follows. That father and son will pass these tests is never in doubt. What we admire is the exemplary way in which their "beautiful patience" manifests itself.

In the following example the Qur'anic quality of "beautiful patience" is brought out by contrast with the biblical account of the same event.

In Genesis, Jacob's sons approach their father with Joseph's bloody coat and say:

> "This we have found; see whether it is your son's robe or not." He recognized it, and said: "It is my son's robe! A wild animal has devoured him; Joseph is without doubt torn to pieces." Then Jacob tore his gar-

ments, and put sackcloth on his loins, and mourned for his son many days. All his sons and all his daughters sought to comfort him; but he refused to be comforted, and said, "No, I shall go down to Sheol to my son, mourning." Thus the father bewailed him. (37:32b-35).

In the Qur'anic account, the brothers also approach their father with the bloody coat, but Jacob's reaction is quite different:

> They said: "Father, we went off to run races with each other and left Joseph with our belongings. But then a wolf came and ate him— yet you will not believe us even though we tell the truth." For they had stained Joseph's robe with an animal's blood. But Jacob said: "No, for clearly your souls have invented this matter. But as for me, beautiful patience. God alone can give help against what you have described to me." (12: 17-18)

It's not that Jacob in the Qur'anic account doesn't fear for his son as much as Jacob in the Bible does. It's that the Qur'anic Jacob has come at least part way into the light of God, and while that light isn't sufficient for him to see fully the extent of the brothers' plotting, he sees enough to make him suspicious and to guard him against what seems by contrast the extravagant grief shown by his biblical counterpart. "Beautiful patience" describes the behavior of a heart illuminated by faith. Through that illumination the heart is fortified against the human tendency simply to react to the surface appearance of things. It's also strengthened to be able to wait quietly till the true meaning of things is revealed. Patience is beautiful because it is aligned with that truth.

But if "beautiful patience" is the first fruit of illumination by God's light, "insight" (*ta'wil*) is the second, and just as important as the first. Actually, one leads to the other. "Beautiful patience" enables the heart to maintain its equilibrium within the hurly-burly of events and their deceptive meanings. Insight is the heart's capacity to interpret the truth of those events from within its God-centered tranquility.

Insight is the quality attributed throughout *Sura Yusuf* to Joseph himself. It comes to him very early in the story, and very early in his life as well — it comes to him, in fact, at the very bottom of the well into which the brothers throw him!

What happens is this.

Unlike in the biblical account, Joseph in the Qur'an is not shown bragging to his brothers about the dream vision in which, in the forms of stars, they prostrate themselves before him. Instead, Joseph tells only his father about the dream. The old man warns Joseph not to let his brothers know about it for fear of arousing their jealousy. But to reassure his son Jacob says: "In this way your Cherisher and Sustainer will choose you and teach you insight into signs and events (*ta'wil-il ahadithi*) and give his favor to you and to my posterity as he once gave it to your ancestors, to Abraham and Isaac; for your Cherisher and Sustainer is Most Knowledgeable, Most Wise."

Soon afterwards, the brothers conspire and throw Joseph into the well. But at that very point God intervenes to provide the boy with the insight Jacob had foretold. "We [God often speaks of Himself in the first person plural in the Qur'an] gave Joseph this inspiration: The day will come when you will tell your brothers the full truth about this affair while they will not perceive it."

And of course, Joseph does tell his brothers the whole truth, not right away in the well, but years later in Egypt, when the brothers are assembled before Joseph and he reveals their malfeasance as well as his own mercy.

Between Joseph's low-point at the bottom of the well and his high-point as merciful vindicator of the wrongs done against him, he passes in the Qur'anic account through many adversities and challenges, the ones we're familiar with from the biblical version: the attempt by Potiphar's wife (in Islamic tradition named Zuleykha) to seduce him, his unjust imprisonment, his interpretation of the dreams of his fellow-prisoners and of Pharaoh himself, his being named to a position of highest responsibility as Pharaoh's chief administrator. In all these crises of fortune, crises that bring him low and bring him high, Joseph never loses the "beautiful patience" which gives space for the insight necessary to interpret events correctly and thus to make decisions that benefit not only himself but everyone else, his family members and the Egyptians alike. There is no partisanship in the way his gifts are used for the common good.

But it's important to stress that for the Qur'an both "beautiful patience" and insight *are* God's gifts, not attributes inherent in Joseph. Like his father Jacob, Joseph has welcomed these gifts; therein lies his own beauty, in that grateful acceptance, rather than in a personal quality he might be tempted to brag about. We see Joseph's gifts drawn on most compellingly in the Qur'an's account of Zuleykha's attempted seduction.

Zuleykha, consumed with passion for the young overseer, maneuvers Joseph into a room whose doors she bolts, locking others out and him in. "Come to me," she pants. Joseph objects: "God forbid! For my Cherisher and Sustainer has made my stay in this land a beautiful (*ihsan*) one. Those who wander in the dark never prosper" (12:23).

What is the basis of Joseph's rejection of Zuleykha's advances? Physical distaste? Smug prudence? Heroic moral fortitude? None of them. To clarify the motive, the Qur'an adds this: "And with great passion she desired him, and he her, so that he might have succumbed had he not seen pledges of his Lord's presence. In this way We turned him away from evildoing and shameful behavior, for Joseph was one of our servants whose heart was transparent" (12:24).

18

The point is not to claim that Joseph is sinless. Joseph himself never makes this claim for himself. He says to Potiphar later on that while he did not give in to Zuleykha, "… I do not want to absolve myself. The soul is inclined to evil unless God gives us His mercy— but this mercy is sure, since God is the All-Forgiving, the Merciful" (12:53).

Joseph's beauty follows from the clarity of his vision. He never blurs the distinction between what lies in his own power and what lies in God's. And he never hesitates to call out to God for strength he knows he does not possess. Zuleykha's physical attractions are too much for him. But he is not so blinded that he cannot see what the Qur'an has described as the "pledges of his Lord's presence" and in that clarity find the wherewithal to resist her.

But there's another way to measure Joseph's beauty, one that Zuleykha herself inadvertently makes possible. The story of how she does so occurs in the Qur'an but not in the Genesis account, though it is found in rabbinic legend.

In the Qur'anic account Zuleykha hears of women of the city murmuring against her, saying that she was wrong to try to seduce Joseph. Stung, she contrives not only to reveal their hypocrisy but to entrap them and Joseph too in a group assault on his virtue. So she invites the women to a feast where she gives them sharp knives. Then she calls in Joseph. The women, overwhelmed by his physical beauty, cut their hands and cry out, "God preserve us! This is no mortal being but the most noble of angels."

On one level, Zuleykha is vindicated, because the women helplessly admit in the extravagance of cutting themselves just how powerfully attractive Joseph is.

Yet the way the women describe Joseph's attractiveness undercuts Zuleykha's obsession with Joseph's physical attractions alone. For their words point to a beauty that while including the physical includes much more as well. When they cry out "God preserve us! This is no mortal being but the most noble of angels," they acknowledge that they are in the presence of spiritual beauty too, and they draw back in awe.

We're not allowed to think this is mere rhetorical overkill on the women's part. Joseph's spiritual beauty is immediately confirmed by the way he reacts to their adoring language. Just as before when pursued by Zuleykha alone, Joseph acknowledges his weakness and appeals to God:

"O my Cherisher and Sustainer, I prefer prison to what they are inviting me to. But unless you turn their plotting away from me, I could weaken, and then I would be just another of those mastered by desire." So his Cherisher and Sustainer heeded him and turned the women's plotting aside, for God is the One who hears, the One who knows. (12:33-34)

Zuleykha up to this point certainly sounds like the villain of the piece, and a frustrated one, a *femme fatale* who has met her match and who must spend the rest of eternity burning with resentment. And since the Qur'an itself says nothing more about her, we can't totally rule out a gloomy end for her, both in this world and in the world to come. Yet a gloomy end just does not seem probable. Because if Zuleykha must be condemned for her sexual plotting against Joseph, how much more must Joseph's brothers be condemned, whose plotting against him is far more wicked than hers. Yet this "most beautiful of stories" allows even the brothers by the end of the story to recognize the error of their ways and to be restored not only in Joseph's good graces, but most importantly in God's. If the brothers can be rehabilitated, doesn't Zuleykha deserve a beautiful future too?

And in fact she receives such a future at the hands of Muslim artists and poets of the Middle Ages (in the first few centuries after the death of the Prophet Muhammad in 632 CE), especially in Iran, under the influence of Sufi mysticism. In paintings and poetry Zuleykha becomes the symbol of the soul's searching for God, while Joseph represents the perfection of beauty and goodness in human form. Zuleykha learns that the lustful behavior she exhibits in the "most beautiful of stories" has to be purified before she can reach her goal of union with Joseph. Purified, but not eradicated; Islam does not favor celibacy. Physical and spiritual beauty combine. Neither is frustrated or at war with the other. Yet human beings tend to turn physical beauty into an idol, and until the erring soul (symbolized by Zuleykha) shatters this idol, it cannot achieve its desire. But Zuleykha does shatter it. And so in the magnificent Persian poem about their relationship, *Yusuf u Zuleykha* , by the Persian Sufi poet Jami (a poem for which, regrettably, we still lack an English translation), she is not only able to satisfy her love for Joseph, but in some miniatures and accounts Joseph even passionately pursues her!

Yet interpretation does not stop there. In Zuleykha's successful pursuit of Joseph, a further allegory develops in which she figures as the human soul in love with God, and Joseph becomes an emblem of God the beloved. Such imaginative elaboration of the "most beautiful of stories" does no violence to the Qur'an. Quite the contrary. It enables those Muslims who love Joseph's and Zuleykha's story to pursue and capture the fullness of its meaning. In doing so they often cite another story, one of the *hadith* or eyewitness accounts of the Prophet Muhammad's own words.

In this famous *hadith*, the Prophet is approached by a mysterious white-haired figure identified as the angel Gabriel. The stranger asks Muhammad to name the fundamentals of the religion which God is revealing to and through him. The Prophet promptly — and to the stranger's satisfaction — names three fundamentals in order of their relation to the outer and inner dimensions of worship. *Islam*, or self-yielding, Muhammad names as the first fundamental, one established through the external practice of the Five Pillars: witness to the oneness of God and to Muhammad's prophetic calling, daily prayer, almsgiving, fasting, and pilgrimage. Next the Prophet names *iman*, or belief: in the angels, in the Day of Judgment, in the prophets, and in their books. And as the third he names *ihsan* — beauty — here meaning spiritual virtue, or transparency of the heart, as a result of which you act always as if you were face-to-face with God, for though you cannot see Him, you know that God can see you.

This *hadith* captures the purity and intimacy of *ihsan* or beauty, at the same time linking it firmly with communal practice and with secure orientation in belief. The story of Joseph and Zuleykha, as elaborated and loved by so many Muslims over the ages, becomes then a symbol of this harmony of the outer and the inner, of the external and internal disciplines of religion — of right practice clarified by the thoughtful grasp of correct doctrine, both of them enlivened by the heart's pursuit of the Beloved. Such harmony is not achievable without the "beautiful patience" and the "insight" with which we see through our own and the world's idols and deceptions into the reality lit by the Light of heaven and earth.

Chapter 1d. The Ugliness of Humankind: Yielding to "the soul inclined to evil"

"But does the Light of God in some way *cause* the darkness? I mean, would there *be* ugliness, would there *be* opposition if there weren't first Light and Beauty?"

That's the question I launched at Dr. Shafiq one day in his office when I managed to catch him between phone-calls. I was conscious of perhaps being unfair to him, throwing him a poser when he was in the middle of juggling complicated demands from this person and that. My own demand just added to the balls he had to keep up in the air.

But he didn't seem annoyed. We had gotten to be close friends; several years had passed since he'd first handed me the glossy card with the Light Verse printed on it in English translation. He knew my subsequent struggles and delights with this verse, my attempts to memorize it in Arabic, as well as my efforts to use it as a point of orientation in my study of the rest of the Qur'an. So he was inclined to be patient with me. But I also knew he loved knotty theological questions. Tricky as they might be, they came, I think, as a relief to him in the midst of a day's quota of knots — or muddles — of the insoluble human kind.

"Revelation isn't all-inclusive," he said, pausing to smile. "I mean, it does not force itself upon us. As Light, Revelation doesn't cause darkness. It exposes our three selves, illuminating the middle one, to enable us to increase the illumination."

And then he had to answer another phone call.

And I had to take it from there.

But over the years he, and other kindly members of the Islamic Center, had provided me with the tools to do that. So what might seem a cryptic answer on his part was actually full of helpful clues.

Take Dr Shafiq's mention of the "three selves." These, I knew by this time, referred to the Qur'an's characterization of the three basic states of the human soul.

Characteristically, the Qur'an doesn't mention these states in a systematic way. This may seem frustrating if what we're looking for in the Qur'an is a treatise in moral theology. The "three selves" emerge, not as part of a continuous discourse on the topic of the human soul, but in widely separated verses, in quite different contexts. The effect is not, however, to confuse the issue but to ground the three possibilities of human response to Revelation in a variety of life situations.

The "three selves" are differentiated according to their reaction to the Light of God. The self most open to that Light emerges from an explicit social-justice context. It is mentioned in a short sura describing the Final

Judgment on tyrants and on all others who oppress orphans and those who are poor. But for those who serve God and care for others, especially the marginalized, the Day will present a quite different prospect. The *sura* reserves its last words for the just ones, or rather to the state of soul that issues in just behavior: "O human soul, you who have attained tranquility of heart — return to your Cherisher and Sustainer delighting yourself and him as well. Come into the Garden" (*Sura al-Fajr* 89:27). Tranquility proceeds from orderliness, harmony, balance. These psycho-spiritual dimensions of a soul are inseparable from its communal or social orderliness, expressed in the righting of broken relationships and the overcoming of social exclusions. And while the word "beauty" does not appear explicitly in this context, its meaning is implicit in the reference to the Garden, the place of *salaam*: of the fullness of physical and spiritual life in harmony with the Creator's will.

As for the self on the opposite end of the spectrum, the soul closed to the Light, we've already heard about it. Joseph refers to it in his reply to Potiphar: "… I do not want to absolve myself. The soul is inclined to evil unless God gives us His mercy — but this mercy is sure, since God is the All-Forgiving, the Merciful" (*Sura Yusuf* 12:53). We get a sense of what this soul is like from the behavior of Joseph's brothers and of Zuleykha, from the consuming envy of the first and the rapacious sexuality of the second. No tranquility, no beauty here but agitation and scheming in dark corners.

Maybe it comes as a surprise to discover that Joseph, of all people, should be referring to his own soul as "inclined to evil" in this instance. Given Joseph's evident holiness as a person transparent to God's light, we'd expect him to think of his soul as the one first described: the soul in tranquility. Humble as Joseph is, he would still have to acknowledge a world of difference between the state of his soul and that of his brothers or of Zuleykha.

But even if this were not the case, if Joseph's soul really were lost to the Light, why would God give mercy to a soul inclined to evil? Of course, God could do such a thing if God wanted. But it would seem that by doing so God would be violating the soul's freedom, by saving a soul bent on *not* being saved. In that case, however, mercy would lose its quality as mercy. Mercy can't be mercy if it's forced down our throats!

The confusion disappears, though, once we introduce what Dr. Shafiq called the "middle one," the soul in between the extremes. Mention of this soul occurs at the beginning of *Sura-al-Qiyamat* or Resurrection. The *sura* begins with two oaths — the "middle soul" is mentioned in the second of them:

> By the Day of Resurrection, and by the soul that reproaches itself—
> Does humankind think we cannot reassemble his bones?… (75:2)

That "middle soul," the "soul that reproaches itself," is the capacity within each of us to rescue ourselves from the "soul inclined to evil" and to strive instead for "tranquility of heart." For like Joseph himself, each of us possesses all three souls. The question before us is: to what extent do we allow the "middle soul" to guide us away from darkness and point us towards light? Joseph, confronting this crisis in his attraction to Zuleykha, immediately reproaches himself and calls out on God's mercy, that he may attain tranquility of heart.

The beauty of Joseph's story isn't that it sets off the proud superiority of a plaster saint, but that it illuminates our capacity to extricate ourselves from our darkest desire, which is to be a god all to ourselves, a little monarch of the kingdom of self-will.

True, Joseph reproaches himself in timely fashion, resisting the evil inclination before it overwhelms him. And even his brothers and, presumably, Zuleykha herself as well, resist their inclination to evil, though the Light of God reaches them a little later in their personal histories than it reaches Joseph in his; their rescues come after a significant and potentially disastrous falling away from the Light. But what of people not so resistant, so well-formed, so "beautiful," as we might say? What of people who allow the evil inclination to take possession of them wholly? What of those whose behavior during life doesn't bring them to the Garden at all but to its utter absence, its utter negation — to utter ugliness?

We could say that the Qur'an was given by God through Muhammad that he might warn humankind of this truly dark possibility, which is the possibility of nothing more or less than hell itself.

Yet putting the Qur'an's purpose that way risks raising hell or darkness or ugliness to equal status with their presumed opposites: with the Garden, with Light, with Beauty. That's not what the Qur'an is saying. Rather, hell, darkness, and ugliness are the consequence of humankind's stubborn refusal to enter into God's creation — the only creation there is — and to substitute one of its own making. The result is not an alternative structure, or anything like it, but collapse, ruin, nullity, despair.

The Light Verse says it best. Or rather the two verses that follow a little later on and which close off this extraordinary series of six verses all told which are imbedded in the middle of *Sura an-Nur*.

What happens in the three verses immediately following the Light Verse is this: From the Light Verse the Qur'an moves to depict and commend the practice of those who live under its illumination. These blessed ones (people in whom the "self-reproaching self" has been active) perform their prayers and serve others faithfully and well. They are rewarded by God's favor far beyond what they can deserve.

Now we come to the two final verses of the set: about those who yield to their inclination to evil. They too receive a reward, though only irony can express what that reward is. For under God's Light, even their supposed good deeds are shown to be unreal, "like mirages in the desert which those who are thirsty think is water until they come closer and discover nothing at all until they discern the face of God in its place, for God will pay them what is owed them — God is prompt in paying accounts" (24:39). But as for their evil deeds:

> Their evil deeds are like the darkest depths
> of the deepest sea
> covered over by wave upon wave
> and clouds above
> layers of blackness piled one atop the other
> so that if one puts out his hand
> he would scarcely see it
> for to the one to whom God gives no light,
> no light ever arrives (24:40).

No passage in the Qur'an captures better than these two verses the emptiness of what it means to reject the Light of Heaven and Earth, to turn away from the Beauty that the Light reveals. In verse 39, efforts merely to *mimic* good deeds produce mirages: the worst, most feared sort of illusion for those who, like the Muslims of Muhammad's day, lived in desert conditions. Here is the image of a dreaded ugliness, as life-giving water dissolves in the heat, to be replaced — too late — by the burning face of the one rejected. But in the last verse, ugliness is perhaps too mild a word for the evil deeds suggested here: betrayals, violence, plots against or indifference to those who are poor and vulnerable. Ugliness at least suggests the presence of the beauty that has been defaced. Ugliness foretells the darkness that threatens to swallow it and everything else. In itself — if ugliness can be said to have any reality at all — it represents the futility of human scheming, and in the form (or no-form) of ruin it may satisfy the pride of ego that brought it about. But verse 40 above depicts evil's end, its self-annihilating goal, in unmaking and dissolution. There is no return from such a self-sought depth of darkness.

None of these dire consequences, however, in any way competes with the Light of God. None belongs to a realm set up over against the world which the Light warms into full being. "God is the Light of heaven and earth." And God's Beauty, so revealed, draws us away from our fascination with evil's ugliness, away and then upwards towards the Garden: the abode of reward for our senses and our spirits alike.

CHAPTER TWO: CHRISTIAN BEAUTY

Chapter 2a. Christ's Beauty: "He is the image of the invisible God"

I'm on Saint George's Island, Florida, in gloriously clear sunshine, sitting on our beachfront motel balcony, trying to read the major modern theologian of Christian aesthetics, Hans von Balthasar: "Everything of beauty found in the world (and with it too the true and the good) is drawn up into a relationship to this inexhaustible standard, where the living God of love is glorified as He pours out his limitless love for the creature kenotically..."[1] But I keep gazing up from the nearly incomprehensible prose about beauty to soak in the beauty of this setting. "Beautiful" is the word anyone would use to describe it: the beautiful weather, the beautiful peace of the morning beach with just a few people strolling along the shoreline, the beautiful sight and sounds of the Gulf coast, with the water's blue stretching to the horizon. I can't take my eyes off of it; it tranquilizes and uplifts the soul.

> In Christ everything in heaven and on earth was created
> things visible and invisible.
> All were created through him;
> all were created for him.
> He is before all else that is.
> In him everything continues in being.[New American Bible]

For Lent, George and I are memorizing this passage and the whole of the magnificent hymn that it's part of, the hymn composed in the first decades after Christ's death and resurrection, then incorporated into the New Testament Letter to the Colossians as 1:12-20. (We're memorizing it in the translation above, from the New American Bible, because this is the translation that has gradually entered our beings over the years; it is part of each Wednesday's Evening Prayer in the daily prayer book that we've used at home together for a quarter century.) Gazing at the stretch of crystal white beach, lulled by the lapping ripples of waves, I hear as an overlay the lines of this hymn celebrating Christ as the one in whom and through whom and for whom all this beauty was created.

What can this mean, I wonder: that all was created in and through and for Christ? Christians believe that Christ was with God from the beginning.

---

1. Hans von Balthasar, *The Glory of the Lord: A Theological Aesthetics, Vol.II.* (New York: Crossroad Publishers, translation 1983; originally 1961-9), 12.

As the opening of John's Gospel puts it, "In the beginning was the Word and the Word was with God and the Word was God." That is, God's plan from before time was to create everything, both in heaven and on earth, in and through and for the communication of God's very self whom humanity would come to know as Christ, God's Word, God's self-communication. Christ would be — as the Colossians hymn adds — "the image of the invisible God."

But how does Christ image the invisible God?

The first chapter of John's Gospel puts the answer most famously:

> And the Word became flesh and lived among us, and we have seen his glory, the glory as of a father's only son, full of grace and truth.... No one has ever seen God. It is God the only Son, who is close to the Father's heart, who has made him known.

For non-Christians, this separation of the one God into persons with different functions is very hard to accept, I know. Particularly problematic is the language of "Father" and "Son"; I in fact have problems myself with both its gendered nature (for God is certainly neither male nor female) and its parenting image (for not all people have experienced their fathers in ways worthy of God). But any human language for God will be problematic, and I understand that the point of the Father/Son language here is the *intimacy* between God the Creator and Jesus the Incarnate God. Hence the metaphor of "close to the Father's heart." In fact, the Greek word here translated "heart" literally means "bosom," which has an even more intimate feel. (Though Jesus and his followers spoke Aramaic, the writings comprising the New Testament were composed in Greek, the common literary language of the time.)

What I do treasure without qualification in this passage is the profoundly humbling image that "the Word became flesh and lived among us." This is the most concise biblical statement of what Christians call the Incarnation: God's choice, out of love for humankind, to take on flesh for a time in the person of Jesus of Nazareth. Like every Christian, I melt in gratitude before this wonder, this gift. Since God in Jesus became one of us, now in Jesus we are invited to share that same intimacy with God.

Furthermore, "we have seen his glory." I can never read or recall this amazing statement without pausing. How am I to picture this "glory"? — whether it's specified as the glory of God's Word or of God's Son or simply of God. As soon as I try to picture what the Bible means by God's "glory," I find myself blinking into a blinding sparkle of cosmic sized question marks. "God's glory" calls up a sense of dazzling splendor and power and triumph, but it's hard to give this sense a shape for the mind to wrap around. This difficulty is appropriate, for in the Hebrew Bible (the Jewish Scriptures which Christianity has adopted under the name of the "Old Testament") God's glory refers to the actual Presence of God, and how can mere mortals apprehend such a Presence? It would overwhelm us, knock us flat down. In fact, the Hebrew Bible relates that God kept the Divine Presence nearly always veiled from human sight, in a cloud, to protect the Israelites from being overwhelmed by its power. When the rare person is given the privilege of entering the cloud and beholding God's Presence, as Moses does on Mt. Sinai, the vision is fearful: "the appearance of the glory of the Lord was like a devouring fire" (Exodus 24:17). Similarly in Psalm 97, "the Lord is king" and "all the peoples behold His glory," but look at the language in which his glory is painted: "clouds and thick darkness all around Him"; "fire goes before Him, and consumes His adversaries on every side. His lightnings light up the world; the earth sees and trembles." Beholding God's glory is clearly a terrifying experience.

Enter Jesus, the "image of the invisible God," in whom "we have seen his glory." In Jesus — and this is the heart of the Christian Scriptures, the "New Testament" — God's terrifying glory becomes infinitely tender. Jesus is God's compassion in the flesh. So in embodying God's power, Jesus manifests God's infinite compassion, God's mercy. In Jesus the glory of God is made visible in acts of healing, forgiveness, transformation of death to life.

All four Gospels — which are the New Testament accounts of Jesus' life by four different authors — relate a multitude of episodes of Jesus' healings. One from the Gospel of Luke is characteristic, not only of how Jesus' acts of healing reveal God's glory but also of how they manifest God's mercy in forgiving human sinfulness.

The scene (Luke 5:17-26) begins as many Gospel scenes do, with Jesus giving a teaching session. Presumably his theme is what it has been elsewhere: "the good news of the kingdom of God" (Luke 4:42). Though Jesus' public ministry has only recently begun, his reputation as a healer and a man of wisdom has already spread, so there is a large crowd gathered to hear him. Among them are sick people hoping he'll miraculously heal them. But also present is a hostile group: members of the religious authority who suspect that Jesus might be guilty of blasphemy, that is of claiming to possess powers reserved to God. This watchdog group (they're designated throughout the Gospels as "the scribes and the Pharisees") has come from all over the region deliberately to keep their eyes on him.

On this particular day, the whole crowd is squeezed into someone's house. Jesus is teaching them, but also "the power of the Lord was with him to heal." The episode continues:

> Just then some men came, carrying a paralyzed man on a bed. They were
> trying to bring him in and lay him before Jesus; but finding no way to
> bring him in because of the crowd, they went up on the roof and let him

down with his bed through the tiles into the middle of the crowd in front
of Jesus. When he saw their faith, he said, 'Friend, your sins are forgiven
you.' Then the scribes and the Pharisees began to question, 'Who is this
who is speaking blasphemies? Who can forgive sins but God alone?'
When Jesus perceived their questionings, he answered them, 'Why do
you raise such questions in your hearts? Which is easier, to say, 'Your
sins are forgiven you,' or to say, 'Stand up and walk'? But so that you
may know that the Son of Man [this is one of Jesus' titles for himself,
adopting a Hebrew biblical honorific] has authority on earth to forgive
sins' — he said to the one who was paralyzed — 'I say to you, stand up
and take your bed and go to your home.' Immediately he stood up before
them, took what he had been lying on, and went to his home, glorifying
God. Amazement seized all of them, and they glorified God and were
filled with awe, saying, 'We have seen strange things today.'

One clarification is in order. The paralytic's "bed" is certainly not a four
poster, nor even a box spring and stuffed mattress. Other translations say
"mat," which would be closer to the customs of the time. So the paralytic
doesn't suddenly receive the superhuman strength to lift a huge piece of
furniture; what he receives from Jesus is a cure for his paralysis. At Jesus'
words, the paralyzed man can miraculously stand and walk. Not only this:
he can follow Jesus' directive to pick up his former bed of infirmity and to
"go home," to go about the normal business of living. No longer a victim or
invalid, he has been integrated into the functioning human community.

But notice precisely what Jesus' words to him were. Jesus doesn't say
"you are cured of your infirmity" but rather "your sins are forgiven you."
In Luke's Gospel, human sinfulness is our greatest infirmity. God's mercy
in forgiving our sins is the same power of love as God's mercy in healing a
physical ailment. And Jesus demonstrates this power, this mercy.

No wonder the religious authorities (the scribes and Pharisees) are
scandalized. And no wonder the ordinary people are filled with "amazement." They are seeing in Jesus the image of the invisible God! They all
"glorified God" — because in the healing power of Jesus they have seen
God's glory.

In John's Gospel, written later and attributing to Jesus a more fully
developed knowledge of his identity as God's Son, it is Jesus himself who
proclaims that his miracles make visible the glory of God. This is in fact
the key point in the dramatic account of what we might call Jesus' ultimate miracle: bringing his friend Lazarus back from death to life (John
11:1-44). The episode begins when Jesus, in another town, receives a message from Lazarus's sisters that Lazarus is ill. They are loyal friends of
Jesus and believe in his healing powers, so they naturally call on him when
their brother is seriously sick. But instead of rushing to Lazarus's aid, Jesus
responds by saying to his companions, "This illness does not lead to death;
rather it is for God's glory, so that the Son of God may be glorified through

it." And he actually hangs around where he is for two more days. Finally, when he is certain in his heart that Lazarus has died, he says to his disciples: "Lazarus is dead. For your sake I am glad I was not there, so that you may believe" — believe, that is, that he himself is the very image and power of the invisible God. "But let us go to him."

When Jesus arrives at Lazarus's village, Lazarus has been already been buried for four days in a cave that serves as a tomb. Lazarus's sister Martha, in her grief, rebukes Jesus for not having come sooner to save her brother's life, and the crowd around her shares her dismay at him. But Jesus responds: "Did I not tell you that if you believed, you would see the glory of God?" And he orders that the rock covering the cave's mouth be removed. Then he shouts "Lazarus, come out!" — and "the dead man came out, his hands and feet bound with strips of cloth, and his face wrapped in a cloth. Jesus said to them, 'Unbind him, and let him go.'"

To bring the dead back to life is surely the most wondrous of God's powers. Jesus performs this miracle literally in the raising of Lazarus, but in a sense all his acts of healing and forgiveness also free people from the bonds of a kind of death, restoring them to a new fullness of life. In the New Testament, infirmities of body (illness) and of spirit (sin) prevent people from the joyous freedom for which God created them. Jesus' call for Lazarus — 'Unbind him and let him go' — is his exhortation to all on whom he bestows his merciful power of healing and forgiveness.

It is also Jesus' exhortation to his followers throughout the ages. Christians believe that the healing, restorative power manifested by Jesus when he lived in the flesh remains active in the resurrected Christ — and also remains active in all who are baptized as Christians "in the name of the Father and the Son and the Holy Spirit" (as the baptismal rite puts it, quoting Matthew 28:19). In baptism, Christians are remade in the image of the Christ who is the image of the invisible God. As Christ's image and embodiment in their own day, Christians are empowered to go forth and continue his healing, forgiving, life-renewing mission. Christians are to be merciful as God is merciful, to forgive as God forgives, to love with God's infinite love — and through this mercy, forgiveness, and love they will be agents of God's healing power in the world. Through them, God's glory will continue to be made visible.

Matthew's Gospel has Jesus express it this way to his followers:

> You are the light of the world. A city built on a hill cannot be hid. No one after lighting a lamp puts it under the bushel basket, but on the lampstand, and it gives light to all in the house. In the same way, let your light shine before others, so that they may see your good work and give glory to your Father in heaven. (Matthew 5:14-16)

Here is another metaphor for God's glory: *light*. It is so rich a concept in the New Testament and in Christian self-understanding that it needs to be discussed in its own chapter. But before we move on, one comment seems called for on the title of this current chapter: *"Christ's beauty: 'He is the image of the invisible God.'"* The word "beauty" has not appeared in my discussion. That's because it is a word that scarcely occurs in the New Testament, and not at all with reference to Christ. Yet theologians from the earliest centuries to the present speak lavishly of "Christ's beauty," which they identify with his "glory" — and also, as we'll see in the next chapter, with his "goodness" and "truth."

Chapter 2b. The Transfiguration: "And his clothes became dazzling white"

The episode called "The Transfiguration" is recounted in three of the Gospels: by Matthew, Mark, and Luke. In all three, Jesus takes his disciples Peter, James, and John to a solitary place on a mountain top. There, "he was transfigured before them, and his face shone like the sun, and his clothes became dazzling white": this is how Matthew relates it. Mark is similar: Jesus "was transfigured before them, and his clothes became dazzling white, such as no one on earth could bleach them." Luke adds an interesting detail, that it was "while Jesus was praying" that this luminous transfiguration of his whole being occurred. Luke's implication is that the intense closeness of Jesus to God the Father in prayer was what shone through Jesus' body so brilliantly that even his clothes became dazzling white.

While watching the transfiguration in wonder, the startled disciples then see the long-dead prophets Moses and Elijah talking with Jesus. All three "appeared in glory," Luke says, using the word "glory" in place of Matthew and Mark's word "transfigured." Peter wants to cling to this marvelous moment, by building dwellings right there for the three glorified figures to remain in. But as soon as Peter utters this offer, "a bright cloud overshadowed them, and from the cloud a voice said, 'This is my Son, the Beloved; with him I am well pleased; listen to him!'" All three Gospel writers express in nearly identical words this astounding affirmation of Jesus' divine mission pronounced by God's own voice. And all relate the aftermath similarly: the disciples keel over in fear at hearing the very voice of God, and when they get the courage to look up again, they find themselves alone with Jesus. The transfiguring, glorifying moment has passed; Jesus is again their familiar companion, master, friend.

What has not passed, for them or for Christians (Christ's disciples) through the ages, is the imaging of Christ as brilliant, all-suffusing light. "I am the light of the world," Jesus says more than once in John's Gospel. John doesn't relate the Transfiguration episode, but he doesn't need to: Jesus walks throughout John's Gospel transfigured in divine light. He is the light shining in the world's darkness, which the darkness — whether of evil, suffering, or death — cannot overcome.

The many branches of Christianity that have developed over the centuries have found various ways of carrying on this symbolism of Christ as the light of our lives. For the Orthodox tradition, the Transfiguration episode is so central that Orthodox Christians picture their closeness to God as a *glow*. That is, just as Jesus in the Transfiguration became aglow with the intensity of his closeness to God the Father, so Christians share in that glow as they imitate Jesus at prayer. Orthodox worship also makes lavish use of candles — as does the worship of many other branches of Christianity. At regular Sunday worship in many Christian churches, two candles remain lit at the two ends of the altar or communion table. The lit candles symbolize the light of Christ as God's Presence always with us and guiding our way. At baptisms, as well, candles play a key role in some Christian traditions. During the baptismal rite, the newly baptized person (or her god-parent if she is a baby) is handed a lit candle with words such as "receive the light of Christ." Henceforth the new Christian will carry Christ's light in her very being, spreading its goodness and mercy through all her actions, all her life.

Most dramatically in my own Catholic Christian worship, on the Saturday night before Easter Sunday each year we light afresh a new large Easter candle. It is the most exciting, hope-filled moment of our church year, as we anticipate Christ's resurrection which Easter celebrates. The liturgy begins with the church in total darkness, symbolizing death's apparent conquest of the world at the crucifixion of Jesus, which we have commemorated on Friday. From a newly made charcoal fire, the priest lights the new Easter candle, saying "May the light of Christ, rising in glory, dispel the darkness of our hearts and minds." Then the priest or other minister lifts the lit Easter candle high and sings "Christ our light." With grateful hearts we all sing in response "Thanks be to God." Then as the Easter candle is carried in procession to the altar, members of the congregation nearby each dip the wick of a small candle into the Easter candle's flame; from their lit candles they pass the flame — the light of Christ — to the small hand-held candles of everyone around them. As we all then stand facing the altar, where the Easter candle now rests, holding our small flame and sensing ourselves bearers of a precious bit of Christ's light, we hear chanted this prayer to God:

> May the Morning Star which never sets find this flame still burning:
> Christ, that Morning Star, who came back from the dead,
> and shed his peaceful light on all humankind,
> your Son who lives and reigns for ever and ever.

"That Morning Star, who came back from the dead/ and shed his peaceful light on all humankind": this resurrected Christ is the joy and beauty of all Christians' faith. In raising Jesus from the dead, God enacted His power and promise of raising all of us to renewed life, out of the death and darkness of sin and sorrow which we all suffer as our human lot.

These images of light — candle, star, the brightness of bleached white garments — have helped Christians over the ages understand what the glory of God means to them personally, how their lives have been utterly changed by the wondrous gift of that glory coming to earth in Jesus and remaining with them always in the resurrected Christ. One particular canticle (or hymn) from the Gospel of Luke (1:68-79), beloved by many Christians, concludes with a verse linking God's gifts of light, compassion, and peace.

> In the tender compassion of our God
> the dawn from on high shall break upon us,
> to shine on those who dwell in darkness and the shadow of death,
> and to guide our feet into the way of peace.

This canticle is included in every day's Morning Prayer in the book called *Christian Prayer: The Liturgy of the Hours*, a four-week cycle of prayers and Bible readings produced by the Catholic church but used by other Christians as well. George and I pray from this book every morning and evening, along with Christians all over the world. Each morning when we recite the verse quoted above, in the prayer space that we've arranged at home, the early sunlight filtering through the blinds literalizes for me the hope expressed in this hymn. Here in a single verse are God's light, goodness, and beauty, blessing the start of my day. God's light is in "the dawn from on high," God's goodness in His "tender compassion" shining His love into our darkness, and God's beauty is in it all — but in a special way in "guiding our feet into the way of peace." For Christians can't hear this phrase without recalling the beloved line from the Hebrew prophet Isaiah (52:7): "How beautiful upon the mountains are the feet of the messenger who announces peace, who brings good news, who announces salvation, who says to Zion, 'Your God reigns.'" Biblical peace is the good news of God's reign, God's absolute power to save us from the forces of darkness and death. Any messenger of this good news walks with beautiful feet.

As I recite Luke's canticle each early morning, the beauty of God's saving care for us is represented further for me by a sculpture that George and I have placed on the floor in front of us in our prayer space. I commissioned it from a sculptor friend who specializes in images of the intricate divine/human relationship. In this particular piece, two gently curving abstract forms represent a mother cradling her baby. Gazing at the mother's spherical body protectively enfolding the fragile child, I see God enfolding all us fragile children in tender compassion. Through the hymn's words and the sculpture's visual representation, I'm drawn to contemplate God's goodness and beauty in offering, day after day with every new dawn from on high, exactly what our hearts yearn for: the goodness of God's compassion and the beauty of the promise of guidance into the way of peace.

My contemplation bubbles gratefully out of the wellspring of over two thousand years of Christian theological pondering about God's goodness, beauty, and light. The earliest Christian theologians, influenced by Plato, called these God's transcendent attributes, along with other divine attributes like oneness and truth. A sixth century theologian known as Pseudo-

Dionysius called them all God's "names," in a treatise he wrote titled *The Divine Names*. Pseudo-Dionysius put Beauty at the core of all the divine names, but he insisted that it is inseparable from the others. "Beauty unites all things and is the source of all things," he wrote. "It is the great creating cause which bestirs the world and holds all things in existence by the longing inside them to have beauty."

This is a marvelously compelling and inviting vision. Beauty is *God's* attribute, Pseudo-Dionysius is making clear; but God is Beauty for *us*, for all creation. All of creation's deep "longing" for Beauty "bestirs the world" into existence and into the heart of the living God. Without this foundational Beauty and our innate yearning for it, neither we nor anything that we know of would even exist. We are formed in and through and for Beauty, which Pseudo-Dionysius goes on to identify with "the Good" and with Christ himself, whom he names "the Beloved" — God's name for Jesus in the Gospel Transfiguration episode.[2] Pseudo-Dionysius's "Beauty" is indeed very much the Christ of the Transfiguration, dazzling white in divine glory. As Pseudo-Dionysius puts it: God has the name Beauty "because it is the cause of harmony and splendor in everything, because like a light, it flashes onto everything the beauty-causing impartations of its own well-spring ray."[3]

The contemporary theologian who has most influentially picked up this ancient focus on Beauty as the core attribute through which God calls all creation to Himself in Christ is the very one I was reading by that Florida beachfront: Hans von Balthasar. That long, difficult sentence of his which I was lured away from by the Gulf Coast's beauty seems a bit more comprehensible now, when I look at it in the light (so to speak) of Christian reflection on God's glory ever since the Gospels' account of the Transfiguration.

> Everything of beauty found in the world (and with it too the true and the good) is drawn up into a relationship to this inexhaustible standard, where the living God of love is glorified as He pours out His limitless love for the creature kenotically into the voice which is empty of Himself, indeed into what is strictly totally other than Himself: into the abyss of guilty, godless darkness and godforsakenness.

It's still quite a mouthful and mindful. But when I meditate on it as tranquilly as I gazed out at the Gulf Coast, I see all of creation transfigured by being drawn into the glorious light of "the living God of love." God's love is not without cost, however — for God Himself. The cost to God is a total self-emptying (this is what the word "kenotically" means). God pours Himself out into a world utterly other than Himself, a world of "guilty, godless

---

2. *The Classics of Western Spirituality, Pseudo-Dionysius, The Complete Works*, trans. Colm Luibheid. (New York: Paulist Press, 1987), 78.

3. Pseudo-Dionysius, *The Divine Names*, quoted by Roberta Bondi, "Surprised by Beauty," *The Christian Century* Aug.29-Sept.5, 2001.

darkness." God pours Himself — his beauty, goodness, truth, and limitless love — into the human form of Jesus Christ, who then becomes the willing, self-sacrificing victim of godless darkness.

This is why the Gospel episode of Jesus' Transfiguration takes place on his journey to Jerusalem, where Jesus will suffer crucifixion and death. On the mountaintop, his glory as the visible image of the invisible God is revealed to his disciples; brilliant divine light suffuses his being before their eyes. But when they all come down the mountain, Jesus alerts the disciples to the darkness to come, warning them that he'll soon "be betrayed into human hands." (This is Luke's wording; Matthew's is similar.)

This betrayal and the events of Jesus' crucifixion which follow from it are the height (or depth) of human ugliness. Yet, strange as this might sound, Jesus' suffering and death — what Christians call his Passion or his Cross — are not without their beauty.

Chapter 2c. The Beauty of the Cross: "Jesu, thy blood and righteousness/ My beauty are, my glorious dress"

George and I were driving home to Rochester, NY, from visiting family for the weekend. As is our custom, I was the driver so that he could read aloud to us (I get carsick reading on the road). That evening — it must have been about thirty years ago — he was reading from the New Testament. For me, these were entirely new texts; I'd scarcely ever looked at the Bible in my life. For George they were a bit more familiar, since he'd been studying the New Testament in recent months. Neither of us had grown up as Christians, but at that time we were beginning to be drawn toward the Christian faith, George in a spirit of open-hearted exploration, I with a lot of skeptical resistance.

He was reading from the Letter to the Romans:

> If we have died with Christ, we believe that we will also live with him. We know that Christ, being raised from the dead, will never die again; death no longer has dominion over him. The death he died, he died to sin, once for all; but the life he lives, he lives to God. So you also must consider yourselves dead to sin and alive to God in Christ Jesus. (6:11)

"That's just clever wordplay," I said irritably. "'Death is life' — it doesn't make any sense. And 'dying to sin' sounds like nonsense. What can it mean that Christ 'died to sin'?" I paused in my cranky scorn. Then more softly I conceded, "But I admit that I don't understand *anything* about Christ."

Now, over a quarter century after my baptism into the death and resurrection of Christ, I read a Scripture passage like this with grateful joy. Like many practicing Christians, I have several Crosses hanging in my home, and I carry a small one in my purse to finger when I need to be reminded of God's presence: when I need the reassurance that God, in Christ's Cross, not only accompanies all my sufferings but also gives me a share in his transformation of them into glorious eternal life.

Yet I know that for many non-Christians, the centrality of the Cross as Christian symbol seems to be a worshiping of death. "Look," they object, "you gaze at this instrument of torture that your God died on. How can such a negative image be an object of worship?"

I sympathize, since I once was equally baffled by the Cross.

Now when I gaze at it, what do I see? I see beauty.

I see, first, the beauty of self-sacrifice, of giving one's very self for another. God's very self is divinity, godliness. But in Jesus Christ he gave up his divinity to become human for our sakes, and not only to become human but to let himself become the victim of human evil — so that taking all human evil into himself, even to the point of his death, he could in Christ's resurrection bring all of humankind into eternal divine life with him.

The beauty of self-giving. We commend it all the time when we see it in another person. My neighbor gave herself over to nursing her father... "how beautiful of her," we admire. A teenager I know cleared out her closet and took heaps of clothes to a drop-in center in a poor section of town... "how beautiful of her," we admire. And here is a contemporary theologian on the beauty of God's self-giving: "God reveals His strength in the weak, His honor in lowliness, and His splendor in the cross of Christ. His glory is not the splendor of otherworldly superior power but the beauty of love which empties itself without losing itself and forgives without giving itself away."[4]

I treasure now these paradoxes that thirty years ago drove me wild. I treasure them because now I know that they aren't simply mind-games. They are the truths that enfold my daily life of stumblings and failings — and, yes, of sin — into God's transformative love. So this is the second facet of beauty that I see when I gaze at the Cross: that in Christ's suffering on the Cross, God gave himself over to our human ugliness and evil so as to transform them into a beauty that I can share in.

In the next chapter, I'll have more to say about the evil of human ugliness. For now I want to stay with how God both enters and transforms it in the Cross. Another contemporary theologian has put the transformative dynamic this way: "For our sake the beauty of God takes on ugliness."[5] And then he continues by quoting one of the earliest and greatest of Christian theologians, Augustine, who said of Christ that "His deformity is our beauty."

How does this dynamic work? How does Christ's deformity (his submitting himself to the grotesque torture of his crucifixion) become my beauty? The apostle Paul, author of many of the New Testament letters that were the first explorations of the meaning of Christ's suffering and death, offers this answer in his Letter to the Galatians (2:19-20): "I have been crucified with Christ; and it is no longer I who live, but it is Christ who lives in me. And the life I now live in the flesh I live by faith in the Son of God, who loved me and gave himself for me."

At our baptism, Christians believe, we die with Christ so as to be raised to new life in Him. We no longer live a separate, sinful existence ("it is no longer I who live"), but Christ now and forever lives in each of us. This is the gist of that passage from Paul's Letter to the Romans which I quoted at the start of this chapter and which thirty years ago so baffled me:

> If we have died with Christ, we believe that we will also live with him.

---

4. Jürgen Moltmann, *Theology and Joy* (London: SCM Press, 1973), 60.

5. Richard Harries, *Art and the Beauty of God* (London: Mowbray, 1993), 58, quoted in Gesa Elsbeth Thiessen, *Theological Aesthetics: A Reader* (Grand Rapids, Michigan: Eerdmans, 2004), 354.

> We know that Christ, being raised from the dead, will never die again; death no longer has dominion over him. The death he died, he died to sin, once for all; but the life he lives, he lives to God. So you also must consider yourselves dead to sin and alive to God in Christ Jesus.

"Alive to God." That means alive *in* God, living within the very beauty of God. Do my daily stumblings and failings then magically disappear? Certainly not! But acknowledging them repentantly, I return over and over to a life shared by the God who, in Christ, suffered the ugliness of death so as to conquer it for all humankind. The eighteenth century hymn that I quoted as this chapter's title expresses this core Christian gratitude for the Cross: *"Jesu, thy blood and righteousness/ My beauty are, my glorious dress."*[6]

"*My* beauty, *my* glorious dress." Yes. But the beauty of the Cross — and this is the third facet of it that I want to address — is that it *isn't* only "mine." The New Testament is crystal clear that Christ's sacrifice was made in order to reconcile all of humankind to one another and to God. The beauty of the Cross is the beauty of *reconciling* love.

Two of my favorite New Testament passages express this felicitously (I want to say "beautifully"). One is the end of that hymn from the Letter to the Colossians (1:12-20) that I mentioned at the very start of this chapter, the hymn that George and I were memorizing for Lent on the Florida seacoast. Remember that the hymn praises Christ as "the image of the invisible God," in whom "all things in heaven and on earth were created." After celebrating Christ as "the beginning, the firstborn from the dead," the hymn closes:

> For in him all the fullness of God was pleased to dwell,
> and through him God was pleased to reconcile to himself all things,
> whether on earth or in heaven,
> by making peace through the blood of his cross.

Here the focus is on the peace made between God and all creation, including sinful humankind. In Christ's blood on the cross, God "reconciled to Himself all things." In my other favorite passage about the Cross's reconciling function, peace among people is the theme. It comes in the Letter to the Ephesians (2:13-16), after an allusion to hostility that had arisen between Jews (who were the first followers of Jesus, since he himself was a Jew) and "Gentiles" (as non-Jews were called). The Ephesians to whom the Letter is addressed were Gentiles, who formerly were "without Christ, being aliens from the commonwealth of Israel." "But now," says the Letter, in this magnificent explication of the Cross's unique reconciling act,

> But now in Christ Jesus you who once were far off have been brought near by the blood of Christ. For he is our peace; in his flesh he has made

---

6. Thiessen, *Theological Aesthetics*, 163.

both groups into one and has broken down the dividing wall, that is, the hostility between us. He has abolished the law with its commandments and ordinances, that he might create in himself one new humanity in place of the two, thus making peace, and might reconcile both groups to God in one body through the cross, thus putting to death that hostility through it.

On one Friday morning each month, I read this passage aloud as part of the Morning Prayer that George and I pray at home from our four-week cycle of prayers and Scripture readings, *Christian Prayer: The Liturgy of the Hours*. Though I've read this passage in the context of Morning Prayer some three hundred times over the years, it never ceases to move me. The image of Christ "breaking down the dividing wall of hostility" between opposing peoples fills me with gratitude and hope. And the image always becomes concrete and personal for me: in it I see whatever hostile groups are clashing with each other at the moment — whether in my personal life or in the political world. I picture these hostile groups, and then I picture Christ "creating in himself one new humanity in place of the two, thus making peace" through the blood of his Cross. Of course, I know that the world is not fully at peace, and sometimes it seems scarcely at peace at all. But this absence of peace is our human failure. We fail to accept the reconciling peace which Christ has already created for us in giving himself as the ultimate sacrifice: in taking all our hostilities into himself and dying from them so that they could die along with him.

This is the beauty of the Cross as reconciling love. And it brings me to the final facet of the Cross's beauty which I'll touch on: the beauty of the resurrected Christ and the eternal life promised to us all through his resurrection. The Cross, for Christians, is not the end of the story. Christians do not "worship" the Cross. Quite the contrary. The core Christian belief is that Christ has "conquered death" (as the common phrasing of Christian worship puts it). God raised Christ from the dead, and now Christ lives forever in the heavenly bliss into which he invites us. He invites us into it even now, in our earthly lives, by dwelling within us to animate in us God's own love — though our imperfect human nature keeps us from letting this divine love live totally through us at each moment. But at our deaths we shall be free of our earthly impediments, and Christ then invites us fully into his resurrected life.

So any image of the Cross carries for Christians not only the beauty of Christ's self-sacrifice and of his reconciling love but also the beauty of the Resurrection. Indeed some Crosses over the centuries have been painted or sculpted actually to represent this resurrection joy and triumph right on the Cross itself. The most famous of these is the crucifix of San Damiano in Assisi, Italy, created probably in the twelfth century by an anonymous artist. The figure of Jesus on this Cross is not at all in pain. Rather, he looks outward and slightly upward with serene bliss, his arms open wide in a gesture of embrace to all who come to him. Surrounding him on this Cross are painted many symbolic figures, representing various elements of Christian belief. These needn't concern us here, except to understand that taken together they represent Christ's glorious triumph over all the evils of the universe, and his promise at the Last Judgment to bring the whole universe into the reign of his glory.

The beauty of the Cross. *"Jesu, thy blood and righteousness/ My beauty are, my glorious dress."* It is a beauty conceivable only in paradoxes. In Christ, God takes on our life (which includes our death) so that we can take on God's eternal life of unconditional love. I can't sum up the paradoxes of the Cross better than by quoting contemporary professor of theology Richard Viladesau's elegant articulation of them:

> The crucifixion as murder was ugly; as martyrdom it was beautiful. Physically it was ugly; spiritually—in its meaning, self-sacrifice for others — it was beautiful. What happened to Christ was ugly and horrid; his willingness to undergo it was beautiful.

And the title of Viladesau's book from which this quotation comes? *The Beauty of the Cross.*[7]

---

7. Richard Viladesau, *The Beauty of the Cross.* (New York: Oxford University Press, 2006), 12.

Chapter 2d. The Ugliness of Humankind: "Doing evil deeds"

> Woe to you Pharisees! For you tithe mint and rue and herbs of all kinds, and neglect justice and the love of God.... Woe also to you lawyers! For you load people with burdens hard to bear, and you yourselves do not lift a finger to ease them. (Luke 11:42, 46)

> Woe to you, scribes and Pharisees, hypocrites! For you are like white-washed tombs, which on the outside look beautiful, but inside they are full of the bones of the dead and of all kinds of filth. So you also on the outside look righteous to others, but inside you are full of hypocrisy and lawlessness. (Matthew 23:27-28)

> Now you Pharisees clean the outside of the cup and of the dish, but inside you are full of greed and wickedness. You fools! Did not the one who made the outside make the inside also? (Luke11:39-40)

These angry outbursts come from the mouth of Jesus in the Gospels. And what has kindled his strong, condemnatory language? Clearly it's the hideous behavior of people who have authority in the community but who use their authority to mistreat others.

The scribes (who were lawyers) and the Pharisees had the role of interpreting religious law for their Jewish community. This role gave them considerable power. What enrages Jesus is their oppressive and hypocritical use of this power. "Tithing," for instance, was the customary way of collecting taxes to support the Temple. Here Jesus castigates the Pharisees for tithing even the tiniest of things (herbs) while neglecting the huge imperatives of religious life: justice and the love of God. Injustice is also at the heart of Jesus' wrath against the lawyers. They interpret the law in its harshest, most burdensome sense while "not lifting a finger" to help people carry these burdens. (What Jesus doesn't explicitly say here, but which his Jewish hearers would be aware of, is that betraying the gracious spirit of God's law is a terrible offense. For the Jewish people, God's law — the Torah — was a beautiful gift, a source of uplifting joy for the community. "Oh, how I love your law!" sings Psalm 119; "I delight in the way of your decrees as much as in all riches.")

Jesus, a faithfully practicing Jew, is infuriated by any betrayals of the spirit of God's love for His people. And the worst betrayal, as he sees it throughout the Gospels, is hypocrisy. For Jesus, what characterizes hypocrisy is its insidious contrast between outside and inside. "On the outside you look righteous" and even "beautiful," he says scornfully to the scribes and Pharisees; but your beauty is like that of "white-washed tombs," which inside "are full of the bones of the dead and of all kinds of filth." Jesus' image is scathing in its vividness. Hypocrites are those who are rotting inside from their ugly deeds while on the outside they show to the world a veneer of beauty's righteousness. His image of the cup and dish makes a similar point. "You Pharisees," he inveighs, are scrupulous about keeping clean the outside of the vessels you eat from, yet in your very innards you are filthy, "full of greed and wickedness."

The ugly behavior of people in power receives Jesus' invective throughout the Gospels. But ordinary folks as well — all of us — are also called to account for the ways we behave toward others. Christians' favorite Gospel passage dramatizing this accounting is Matthew 25:31-46, where Jesus describes in gripping and poetic detail what will happen at the Final Judgment, when he will come in his glory as king to judge all people of all time.

> All the nations will be gathered before him, and he will separate people one from another as a shepherd separates the sheep from the goats, and he will put the sheep at his right hand and the goats at the left. Then the king will say to those at his right hand, 'Come, you that are blessed by my Father, inherit the kingdom prepared for you from the foundation of the world; for I was hungry and you gave me food, I was thirsty and you gave me something to drink, I was a stranger and you welcomed me, I was naked and you gave me clothing, I was sick and you took care of me, I was in prison and you visited me.'

These righteous people are understandably puzzled, since they don't recall ever doing these good deeds for Jesus. So he explains: "Truly I tell you, just as you did it to one of the least of these who are members of my family, you did it to me."

Then the king turns to those whom he has thrust, alas, to his left side, and with powerful poetic parallelism he berates them:

> You that are accursed, depart from me into the eternal fire prepared for the devil and his angels; for I was hungry and you gave me no food, I was thirsty and you gave me nothing to drink, I was a stranger and you did not welcome me, naked and you did not give me clothing, sick and in prison and you did not visit me.

Those hearing this condemnation are as puzzled as were the righteous; they don't recall ever ignoring or demeaning Jesus. And he gives them the parallel but opposing reply that he gave to the righteous: "Truly I tell you, just as you did not do it to one of the least of these, you did not do it to me." The scene concludes with the king's uncompromising words of final judgment: "And these will go away into eternal punishment, but the righteous into eternal life."

Christians today hear Matthew 25:31-46 read often during their worship, and never without a shudder. Always the familiar words are a wake-up call, a reminder: that the ways we treat one another — especially the most vulnerable among us, "the least of these who are members of my family" —

matters absolutely and ultimately. How we will spend eternal life depends on whether our behavior to others has been beautiful or ugly.

Christians' understanding of their responsibility for choosing between ugly and beautiful behavior begins with the biblical narrative of the Garden of Eden. As the story is told in Genesis (the opening book of the Bible), Adam and Eve disobey God's prohibition against eating from the tree of the knowledge of good and evil. As punishment for their disobedience, God not only expels them from the Garden forever but also consigns them to a life of toil and pain: the woman to pain in childbirth, the man to arduous work tilling the rough ground for his food. Furthermore, their days will end in "dust"; they will die. Christian theology calls this event "the Fall," because Adam and Eve fell away from God's grace. And the disobedience that caused their Fall came to be called "original sin."

Over the centuries, Christian theologians have developed varying ways of understanding how all of humankind participates in the Fall and in original sin. Clearly we humans have a propensity to sin, individually and collectively. But did we inherit this propensity genetically from Adam and Eve, our first parents? Or is the Genesis narrative a way of explaining what is obviously a human characteristic: the tendency to fall away from a harmonious relationship with God and with one another? These are not questions that can be answered; they are matter for theological speculation. But what is unquestionable is that we do live in a world where individual and collective evil are powerful forces. A frequent way for Christians to put this is to say that we live in "a fallen world."

A fallen world — but also a redeemed world. Because for Christianity the Fall is not the end of the story. God sent His Son Jesus into our world to save us from the damning consequences of our sinfulness. God became human in Jesus — was "incarnated," we say — in order to suffer the Fall's effects in his own flesh, even unto death, and then rise from this death into the everlasting life of God's glory. With Jesus, the human narrative takes on a new trajectory. We were created initially in the image of God; then through disobedience we fell from God's grace and became disfigured by sin; but in Christ we are re-made in God's image. As the First Letter to the Corinthians in the New Testament puts it: "Just as we have borne the image of the man of dust [Adam], we will also bear the image of the man of heaven [Christ]" (15:49).

Bearing Christ's image doesn't mean, however, that we automatically behave in holy ways. Not at all! It means that we have the power to choose Christ-like behavior, to act in the beautiful spirit of Christ, to treat all people (remember Matthew 25) as if they were God Himself: feeding the hungry, clothing the naked, visiting the sick and imprisoned. So the New Testament Letters, which were instructions to particular newly-forming Christian communities, praise good behaviors and strongly condemn the bad. Often the opposition between bad and good behavior is put in terms of "death" versus "life," or the "old self" (in Adam) versus the "new self" (in Christ). Here, for instance, is an instruction from the Letter to the Colossians (3:5-10):

> Put to death, therefore, whatever in you is earthly: fornication, impurity, passion, evil desire, and greed (which is idolatry). On account of these the wrath of God is coming on those who are disobedient. These are the ways you also once followed, when you were living that life. But now you must get rid of all such things — anger, wrath, malice, slander, and abusive language from your mouth. Do not lie to one another, seeing that you have stripped off the old self with its practices and have clothed yourselves with the new self, which is being renewed in knowledge according to the image of its creator.

In fact, so tightly is the injunction against evil behavior interwoven with God's gift to humankind in Christ, that the New Testament Letters move seamlessly between the two topics. As example, I want to take an earlier part of the Letter to the Colossians, a part including that passage with which I began this entire section on Christian beauty. On the Florida seacoast one winter during Lent, I mentioned, George and I were memorizing the hymn from this Letter which exalts Christ's beauty as "image of the invisible God." I returned to this hymn in Chapter 2c, when discussing the beauty of the Cross, because the hymn ends with the image of God reconciling all things to Himself through Christ, "making peace through the blood of his cross." Now, finally, I want to put these pieces together and add what follows right after them in the Letter to the Colossians. Because what follows immediately from Christ's reconciling self-sacrifice is an injunction directly to us: that we also must now be reconciled and turn from our evil ways. Here then is the whole of Colossians 1:15-23, as it is printed in prose in the New Revised Standard Version translation:

> He [Christ] is the image of the invisible God, the firstborn of all creation; for in him all things in heaven and on earth were created, things visible and invisible, whether thrones or dominions or rulers or powers — all things have been created through him and for him. He himself is before all things, and in him all things hold together. He is the head of the body, the church; he is the beginning, the firstborn from the dead, so that he might come to have first place in everything. For in him all the fullness of God was pleased to dwell, and through him God was pleased to reconcile to himself all things, whether on earth or in heaven, by making peace through the blood of his cross.
>
> And you who were once estranged and hostile in mind, doing evil deeds, he has now reconciled in his fleshly body through death, so as to present you holy and blameless and irreproachable before him — provided that you continue securely established and steadfast in the faith, without shifting from the hope promised by the gospel that you heard,

which has been proclaimed to every creature under heaven.

We have done "evil deeds." We are capable of continuing to do them. But through God's mercy we are also capable now of holiness. As the contemporary painter Makoto Fujimura wrote in response to the World Trade Center attacks on September 11, 2001, "We are the children of God in a disfigured age. Our call is to love in that condition. Our call is to see through the disfigurement and tragedy. This is the heart of the New Creation." And he added: "Theologically, the whole world, after our expulsion from Eden, is ground zero. But art can refill the world with the aroma of grace."[8]

Disfigured, evil, estranged and hostile: yes, humankind lives with this ugliness — such as the U.S. attack on Iraq, slaughtering thousands of innocents. But we also live in the New Creation, in the beauty of God's reconciling love in Christ. Let's pause here, at rest in the beauty. Let's put this beauty in dialogue with the beauty at the heart of Islam. When we return to Fujimura's art and words in Part Two, we'll have ample space to explore how, as he posits, "art can refill the world with the aroma of grace."

8. Makoto Fujimura, "Being a Child of the Creative Age," Refractions Essays blog, posted March 3, 2007 at www.makotofujimura.com.

Dialogue: A Muslim and a Christian compare their beauties

Muslim: So here we are in dialogue about our beauty. Our beauties. The beauty at the heart of Islam; the beauty at the heart of Christianity. Shall we begin with our affinities or our differences?

Christian: How about the affinities. Because they are dazzling, even (dare I say?) luminously beautiful.

Muslim: You're thinking about the Light?

Christian: Yes, I'm thinking about the Light. I'm seeing the Light. I'm capitalizing it because for both of us it is *God's* light, no? God's beauty shines for us as light. As the Light beyond lights. Would you agree?

Muslim: Naturally. We've heard the Qur'an's "Light Verse": "God is the light of heaven and earth.... Light upon light!" And we've heard from your ancient philosophers, like your Pseudo-Dionysius writing that God's name is Beauty "because Beauty is the cause of harmony and splendor in everything, because like a light, it flashes onto everything the beauty-causing impartations of its own well-spring ray."

Christian: Yes, but of course the authority backing up those two quotations isn't at all equal. The "Light Verse" comes from the Qur'an. Probably most Christians don't even know who Pseudo-Dionysius is.

Muslim: I suspected that. But I didn't want to mention the way Jesus is talked about in the Gospel of John as the "the light of the world" because right away we'd get stuck in our differences (my not believing that Jesus is divine), and we agreed not to do that here in the beginning.

Christian: So we did, and I appreciate your tact. I also appreciate the fact that the quotation from Pseudo-Dionysius paints a picture of God's beauty similar to the one in the "Light Verse." Is that another reason why you quoted it?

Muslim: It was. And also because both passages paint their pictures with wonderful energy of language. I like thinking of Beauty as "flashing" its "well-spring ray" upon everything. Yes, Dionysius may have a mixed metaphor there — flashing light and a watery well-spring. But the mixing of metaphors gives a vivid feeling of the sheer power of God's beauty. And that's important, because God's beauty isn't cool and aloof. It scintillates, even flows with creative force.

Christian: Scintillates and flows — I like that. But God's beauty doesn't do all this scintillating and flowing just to please itself. God's beauty acts with purpose.

Muslim: I agree. For example,...

Christian: Wait! Let me spell out what the purpose seems to me to be, and then you tell me if it's what you have in mind. Alright?

Muslim: Sure! Go ahead.

Christian: Well, then, here goes: the purpose of God's beauty — which the Qur'an and Pseudo-Dionysius (in fact, the whole of Christianity's 2,000 years of tradition and practice) both speak of in terms of light — isn't simply to illumine the things of this world, including the people in it. Beauty's purpose is to bring about a kind of responsive beauty in those things. That's why Dionysius talks about beauty's being "the cause of harmony and splendor in everything," and about the light's "beauty-causing impartations."

Muslim: And the "Light Verse"? Exactly how is it similar? I'm teasing you here. I'm curious to see how far Christianity can go in accepting the "Light Verse."

Christian: Oh, all the way! There's nothing about the "Light Verse' that gives me problems. Just the opposite. I love it! What I especially love about the "Light Verse" is the way it lays out a kind of trajectory for God's beauty, moving step by step from beyond heaven and earth, descending to kindle an oil lamp which becomes the human heart, producing an answering light in that heart, a light that illumines the path back to the source of the light, to God's Divine Essence.

> God guides to God's light
> The one God wills to guide
> And the one who wills to be guided ...

There's nothing about that descending movement of the Light and the ascending movement in response that Christians can't accept. The idea of guidance towards the Light is powerful for me too. In fact, Christians through the ages have evoked this image every time they recite in their prayers that canticle from Luke's Gospel that we heard some of. Remember, the last verse goes like this:

> In the tender compassion of our God
> the dawn from on high will break upon us
> to shine on those who dwell in darkness and the shadow of death
> and to guide our feet into the way of peace.

Muslim: That's beautiful, and very Qur'anic, I mean not only in the image of guidance, but in the reference to God as compassionate—*ar-Raheem*. But you'd interpret the Light of that dawn as Jesus himself, wouldn't you?

Christian: Yes, I would, but let's hold off on that a little longer, alright?

Muslim: I agree. I just asked that for clarification. You see, I've resolved to try to think about God as Christianity does. It isn't easy, let me tell you, because of the centuries of polemic between us. All that negative baggage makes it hard to stand in your shoes looking towards God from your perspective without feeling I'm betraying my own perspective. Even talking about my beliefs as a "perspective" seems a betrayal.

Christian: I know what you mean. I have the same struggle when I try to stand in your shoes. But how can we dialogue unless we take risks like this?

Muslim: We have to take them, we're both convinced of that. But let's build our bridge solidly first before putting weight on it.

Christian: Using our affinities like bricks in that bridge, right? Well, here maybe is another, something else that came to mind as I was reciting the "Light Verse" just now, I mean the part about how God wills to guide certain people to his Light and about how some of us are willing to be guided. What struck me is that this implies there are some who refuse to be guided.

Muslim: I see where you're going. But it's more than an implication. It's a real and terrible possibility. We both use the same metaphor for it: darkness.

Christian: Fine! Brick upon brick. Here's another: We both say that Judgment awaits those who disappear into the darkness. We both speak of Hell — and of course also of Heaven: places of eternal separation from God and places of eternal connection with Him. And we both speak of our free will — our power either to receive God's beauty or reject it — as itself a gift of God.

Muslim: Yes, although the Qur'an doesn't put it that way. It says that this gift is God's *ruh* or spirit, an attribute of God bestowed upon us. It's an energy of self-guidance, you might say, which in God always turns itself in the right direction, towards the Light. But in human beings it often veers off course. Although...hmm...

Christian: What's the matter?

Muslim: Just the way I said that. Misleading. I made God sound like a human being, an exceptionally good one, to be sure. But still a human being. I know I talked that way only to make a point, but I'm still uncomfortable. It comes too close to what the Qur'an calls *shirk*, idolatry. No problem for you, though, because while for us both Jesus was a human being, for you, though, Jesus was, well...

Christian: "God," you mean...

Muslim: Yes, but...

Christian: Wait. Back up. We're not ready to go there, not yet. There's still an important affinity we need to lay down before that.

Muslim: Which is?

Christian: Well, whether we call it free will or *ruh*, we're still talking about a power God has given us to become like Him in beauty. Call it a principle of correspondence. We might not be able fully to explain how the principle works, but we both believe that it does work. For example, the way you talk about the Beautiful Names— these for you aren't simply attributes of God that you sit back and admire from a distance. They're qualities that God allows you to emulate. Isn't that so?

Muslim: I see what you're getting at. Of course it's so. And if I'm not mistaken, this is the way Jesus works for you — or one way he works for you. As the source of divine attributes which you then imitate after your own fashion and capacity.

Christian: Yes, that's right. Jesus is my model for imitation. But he is more than that; my belief is that he actually dwells within the life of every Christian. So maybe it's here that we have to change direction and look at the way my understanding of beauty is different from yours. For example, my way of understanding is more... it has greater...

Muslim: What's the matter? Why are you hesitating? No... don't say a word. I'll bet it's the same question that's been haunting me throughout this dialogue. What's making us both hesitate is the challenge of expressing a difference without at the same time expressing a judgment.

Christian: And there's the opposite trap we can fall into if we tiptoe around our differences, either by failing to name them fully or else by pretending that they don't really matter. We're caught between a rock and a hard place.

Muslim: You really think we're at an impasse here? That God wants us to freeze in fear of our first difficulty? I keep thinking of a verse from the Qur'an that says, "We have made you different tribes and nations so that you might come to know each other. The noblest of you are those most conscious of God." The point of that verse is to encourage us to look at our differences as opportunities for greater self-understanding, not as threats to our security. So that's why I'm urging you to complete the sentence you started a little while ago. "My way of understanding beauty is more..." or something like that. If your way of expressing the difference forces you into a judgment on me, then I'll help you get past it. And you'll do the same for me, because as I said, I face the exact same problem when I try to talk about my difference from you.

Christian: Thank you. Well then, as you were speaking I kept thinking about the risen Christ coming to his fearful disciples, saying, "Peace be with you." Now right here...

Muslim: Excuse me for interrupting. But that phrase, in Arabic, is *Assalaam aleykum.* " This is the same phrase with which Muslims greet each other.

Christian: Fascinating! Because Jesus almost certainly spoke Aramaic, a Semitic language very close to Arabic. So probably Jesus' words to his disciples sounded a lot like the words Muslims use with each other.

Muslim: Very likely! And the Arabic words for "Source of Peace," one of the Beautiful Names listed earlier, is *as-salaam*, the One who brings peace and wholeness.

Christian: This brings me right back to the point I was trying to make. God's beauty comes to me now in the form of peace, *salaam*: initially as release from fear, but then further as Christ's breathing the Holy Spirit onto and into his disciples. So that henceforth God's beauty invites me to participate in the very life of God. And through God's grace and my own assent to that grace, I am able to know *salaam*, because this *salaam* is God's very own. But you would never say that this attribute becomes part of you in the same way as Christ's peace through the Holy Spirit becomes part of me, would you? You wouldn't say (as I do) that God's peace "dwells within you."

Muslim: No, I definitely would not. I could not describe the action of *as-salaam* as — how do you say it? — as "inviting a participation in God's life." Well, words get in our way here. I could say that it all depends on what you mean by "participation." I certainly can't accept that the prophet Jesus is part of God or is God or however you say it. Nor can I accept that the holy spirit is God. The spirit is a power or attribute of God, as I said. Or more accurately a way of being God or acting as God, but no more.

Christian: But even so, for humankind, the result of sharing that activity is to be able to exercise God's *ruh* as human moral choice? God's doing transformed into human doing?

Muslim: I'm a little uneasy with putting it that way. Moral choice exists, but it is at the same time God's gift. So in the deepest sense I would have to say that *all* is God's doing, even our capacity to exercise God's *ruh*. That is why the Qur'an says, and we repeat in all our prayers, "There is no god but God." Yet saying so does not deny human free will.

Christian: Hm. May I should approach this from another direction. Would you speak of a sharing in God's beauty through an activity of God rather than through the person of God?

Muslim: Hmm. These words get slippery. "Activity," "person"... something like that, I suppose. Listen: I think we're bumping up against a theological door we're not going to be able to open very much farther.

Christian: At least not directly, and not now. I agree. But it isn't the only door. Let's go in a more promising direction: back to the sentence you wanted me to finish: "My way of understanding beauty is more..." Let's see where we can go with it.

Muslim: Go ahead! I've been waiting for this.

Christian: My way of understanding beauty is more...personal than yours, more intimate, more... heartbreaking...

Muslim: Let me help you out. I think there are a lot of problems with what you say here. But there's at least this. I understand that God's beauty for you is inseparable from the life, death, and resurrection of Jesus Christ, whom you call Son of God. I understand that God's beauty emerges for you from the details of a divine life lived also as a human life. And that this human life ended terribly, in the shame and torture and ugliness of crucifixion, but that it rose transformed in light through resurrection. And that all believers are invited to rise in this light with him. So when you use words like personal, intimate, heartbreaking, you're getting at your sense of identification with this divine life lived in a vulnerability just like that of any other person. Am I on the right track?

Christian: Yes, you certainly are. But now I'm uncomfortable with the way I used "more," as in *more* personal, *more* intimate... because I don't think it's a case of my way of understanding God's beauty as *more* personal or more intimate or more whatever than yours. I think it's more accurate to say that the personal quality, the intimacy, is of a different kind. Or at least that these qualities have a different tone.

Muslim: Explain.

Christian: Well, one way to say it might be this: your understanding of God's beauty as personal and intimate seems to me more serene, more distanced than mine tends to be. Why would this be?

Muslim: I'd say it has to do with the way God speaks in the Qur'an. His voice isn't a disembodied one, coming out of nowhere. The Qur'an speaks to the heart, to the Prophet Muhammad's heart first, but then to all humanity's. And it speaks to specific situations and specific needs. Often those needs are the Prophet's own, as he struggles with those who resist God's word. And for Jacob and Joseph in the Qur'an, God's presence is certainly intimate. Yet though God does speak intimately to humankind through the Prophet, God's voice in the Qur'an comes from an unimaginable distance above his creation, from a divine realm of timeless perfection and omniscience. It's through God's mercy — God as *ar-Raheem* — that God enters into humankind's present confusion and forgetfulness and willful blindness.

Christian: Ah, now I see. Whereas for me, God as Jesus Christ enters right directly into the tumult of the human condition and speaks to us from his own direct experience there as a human being.

Muslim: Yet your beauty has serenity, too. The tone of your Gospel of John catches some of that serenity in its portrayal of Jesus as present at the creation and actually as the creative principle, what you call the *logos*, the Word. How does the Gospel of John start? "In the beginning was the Word..."?

Christian: Exactly. And I do see how the Gospel of John could sound Qur'anic. But there's still another element in my relation to God's beauty that we haven't talked about yet, an element I don't seem to share with you. I'm speaking of the heartbreaking quality of Jesus' suffering and death on the Cross. Am I correct in saying that almost by definition you cannot speak of God's beauty as having a dimension of suffering?

Muslim: That's correct. I cannot associate God with suffering. That would be *shirk*, that would be breaking down the barrier between creator and created. And yet it's not correct to say that I don't understand how beauty could express a dimension of suffering. The sufferings in the life of the Prophet Muhammad, peace and blessing be upon him, are beautiful and inspiring because of the gracious way he bore them. And Shi'a laments for the martyred grandson of the Prophet Muhammad, Husayn, certainly catch, and catch beautifully, a heartbreaking tone. Yet what's lamented isn't God's suffering, but the exemplary and redemptive suffering of Husayn, victim of the very evils of tribalism, greed, and envy the Qur'an warns me about. For me, there's much in the beauty of these laments that reminds me of the way you speak of the beauty of the Cross.

Christian: Thank you for the correction. But words are tripping us up again, aren't they. Your use of the word "redemptive," for example. I'm sure we mean different things by it.

Muslim: We do. But can we wait to talk about what the difference is?

Christian: Alright, but let's not forget it.

Muslim: "Forgetting" is not something I can easily do! Another name for the Qur'an is *al-dhikr*, the Remembrance. And God in the Qur'an says, "I'll remember you if you remember me." Remembering too is beautiful!

Christian: I agree.

Muslim: And if we look at the use of the rosary in the two traditions we might see further resemblances in our ways of enlisting memory in our desire for union with Truth.

Christian: How do you mean?

Muslim: We use our beads to remind that part of our heart, which is in time and space, of its everlasting spiritual counterpart. By the remembrance through repetition of the Beautiful Names, and especially the name Allah, we rhythmically remind our lower selves of our true perfected nature, veiled by our distracted lives. We call that perfected nature our *fitrah*, or primordial norm.

Christian: Just as Roman Catholics and others use our rosary to remind us of how we are perfected through union with Christ, in suffering, death, and glorious resurrection.

Muslim: Such different understandings of perfection, but such similar longings for it.

53

Christian: May we both reach our heart's desire.
Muslim: *Ameen* to that.

Moving On:
And what does this have to do with
the life of the arts and the art of life?

Here we are in our own voices now, George and Peggy, offering some thoughts on how the beauty of these two faiths opens up into the lives of the faithful. "God made everything that he created beautiful," says the Qur'an in *Sura al-Sajdah* 32:7. So, "act beautifully, as God has acted beautifully towards you" (*Sura al-Qasas* 28:77). And a *hadith* elaborates: "God is beautiful and He loves beauty." Commenting on this *hadith*, Muslim scholar Seyyed Hossein Nasr says that "to beautify things is to see God's beauty reflected in things and therefore to turn to God."[1]

"Act beautifully." "Beautify things." These are Islam's imperatives. For Christians, the imperative — no, "inspiration" would better catch Christianity's tone — the inspiration comes from two foundational biblical motifs. First there is the creation narrative at the very beginning of the Bible. After creating the earth and the waters, the sun and the moon, the animals and birds and plants, God says in Genesis 1:26 "Let us make humankind in our image." And 1:27 follows with: "So God created humankind in His image." Christian artists hear this foundational statement as charging them to live and act in the image of their Creator — that is, to become creators themselves. As Christian poet and essayist Luci Shaw puts it in an essay called "Beauty and the Creative Impulse," "God made us human beings in his image; we participate in creative intelligence, giftedness, originality." Therefore, "we were each, in the image of our Creator, created to create, to call others back to beauty."[2]

By no means does this imply, however, that human creativity is equal to God's. In her book *Breath for the Bones*, Shaw explains the distinction. "Though we cannot produce something out of nothing, as God did, we can combine the elements and forms available to us in striking and original ways that arise out of the unique human ability (designed and built into us by God) to imagine, to *see pictures in our heads…* to hear sounds and rhythms and recognize patterns and to translate them into forms that will

---

1. Seyyed Hossein Nasr, "Islamic Art" in *Islam and the West*, The Modern Scholar Series (Prince Frederick, Maryland: Recorded Books, 2004).

2. Luci Shaw, "Beauty and the Creative Impulse," in *The Christian Imagination*, ed. Leland Ryken, (Colorado Springs: Waterbrook Press, 2002), 90, 99.

strike a chord in the hearts of other human beings. In art and creativity, we make visible to others the beauty and meaning God has first pictured, or introduced, into our imaginations."[3]

The second foundational biblical motif inspiring Christians to creative work is one we're already familiar with from Chapter Two. It's the core belief formulated in Colossians 1:15, that "Christ is the image of the invisible God, the firstborn of all creation." And further that "all things have been created through him and for him" (verse 17). Christians are baptized into the very life of Christ and hence are commissioned to carry on his life in their own environments and through their own particular God-given gifts. The Catholic Archbishop of Mechelen-Brussels, Godfried Cardinal Danneels, talks about Christian creativity in an interview in the journal *Image* (#54: Summer, 2007, 3-33). Recalling that Jesus is "the image of the invisible God," Danneels notes that art, too, "is saying what can't be said and seeing what can't be seen." Through faith we are enabled to "see," in a sense, "what is not visible. But we can't do without what is visible." We need art, he stresses, because "art gives us the power to bring forth something that the senses wouldn't otherwise perceive."

Interestingly, Professor Seyyed Hossein Nasr made a similar point in his interview for the book *The Inner Journey: Views from the Islamic Tradition*. "The function of art, according to its Islamic conception, is to ennoble matter," Nasr said. "Islam as a religion emphasizes beauty and as a civilization was always based on the attempt to create beauty. Beauty is a way of access to God."[4]

We cannot, Nasr insists, flourish without beauty, the beauty that God calls on us to make, to enact, to live. Christian theologians and artists would wholeheartedly agree. Nasr's elaboration of this point would be largely comfortable for Christians, too, though Nasr puts it in a characteristically Muslim way, with his evocation of memory, of Paradise, of God's infinity.

> There is something in us that seeks beauty, and the reason for that is twofold. First of all, we still carry within ourselves the perfect nature with which we're created...paradisiacal nature...something of the memory of the Edenic state. And therefore we have a kind of thirst for what we really are. We are looking for ourselves, and that self was always impregnated by beauty. It was inundated, that self in Paradise, by beauty. Secondly, as a consequence, we cannot evade being what we are, there is something of the infinite in us, our being opens up to the infinite...Beauty is really a kind of echo of that infinity. Beauty for a moment breaks the bond of limitation, breaks the chain with which we are shackled, and therefore our soul thirsts for beauty.

---

3. Luci Shaw, *Breath for the Bones* (Nashville: Thomas Nelson, 2007), 18.
4. William Chittick, ed., *The Inner Journey: Views from the Islamic Tradition*. Parabola Anthology Series. (Sandpoint, ID: Morning Light Press, 2007), 71.

Christians would want to qualify "the perfect nature with which we're created" by pointing to our sullying of this perfection by our fall from grace in the Garden. And they would add, as Cardinal Danneels does, that "the greatest artist was Jesus. With his whole life he pointed to something greater, something deeper — to the truth.... Such beauty disarms us when we find it. It shows us our own possibility and opens us to what lies beyond ourselves."

But there is a deep resonance between the two faiths in the centrality that they give to beauty — and to the arts as making visible the beauty whose only fullness can be God. For both faiths, art's mission is to call and recall us to the infinity that is the true reality and meaning of our lives. As Nasr eloquently phrased it above: beauty is "a kind of echo of that infinity."

Nasr draws on the tradition of one of Islam's greatest philosopher of the spirituality of beauty, Ibn 'Arabi, who lived in 12th-13th century Andalusian Spain and was a poet himself. Ibn 'Arabi's vision of the artist as God's instrument for making visible God's beauty is expressed in these lines from one of his poems:

When my Beloved appears to me,
with which eye do I see Him?
With His eye, not with mine:
for none sees Him but Him![5]

Since for Ibn 'Arabi, God constructed the universe as a work of art, the artist (the poet in this case) is uniquely gifted in expressing this artistry in terms that human beings can grasp and respond to.

The prolific Christian writer Madeleine L'Engle, who died in 2007, had a similar sense of her art unfolding naturally from her faith. In *Walking on Water: Reflections on Faith and Art*, she wrote: "My feeling about art and my feelings about the Creator of the Universe are inseparable. To try to talk about art and about Christianity is for me one and the same thing, and it means attempting to share the meaning of my life, what gives it, for me, its tragedy and its glory. It is what makes me respond to the death of an apple tree, the birth of a puppy, northern lights shaking the sky, by writing stories."[6]

As L'Engle continues her reflection, there is a particularly Christian cast in her statement that "to paint a picture or to write a story or to compose a song is an incarnational activity." But while "incarnation," as we've noted throughout Chapter Two, holds for Christians the entire belief that

---

5. Ibn 'Arabi, *Futu'ha't al-Makkiyya*, quoted in Pablo Beneito, "On the Divine Love of Beauty," *Journal of the Muhyiddin Ibn 'Arabi Society*, Vol. XVIII (1995): 1.

6. Madeleine L'Engle, *Walking on Water: Reflections on Faith and Art* (New York: Bantam Books, 1980), 16. The quotations that follow are from pp. 18-28.

God became human in Jesus Christ, so that it is through Christ's incarnation that all matter and all human shaping of matter is ennobled, Islam's conception of art's purpose is also, as we heard Nasr say just above, "to ennoble matter." And while L'Engle goes on to see Mary's conception and birthing of Jesus as the model of the artist's relation to God, she does so in terms that are comfortable and even key for Muslims: *obedience, service,* and *patience.*

> The artist is a servant who is willing to be a birthgiver. In a very real sense the artist (male or female) should be like Mary who, when the angel told her that she was to bear the Messiah, was obedient to the command.... The artist must be obedient to the work, whether it be a symphony, a painting, or a story for a small child. I believe that each work of art, whether it is a work of great genius, or something very small, comes to the artist and says, 'Here I am. Enflesh me. Give birth to me.' And the artist either says [as Mary did in the Gospel of Luke], 'My soul doth magnify the Lord,' and willingly becomes the bearer of the work, or refuses; but the obedient response is not necessarily a conscious one... As for Mary, she was little more than a child when the angel came to her; she had not lost her child's creative acceptance of the realities moving on the other side of the everyday world."

Those "realities moving on the other side of the everyday world" are the realities of God's being, the "infinity" that Nasr spoke of when he said that "beauty is really a kind of echo of that infinity." How to hear that echo, how to listen for God's voice reverberating through our own beings, is for L'Engle the essence of the creative process.

> When the artist is truly the servant of the work, the work is better than the artist; Shakespeare knew how to listen to his work, and so he often wrote better than he could write; Bach composed more deeply, more truly than he knew; Rembrandt's brush put more of the human spirit on canvas than Rembrandt could comprehend. When the work takes over, then the artist is enabled to get out of the way, not to interfere. When the work takes over, then the artist listens. But before he can listen, paradoxically, he must work. Getting out of the way and listening is not something that comes easily, either in art or in prayer.... I must pray [the words of prayer] daily, whether I feel like praying or not. Otherwise, when God has something to say to me, I will not know how to listen."

"Someone wrote," L'Engle continues, that 'the principal part of faith is patience.'" *Beautiful patience!* We recall from Chapter One that this is a key Muslim virtue. For L'Engle this virtue must operate in faith and in art alike. "We must work every day, whether we feel like it or not, otherwise when it comes time to get out of the way and listen to the work, we will not be able to heed it."

The discipline of art as prayerful work: as we'll find in Chapter Three, this is the discipline of those Muslims who, for instance, devote themselves to chanting the Qur'an in particular traditional styles, or the discipline of other Muslims who painstakingly transmit the Qur'an's holy words through calligraphic art. For Christians, the art form which most consciously melds prayer into its creative process is the icon-painting tradition of Eastern Orthodox Christianity. In this tradition, Jesus or Mary or one of the saints is painted — but not representationally. Rather, it is the *quality* of holy life that the iconographer tries to transmit, through his own discipline of prayer and effort to "get out of the way" of the work (as Madeleine L'Engle put it). The icon in the Eastern Orthodox Christian tradition becomes, L'Engle writes, "an open window through which we can be given a new glimpse of the love of God."

"All true art," she adds, "has an iconic quality." *True art*: it's a phrase we must pause over and ponder. Not all that passes for art has either truth or beauty or goodness. But how to distinguish true art from false, good art from bad, beauty in art from mere prettiness?

We can start with a few basic criteria. Art that is merely pious and sentimental — that simply repeats the formulae or familiar images of a faith — is bad not because it's evil but because it doesn't move us anywhere new. One reader of a blog that Peggy writes for (at www.imagejournal.org), Heather Goodman, commented helpfully on this distinction: "one of the key differences between sentimentality and beauty is the ability to transform. While sentimentality indulges emotions (and we leave unchanged, happy only to have laughed or cried), beauty moves us. We have to do something with it, to respond to it in some way." So beauty in art is transformative; it elicits a response in us that will be unexpected, fresh — opening that window that L'Engle spoke of "through which we can be given a new glimpse of the love of God."

All the art that we'll be discussing in the following chapters is "good art" in the transformative sense suggested above. It is good both aesthetically and morally; indeed, a point of Parts II and III alike is that the "truly good" — whether of art or of human behavior — manifests the inseparable aesthetic and moral dimensions contained in the concept of beauty offered in Part I. This is why we'll be able to speak of "art's beauty": because the art we're presenting reaches toward the beauty of the God who longs to draw all his creatures and their creations to Himself.

Art that is true, good, beautiful: it has that "iconic quality" noted by L'Engle. It opens a window onto the wonders of the God who for Islam carries names that include The Truth, The Beneficent, the Beautiful One. So to lead us into these arts, a poem specifically *about* an icon seems appropriate. American Orthodox Christian poet Scott Cairns has written many poems about icons. In this one, called "Nativity," he is standing before an icon depicting the traditional image of Mary holding the newborn Jesus. The poem begins:

As you lean in, you'll surely apprehend
the tiny God is wrapped
in something more than swaddle. The God
is rightly bound within
His blesséd mother's gaze — her face declares
that she is rapt by what
she holds, beholds, reclines beholden to.
She cups His perfect head
and kisses Him, that even here the radiant
compass of affection
is announced, that even here our several
histories converge and slip,
just briefly, out of time....[7]

"Our several histories converge and slip,/ just briefly, out of time." This is what good art informed by faith does for us: it takes us "just briefly out of time." It takes us to those "realities moving on the other side of the everyday world," which Madeleine L'Engle spoke of. It takes us to our true self, as Seyyed Hossein Nasr described it, to our "paradisiacal nature" which "was always impregnated by beauty" but which we so easily forget.

"If religion is not beautiful, it is not religion," writes scholar Khaled Abou el Fadl in *The Search for Beauty in Islam*.[8] If our lives are not beautiful, they are not religious lives. And art? As we'll see in the chapters that follow, art informed by religious faith transmits the beauty of that faith — with all the surprising, even startling dimensions of that beauty.

7. From sequence "Two Icons," *Compass of Affection: Poems New and Selected* (Brewster, MA: Paraclete Press, 2006).

8. Khaled Abou el Fadl, *The Search for Beauty in Islam* (Lanham, MD: Rowman & Littlefield, 2005) 84.

PART II. ART IN ISLAM AND CHRISTIANITY

CHAPTER 3: ART INFORMED BY MUSLIM FAITH

Chapter 3a. The Beauty of Voice: The Qur'an as God's Art

I first experienced Islam as a voice.

It took a long time before I began to experience that voice as beautiful, so undeveloped was my ear for its particular beauty. But once I began (by God's grace) to teach my ear to listen, I caught beauty's first echo. Because beauty draws us to itself, I kept listening, and my capacity to listen improved. It continues to improve — into ever-deepening awareness of God's presence to us through that voice.

The voice I speak of is the voice of the Qur'an. As I said in Part I, the Qur'an is preeminently "the reciting," the vocal transmission through the Prophet Muhammad of God's own words, in Arabic, as addressed to the local community of Muhammad's hometown of Mecca, but also to every community of the world, past, present, and still to come.

The Qur'an, as the vehicle for the beautiful revelation of God, could be thought of as one of the many forms of God's art. As a voice, the Qur'an calls for response, a voice in answer, but ideally a voice as beautiful (given human limitations) as its own. The art of Muslims (the effort to form that beautiful response) is therefore essentially vocal, even when expressed visually, in calligraphy, primarily, but also in decoration and architecture. The art of Muslims serves the primacy of what is heard: not simply to recall what is taken in through the ear, but to make manifest the ways what is heard softens and changes the heart.

I can pinpoint exactly when and where I first realized that the Qur'an was God's art, or creation.

It hit me as soon as I opened the door of the Islamic Center of Rochester on a certain Saturday afternoon in the summer of 1994. I was stopped right there on the threshold by someone chanting the Qur'an in *tajwid*.

How to convey the expressive quality of *Tajwid*? "Operatic" is entirely misleading. If you've had the luck to hear beautiful renditions of Gregorian chant, you'll have some idea of the tonal purity and disciplined freedom of *tajwid*. *Tajwid*, we might say, is the exploration by the human voice of the Qur'an's vast potential for vocalization. Yet even "vast" is too small a word. And "potential" when used of God's revelation is nonsensical. There is no limit to the Qur'an's nuances and ramifications. It is God Himself who speaks in the Qur'an. It is God's voice we hear, God's and no other. Yet here too words fail.... For while no one else speaks in the Qur'an, unless God Himself reports that speech, the Qur'an itself is not God's speech directly, but God's speech as recited. It was recited first, according to tradition, by the angel Gabriel to the prophet Muhammad, then recited through the instrumentality of Muhammad's human voice to Muhammad's companions, and then through the voice of every other reciter till the very last reciter of all reciting to the last human listener.

Yet these recitings, while moving forward in time, are not dependent on or coextensive with time, because their source is eternal. The last reciting loops back to the first for all are comprehended by God. That is why the word *qur'an* refers to the action of reciting rather than its result, to the presentness of God's in-breaking Word rather than to its trace or text. The Qur'an or the Reciting is a living breath, first God's, then the angel's, then Muhammad's, then ours, then God's again. The Qur'an is a divine exhalation and inhalation.

The passage of that divine breath reaches down even into dusty corners.

It reaches down even into the corner at the back of Rochester's Islamic Center where for the previous two years I had been trying to imitate the dry, methodical, droning, metronomic *tartil* or schoolbook style of reciting practiced by my heroically patient Qur'an teacher, Siddiq. He and I had been grinding along through the Qur'an for months in *tartil*, he setting the plodding pace for each line and then correcting me again and again for not pronouncing correctly the many and varied gutturals and palatals, for not holding the vowel sounds out for the required beats, for not properly thickening tongue and throat around double consonants.

So when the sounds of *tajwid* reached my ear on that afternoon at the Islamic Center, the Reciting — the Qur'an — assumed a totally different dimension, or rather seemed to come from a different place. It seemed to come not from a schoolroom and a rulebook, but from a light-filled region between heaven and earth. It was not played on a broken or unsuitable human instrument, but through the most supple of membranes. This Qur'an was a breathing with God, in conversation with Him.

"Oh, so *that's* what it sounds like," I nodded to myself as I stood listening in the Islamic Center's foyer. "*That's* what it's supposed to be." I meant that the reciting possessed an expressiveness, at once completely familiar and completely free, completely by-the-book and completely liberated by the reciter's own capacity for projecting the Qur'an's voice through his own into the listener's present moment. It sounded something like the way the Reciting must have been heard by those who heard it chanted first by the Prophet Muhammad himself.

To facilitate its journey through time and the human body, the Qur'an passed and passes through language, or rather, through *a* language, Arabic, as Arabic was purely pronounced and spoken in seventh-century Mecca by the Qureysh tribe of which the prophet Muhammad was a distant member through a minor clan called the Hashim.

This was an astounding mercy on God's part, to pass through that language at that time and place, and through that particular person's, Muhammad's, heart and voice. But God's doing so was no more merciful than God's calling out to the entire seed of Adam at the dawn of our creation, *alastu bi rabbikum* (*Sura al-A'raf* 7:172)? "Am I not your Lord and Sustainer?" Then God reminded us, in the present, of the unanimous assent we all gave to this primordial interrogation and of his having provided each of the human communities that arose afterwards with its particular prophet. The task of each of these prophets was the same: to warn us to remain faithful to our original pledge of allegiance to God and God alone.

To the nomads of Arabia — scattered tribesmen lost in the desert, previously of little account — God sent out the last of these prophetic re-minders, the person the Qur'an itself calls the "seal" of the prophets, Muhammad, with the particular instruction this time that the divine Word be preserved faithfully and exactly as if it had just come from the lips of the Almighty himself. The nomads might have been last in line, but they were honored with the high responsibility of making sure that God's *kalam* or Word would remain God's. It must never be reshaped into a merely human word.

Yet it was again a sign of God's mercy that the Word thus recited to the prophet and to his people for safekeeping did not come to them in supernaturally overwhelming fashion, crushing their hearts and wills under the weight of its divine insistence and unnegotiability. The Qur'an makes this point in its own ironical fashion: "If We had sent this Qur'an, this Reciting, down upon the mountains, you would have seen them humble themselves and split in pieces for fear of God. These are the parables We set before humankind. Perhaps humankind will take them to heart" (*Sura al-Hashr* 59:21).

But no, there will be no mountain-splitting. The Qur'an builds its case instead on the artistic quality, indeed, on the inimitability of the work itself. It challenges competitors to "bring forth one sura like those of the Qur'an if they can" (*Sura al-Baqarah* 2:23); but clearly they cannot do so "unless they call on God to do it" (*Sura Yunis* 10:38).

This was another sign of divine mercy, that God would allow his Qur'an or Reciting to enter into competition with the poetry of creatures. Yes, the Qur'an insists that it is the winner in this competition. But it wins not on the basis of the author's infinite superiority to all comers. That would be a crushing trump card to play, though God could have played such a card if He had wanted to.

The Qur'an also insists that the Prophet Muhammad himself is not to enter that competition. "We have not taught him to be a poet," the Qur'an asserts (*Sura Ya'sin* 36:69). As the Qur'an says of itself, "It is the speech of a reliable messenger, not that of a poet" (*Sura al-Haqqah* 69:40-41). The Qur'an's point here is not to diminish the Prophet or poetry but to defend the Qur'an from the imputation that it is merely a human product, that it is merely a contrivance, however special and inimitable, that it is merely art— or art merely.

For the Qur'an *is* art. What it is *more* than art follows only if we believe that it is *God's* art. This belief is the key. The Qur'an warns us again and again that for our own good we should believe it to be so. In fact, the Qur'an does little else than warn us to believe it to be so. But we are not compelled. "Let there be no force in religion," the Qur'an says (*Sura al-Baqarah* 2:256).

What kind of art is God's art?

The Qur'an calls its art a "sign," the last of many God has sent to humankind over the centuries by the agency of the prophets. But while each sign points to the same truth— that you shall worship God and God alone and you shall care for all of God's creation—, certain signs to certain prophets bear a particular manifestation of God's creative power. Moses before Pharaoh was able to turn a staff into a snake. Jesus was able to cure the sick and raise the dead. Muhammad was able to recite the Qur'an.

The Qur'an, God's art, is art as miracle. Like the other miracles, the Qur'an is God's shaping of human materials into a form that calls us back to relationship with Him. It is a powerful shaping, because it is of God, and it is a beautiful one, because it is meant to attract us to what is good and holy. It is a profoundly relational shaping, because the materials in question are our own bodies and hearts. Miracles are not performances. They are invitations. The Qur'an, the Reciting, is invitation par excellence because it is designed for our participation. It was never intended as a private communication to the Prophet. The very first word sent down to him was *'iqra*, which means "recite," in the command form of the verb. It was always to be — and still is — shared speech, that is, shared *speaking*. It was always to be — and still is — an offer, an opportunity to breathe as God might breathe, to use the voice and throat and body as God might use them. We accept this offer in order that we might come closer to God and to our fulfillment as God's creation.

But like all invitations, all miracles, it can be refused. Pharaoh refused it, and so did the Pharisees. As Father Abraham said to Lazarus in the Christian Gospel of Luke, "If they do not listen to Moses and the Prophets, they will not be convinced even if one should rise from the dead" (Luke 16:31). In at least one place the Qur'an says something quite similar. The Prophet must have come to God in grief and frustration that he had not been able to persuade the people of Mecca with his recitings. God responds to Muhammad as follows: "If it distresses you, O Prophet, that they turn their backs on you, then go — if you are able to seek out a hole in the earth or a ladder into the heavens from which you can bring them back a Sign, then go ahead and try it. But it will be in vain. For remember that if God had willed, God could have gathered them together into His guidance. So do not be one of those driven by ignorance and impatience" (*Sura al-An'am* 6:33-35).

In only the merely human sense of the word "art," the Qur'an submits itself to the receptivity or lack of receptivity of its audience. This audience includes not only those who reject it but also those who, claiming to believe it, appropriate it ideologically. The Qur'an *will* not defend itself from scorn, neglect, ideological misinterpretation, or abuse.

It will not defend itself because it need not. As God's art, and therefore as a manifestation of God's infinite mercy, the Qur'an is infinitely patient. It waits for those for whom it sounds a note of longing that stirs the tongue and captures the heart. Then the Qur'an opens in beauty, and the reciter is drawn towards the light of heaven and earth.

Chapter 3b. The Beauty of Voice: The Adhan (Call to Prayer) as Epitome of Muslim Art

Minarets. Turbans. Domed buildings. Head scarves. The star and crescent...

Perhaps the most easily recognized public signs of Islam.

Yet the most important of these, the sign most representative of Islam has not yet been mentioned —

The Call to Prayer.

We have all heard it, usually in the background of TV travelogues through Muslim lands. We hear it as a high, penetrating voice soaring from a minaret far above the surrounding hubbub of busy streets. The words are mysteriously incomprehensible: exotic, attractive, haunting, mesmerizing, threatening, depending on our state of mind. We hear only a phrase or two before the travelogue's voice-over intervenes, though the Call drones on in the background, muted but still powerfully insistent...and yet not without a certain melancholy at its close.

If you're like me, you always suspected there must be more to the Call to Prayer than a predictable "teaser" for a TV documentary. But what that "more" was, who could tell? For years I concluded my thoughts on the subject with a shrug. The Call to Prayer belonged to that vast world of Orientalia forever closed to me.

That all changed once I actually got to know Muslims and began studying Arabic and observing Muslim prayer. I heard the Call to Prayer often, live and in its entirety, without intruding voice-over. I learned its words. It was no longer incomprehensible.

But it wasn't until just recently, when I was asked to chant the Call to Prayer myself at an interfaith event, that I came to know it intimately. And in that intimate knowing to discover how it could serve as an epitome of the art of Muslims.

Preparing for my debut as *mu'adhdhan* (= Caller of the Prayer, often transliterated *muezzin*) I listened again and again for two weeks to the rendition of the *adhan* by the young and much-honored Turkish Qari Mustafa Ozcan Gunesdogdu included on the CD that accompanies Michael Sells's *Approaching the Qur'an*. (This recording is also available online by searching Gunesdogdu's name.) I did not try to match Qari Gunesdogdu's artistry. The very idea was ludicrous. I do not possess his astonishing vocal gifts. I possess neither his command of tonal range nor of melismatic invention (melodic transformation of the open vowel), neither his breath control nor his sheer vocal power. But I thought I could capture some of the fervent spirit of Gunesdogdu's performance by allowing that performance to find, through imitation, whatever home it could within my voice and body.

Yet even if I had possessed all the vocal gifts in the world, I wouldn't have the right as a Christian to call the *adhan* as a Muslim would, that is, in order to gather other Muslim faithful for one of the five daily prayers. I was asked instead to call the *adhan* mid-way through the interfaith gathering mentioned above, as a way of inducing the conference-goers to return to their chairs after break-time for the Q&A period. I agreed to do this provided that the Muslim presenter saw no offense and provided I would be allowed, at the outset of the day's program, to explain what I would be doing later on and why. The "why"— above and beyond the need to get people back in their chairs— was this: I would be trying to model, as I explained it to those assembled, a way of "passing over" to the religion of the Other by taking into myself the voice of the Other's call to worship.

By one measure my performance was brilliantly successful. It silenced the chatter at the coffee-urn almost instantly, and by the time I finished, all were back in their seats. By another measure, though... well, let me report what the Muslim presenter graciously remarked afterwards. She said that she "honored my effort." I smiled at her terms of praise, grateful for them but aware at the same time of how far short I had come from what we both knew was the ideal.

Yet the two weeks of practicing the *adhan* were all the reward I needed.

Those weeks had persuaded me that in the *adhan* I was hearing the true art of Muslims, and even the first historical example — as well as an epitome — of their art. If Muslims have been called into being in words and through voice, their answer must come in words and through voice as well. The art of Muslims at its most authentic replies to what is artistic in the Qur'an itself. But the art of both, of God and humankind, is at the service of a value higher than any mere crafting. The art of the Qur'an summons the Muslim to beauty, and the Muslim responds by a beautiful making of his or her own. Crafting becomes beautiful in the radiance of what motivates it.

But crafting, for us human beings, certainly, is a humble process; and the *adhan*, at least according to Sunni accounts, has humble historical antecedents as well.

The *adhan*'s very existence follows from a practical need: How to call the young Muslim community to prayer at the five ordained times: after dawn, at noon, before sunset, after sunset, and at night.

The need arose only after the Prophet and his community accomplished their *hijra* or emigration from Mecca to Medina in the year 622 of the common calendar (year 1 of the Muslim calendar). Dispersed as the members of the community became throughout this large comparatively fertile agricultural area, they found it hard to gather at agreed-on times. What to do? The Jewish and Christian communities they were familiar with used bells or wooden clappers for this purpose. Maybe the Muslims should do the same?

One story has it that Abd Allah Ibn Zaid, a companion of the Prophet Muhammad, then heard the words of the *adhan* in a dream. Waking, Ibn Zaid went to the Prophet to tell him the dream and get his opinion — since dreams can be deceptive. The Prophet not only approved the words of the *adhan* but asked Bilal ibn Ribah, a black Ethiopian and former slave, to be the first to use those words to call the community together. The Prophet did so partly because of the power and beauty of Bilal's voice, and partly also because of Bilal's extraordinary fidelity. Back in Mecca, Bilal had endured the Qureysh's attempt through torture to force him to recant his faith. Now, in Medina, newly freed and equal to all others in the new community, Bilal could be honored for the strength of his personal witness. In addition, the evidence of Islam's radical transformation of tribal, racial, and caste taboos could be displayed in this honor given Bilal, of being the first to chant the *adhan*.

Bilal sets the gold standard for all who have chanted the *adhan* in subsequent ages: not just for his vocal command, but also for his purity of heart and commitment to the faith. The qari, as *mu'adhdhan*, should embody in his person the values which the *adhan* conveys.

What are those values, then, that the *adhan* conveys?

The words expressing these values are actually few:

God is beyond all measure of greatness (*repeated four times*)
I witness that there is no god but God (*twice*)
I witness that Muhammad is the messenger of God (*twice*)
Come alive to the prayer (*twice*)
Come alive to fullness of being (*twice*)
God is beyond all measure of greatness (*twice*)
There is no god but God (*once*)

Let's look at the *adhan* phrase by phrase, because the values expressed in the *adhan* do not emerge from an abstract moral framework, but from a dramatic encounter of creature with creator, an encounter imaged in the flow of meaning within the *adhan* itself. This flow of meaning follows a trajectory beginning in the *adhan*'s first phrase and ending in its last, though just as important as the *adhan*'s words for this developing meaning are the silences between each phrase. (Qari Gunesdogdu's silences in the recording of the *adhan* mentioned above are potent.)

The *adhan* begins with a wake-up call, *Allahu akbar,* often translated "God is great." A more accurate (if awkward) translation would be, as above, "God is great beyond all measure of greatness." The Arabic adjective in its intensive form, used in this case for the adjective "great," states that a thing exists in its own category, without rival and invulnerable to comparison with anything in our world. But the effect of the intensive form as used in the *adhan* is not to thrust God outside our limited world, but rather to make God's greatness in our world all the more astonishing for its manifesting itself in never-ending abundance and generosity.

The *adhan* awakens us to wonder at God's greatness not only through the cognitive content of its words but further through the musical way in which the phrase *Allahu akbar* is chanted here at the beginning of the *adhan*.

The phrase is repeated four times, in two pairings. The first pairing of the phrase (*Allahu akbar* repeated once) is chanted forcefully. The phrase in its clear simplicity becomes a clarion call, an assertion. Then there follows a significant pause, allowing for a deepened understanding of the phrase just chanted. As a result, when *Allahu akbar* is chanted in its second pairing, it acquires a different feeling, not assertive now, but celebratory. To achieve this new mood in the repetition, the open vowel "a" of the name for God, Allah, is greatly extended so that it can be elaborated lovingly with melismas across a tonal range of an octave or more. This time, the tone begins higher and moves lower, completing an arch of rising and falling sound. The effect of the repetition is to convey the fullness of the wonder that should be ours at God's creative generosity.

The assertion-reflection pattern repeats itself in the two phrases that follow, which together constitute the first "Pillar" of Islam, the Witnessing or *shahadah*. For example, the chanting of the first of these phrases, "I bear witness that there is no god but God," rises through a narrow tonal range without ornamentation. But when repeated (after that thought-drenched pause), it arcs downward through cascading melismas (all emerging out of the open "a" vowel echoing across the phrase, in the Arabic words for "no" and for "but" as well as for "God") and comes to rest on the initial tonal center. The mood or emotion changes correspondingly. The first time we hear the phrase "I witness that there is no god but God," we hear it as a mighty declaration, brimming with confidence and vigor. The second time, after the pause, we hear the phrase as if echoing in our conscience. The full meaning of what we have just witnessed to (for the believers now gathering in response to the Call are enjoined to echo its words quietly to themselves, phrase by phrase) now dawns on us. What does it mean for us at this moment, what will it mean for us in the future, to submit our will totally to God's? It means to put absolutely nothing in the way of that submission, not money, not power, not prestige, nor any other trick or deception of the ego. Thinking back to our discussion of Jacob's and Joseph's "beautiful patience" in Chapter 1c, we can hear how the *adhan*'s repetition of phrases encourages a similar reflective submission to God's will.

Again, an enhancement or deepening of meaning occurs in the second phrase of the *shahadah*, "I witness that Muhammad is the messenger of God." The first time we hear this phrase, we hear it as a bold declaration. The second time, we hear it in our conscience, as we reflect on what it means and will mean for us faithfully to emulate the Prophet's virtues. (In Chapter 5a we'll look more closely at how the Prophet's personal example becomes the model par excellence for beautiful living.)

Those bold statements of personal witness are then followed in the *adhan* by the invitation first to become a community in worship and then to receive our reward. "Come alive to the prayer" and "Come alive to fullness of being" together make up what we might call the climax of the *adhan*. Each of these phrases, like the previous ones, moves from a declarative to a reflective mood. The first "Come alive to the prayer" summons us to the imminent moment of prayer; the second recital of the line invites us to consider what this "coming alive" in prayer might mean for us — our transformation in the light of God's loving interaction with us. The first "Come alive to fullness of being" pushes the boundary of our anticipation beyond the present moment. It arouses our imagination to anticipate the rewards in store for those who live out their witness faithfully. The second deepens our understanding that those rewards are not handed out automatically, and are not always manifested during our earthly lives, but that they are promised full measure and flowing over in the world to come. Common to both summonses, however — common to "Come alive to the prayer" as well as to "Come alive to fullness of being"— is the positive value placed on human energy. When firmly in service to God and God's creation, human energy becomes more and more exuberantly creative and liberating. Not even death can contain it.

Now, after the climax, do we find a triumphant close?

Not exactly.

The *adhan* does end with the same phrases it began with: "God is beyond all measure of greatness" (twice) and "There is no god but God" (once). The repetition might suggest that simple symmetry is the purpose and effect here. But simple symmetry is not what we get. We do not in fact end where we started. This final "God is beyond all measure of greatness," unlike the first one at the beginning of the *adhan*, is not a clarion call. Chanted this time in a subdued, humbled manner, the phrase becomes a sobering reminder to those still scaling in imagination the heady heights achieved in the previous "Come alive to fullness of being" that, overshadowing even our noblest responses to God's generosity to us, is God Himself. God is not only "beyond all measure of greatness" but beyond even our proclamation of that fact.

The subdued chanting of the phrase at this point reflects the de-centering of God from human reference and from human capture even in prayer. The final chanting of the phrase "there is no god but God" reinforces the effect. The phrase, unrepeated, breaks all connection to us by breaking free of our assertion of witness. (There is no "I bear witness that..." introducing the phrase.) We are delivered back to a chastening hush where nothing more can be known of God than that there is no other than He.

I said above that in the *adhan* I was hearing not only the true art of Muslims, but also the epitome of it. What I meant was that the artistic elements of the *adhan* I have touched on here can be found in the art of Muslims ever since. But these elements, ranging from expressions of joyful wonder to those of sober reflectiveness, are not present in a rigidly formal way nor unmixed with each other. Nor are they the only expressive elements that are allowed in Muslim art. As I said above, the *adhan*'s artistry — and Muslim artistry generally — emerges not from an abstract moral framework but from a dramatic encounter of creature with creator, and specifically with the creator's beauty. The *adhan* itself does not explicitly say so, but its very nature testifies to the fact that beauty is God's and God's alone, offered to humankind not as an idea to be contemplated but as a light to be followed. God's beauty incites human beauty, in the form of lives lived beautifully, whether in artistic creation or virtuous behavior, or (ideally) both. "Come alive to fullness of being," the *adhan* calls. The art of Muslims has echoed that call every since.

In the chapters that follow, we'll look at some of the varied imaginative ways in which Muslim artists have responded to God's art of the Qur'an. Even during the Prophet's lifetime, but with increasing vigor afterwards, Muslim art began to develop in ways undreamt of by Abd Allah Ibn Zaid, who first heard the *adhan*'s words, and by Bilal, who first chanted them. That development has continued over the centuries right up to and including the present day. The *adhan* suggests a range of artistic possibilities and responses which subsequent Muslim artists continue to draw on and extend.

The responses move, ideally, in a trajectory beginning in joyful wonder at God's creative generosity. Wonder begets personal witness to the God who calls each one of us into being. It calls us also to personal witness to the Prophet thanks to whom that call came to us, through what we can call the art of the Qur'an. We then give our worshipful attention to the beauty that embraces the whole of humanity, not just the individual. Worshipful attention awakens us to God's intimate presence as well as to the future awaiting us. Our imaginations come alive in hope for reward, if not in this life, then certainly in the next. The trajectory of these responses traces for the most part an eagerly positive movement, but also one tempered and chastened by silence, modesty, and humility.-

No single Muslim artwork expresses all of these responses in a programmatic way. Yet some can be said to emphasize one response more than another. In the following four chapters we'll look at examples of artworks that emphasize expressions of wonder, of worshipful attention, of joyful witness, and of hope. But these categories are elastic, serving merely as guidelines. For the greatest Muslim artworks in some way really do contain all responses. That is because the ultimate source of beauty, to which all Muslim art pays tribute, is one. "There is no god but God." God's *tauhid* or unicity is absolute. Beauty herself is one and indivisible, though among us she must appear in various forms.

Chapter 3c. Generosity and Wonder: Muslim Architecture and More

Kareem Abdul-Jabbar.

As a Boston Celtics fan during the 1970's, I felt nothing but fear and trepidation when I heard that name pronounced.

Known as Lew Alcindor before he converted to Islam, Kareem became one of the greatest NBA basketball players of all time. My stomach would knot in agony as Kareem employed his patented and indefensible "sky hook shot" against the Men in Green during the Celtics' epic NBA playoff battles with Kareem's Lakers.

Yet decades later, how differently I heard that name, once I understood what its words actually referred to: "The Most Generous One (=Kareem), Servant (=Abdul) of the One Who Restores to Wholeness (=Jabbar)."

While these Names, Kareem and Jabbar — for they are two of the 99 Beautiful Names of God — might have made joyful sense to Lakers fans on a secular, competitive level, they took on their deepest positive meaning for me only when I was able to detach them from the servant (the "Abd" in "Abdul-Jabbar") and reconnect them securely to God, their true referent. Once reconnected, "Kareem," the "most generous one," no longer referred to the bastketball player's scoring of huge numbers of points but to God's attribute of giving forth continually from the divine inexhaustible bounty. "Jabbar" referred not to the basketball player's team spirit but to God's specific concern to find or complete or restore whatever might be lost or missing or broken in God's creation. Both names, when connected to God, captured an aspect of the meaning of the divine "generosity," though only "kareem" is usually translated that way.

Other Beautiful Names capture still different aspects of the meaning of that divine "generosity": for example, *al-wahhab* (the bestower) or *ar-razzaq* (the provider). But the Names carrying the richest aspects of God's generosity are the two most noble names of all, after the name Allah. These are the two names which follow the name Allah in the phrase "in the name of Allah, the Most Beneficent, the Most Merciful" that appears at the beginning of all of the Qur'an's *suras* but one. Muslims use this same phrase (known as the *bismillah*) to evoke God's blessing before every action they take.

Both of these names — the Most Beneficent, the Most Merciful, *ar-Rahmani-ar-Raheem* — are derived from a single Arabic root meaning "womb." Both refer to what we can think of as aspects of the profoundly maternal nature of God: *ar-Rahman*, the Most Beneficent, referring to God's constant creativity, and *ar-Raheem*, the Most Merciful, referring to God's constant care for what God constantly creates.

I stress "constant" because that is how Islam understands God's creativity. Creativity is ongoing. "God never sleeps, nor does He slumber...," says *Sura al-Baqarah*, 2:255. There never was nor can there be a day of rest, a Sabbath for God in Islam. Nor can there ever be in Islam a "deistic" interpretation of God's creativity (an interpretation that suggests that God at the beginning wound up the creation like a clock and then drew apart, to allow it to run on its own). No: "It is God who initiated creation and God who continues it..." (*Sura Yunus*, 10:4). Muslims view creation not as a thing finished but as the living sign of God's unfailing commitment to keep it in being and to perfect it. Creation is not so much an object to be looked at as an object to be looked through, in the sense in which it reveals for our reflection "signs" (*ayat*) of the maternal care constantly bringing creation into being and nurturing it from moment to moment as it moves towards the fullness of its beauty in the World to Come, the Garden. (More on the Garden in Chapter 3f.)

I'll admit that I've had trouble picturing God's creativity in this way: as an ongoing, uninterrupted and uninterruptible divine enterprise proceeding from God's own beauty and directed towards the eventual emergence of a beautiful creation. My difficulty may stem from my inculturation in a Newtonian universe of fixed objects. Whatever the source of my difficulty, however, its hold on me began to lessen when I tried to imagine God's creativity as the Arabs of the Prophet Muhammad's time would have imagined it, most likely at night, under the desert stars. I've never been in Arabia, so I cannot claim to have seen the spread of the heavens from that angle. But I've stood out at night in deserts of the American Southwest, where the stars seem to vibrate in vast swaths over one's head. I could imagine there, in those glimmering expanses, a God who truly never slumbered, never slept.

Yet my most vivid vision of God's constant creativity is a childhood one. I was about ten years old, and had just gotten for my birthday a kit for a reflecting telescope. After assembling it, my father and I carried it far back in the lot behind our house so that we could look at stars and the planets without interference from houselights. Although the ground we were walking over was very familiar to me — the site of innumerable games with my friends —, it all now seemed new. I had never been out there so late in the evening before, and in such darkness. There were neither house lights nor moon to orient and comfort me.

But of course, my dad was with me.

And there were stars, countless numbers of them spread lavishly across that familiar dome of sky which I had always assumed to be solid, like the high ceilings in our Victorian house lost somewhere in back of us in the inky shadows. (All this occurred in upstate New York, in the years before air pollution.) As I peered through the telescope's eyepiece, more and more bits of stellar light swam into view. The dome's solidity, I began to realize, was an illusion, or at least only a temporary cover. Revealed behind it and infinitely far above it was the mysteriously pulsing grandeur of heaven itself. There seemed to be no end to this grandeur. With my dad's help I identified certain anchorages in this black, swarming sea: Venus and Jupiter and Cassiopeia and the Pleiades among them. But the impression that comes back to me is not one of fixity but of unfathomably constant movement. The world above my head seemed more deeply alive than the world immediately around me. Something, or someone, seemed to be bringing the infinite world of lights into being and then to be sustaining them in their courses, and to be doing so right then as I looked on open-mouthed from my perch on another bit of pulsing light itself emerging from the divine generosity and kept in being by one merciful divine touch after another.

I made no such theological interpretation of this vision at the time, and my dad, positivist to the core, would not have encouraged such speculation. But seeing my experience of the heavens now through the lens of the Qur'an, I find it easy and fitting to interpret it as an experience of God's generosity, of His Beneficence and Mercy. At the root of the experience was wonder, a child's wonder to be sure. But the wonder lives in me still. Desert landscapes, as I've said, can reawaken it. But so can the architecture of Muslim mosques and shrines.

Two examples of Muslim architectural artistry do this for me with special effectiveness, since they evoke wonder at God's creative generosity in contrasting, complementary ways: the *qubbat as-sakhrah*, as Jerusalem's Dome of the Rock is called in Arabic, and *la mezquita de Córdoba* (the Mosque at Córdoba, Spain). Through its symbols, the Dome of the Rock evokes wonder at the vertical dimension of God's generosity; while the Mosque at Córdoba evokes wonder, through its own symbols, at the horizontal.

But wouldn't any large-scale religious architecture be suited to the task of awaking wonder at God's creative generosity? Yet size alone is not enough. Mere artistic bigness is oppressive. It can feel as inflated as the egos that produced it. What is required is a way of working with large forms so that they become symbols of what is not merely great but *akbar*, "that which is great beyond all measure of greatness." What is required are symbols of God's Presence in God's overflowing creative generosity, the divine quality hinted at in the double epithets *ar-Rahman*, the Most Beneficent, and *ar-Raheem*, the Most Merciful. Yet how are limited creatures such as ourselves to invent such symbols? We know from a line in the Light Verse discussed in Chapter 1a that "God speaks to humankind in symbols." God does this as a concession to our weakness, since we cannot know or approach God directly. But can we mere creatures — sustained in being from second to second as we are by God's generosity — possibly find a language of symbols with which to answer?

The Qur'an assures us that an appropriate response, even conversation of a kind on our part, is not only possible but greatly desired by God:

> When any of my servants ask for me, tell them, O Prophet,
>   that I am near.
> I respond to the cry of those who cry out to me every time they cry
>   out to me,
> And then they are in turn to respond to me and trust in me—
> Perhaps they will choose to be rightly guided. (*Sura al-Baqarah* 2:186)

Our symbols work differently from God's, of course. God's symbols enable us to grasp in part a reality that overwhelms us. Our symbols enable us to express our longing for what we cannot grasp. God meets that longing if it emerges from a sincere recognition of God's qualities — in this case, of God's generosity, as expressed through God's Beneficence and Mercy.

Wonder at the vertical dimension of God's generosity. How does the artistry of the Dome of the Rock actually evoke this wonder? Alas, I've never been able to visit the Dome to judge the effect for myself. But I've done perhaps the next best thing. I've pored over Oleg Grabar and Said Nuseibeh's magnificent book, *The Dome of the Rock*. The book's text and photos persuade me that I have actually set foot in the Dome. They persuade me also that the Dome is experienced as a vertical emblem of God's generosity. The Dome's inner columns direct the eye upwards, not horizontally. The divine generosity suggested is therefore different from that of the Mosque at Córdoba, as we'll soon see. It is not so much a generosity filling to overflowing the face of the earth. Rather, it is a generosity that fills the heavens above with its panoply of stars and all that lies beyond them. The beautiful name for God that we hear in *Sura Fatihah* 1:2 — Cherisher and Sustainer of all the worlds (*rabbi-l 'alamin*) — takes on fresh meaning.

I was confirmed in this feeling when I came upon a photo in Grabar's book that focuses up from floor level to show the gilded tiles lining the inside of the Dome's cupola. These tiles, glowing golden in the oblique afternoon light and arranged in ascending rings within rings across the cupola's inner surface, suggest not so much individual stars in the firmament as infinity itself. Yet this infinity is overcome, relativized, by the point of convergence at the cupola's peak. The Dome's architects, I thought, were not attempting to reproduce or imitate the starry heavens that the prophet Muhammad and the early Muslim community must have gazed on or that even I had gazed on in my back yard. They were attempting to transform the resplendence we saw with our eyes into a symbol of the divine generosity that never ceases to produce it.

Other artifacts within the Dome enhance the impression of the divine generosity's vertical dimension. The Dome was built in part to enshrine the

View from the inside of the Dome looking upwards.

very peak of Mt. Moriah, whose stony tip protrudes from the Dome's floor. Because of this, the cosmic panoply above is anchored, held in place, at the very spot where the vertical and horizontal intersect. For as the name Mt. Moriah suggests, this is no ordinary spot. Moriah is the site not only of Abraham's near sacrifice of Isaac, according to Jewish and Christian tradition, but also of the First and Second Temples. The Qur'an adds that it was the starting place of the Prophet Muhammad's *mi'raj* or night journey through the heavens to the Throne of God. Legend has it that the imprint of the Prophet's foot as he swung up on the back of his mythic steed Buraq can still be seen in the rock's surface. Moriah has always been and continues to be a launching place for heavenly longing and wonder.

None of this deeper wondering towards the origin of all generosity would have been possible if specific artistic elements hadn't encouraged the effort. Many of those elements are named and discussed in *The Cultural Atlas of Islam* by Isma'il and Lois Lamya' Al Faruqi.[1] The Al Faruqis argue that God's generosity is uniquely expressed by Muslim artists' capacity to produce patterns that give the impression of infinity (like the arrangement of tiles lining the Dome's interior cupola or the repetition of arabesques adorning the Dome's inner colonnades). "It is these infinite patterns, in all their ingenious variety," the Al Faruqis say, "that provide the positive aesthetic breakthrough of the Muslims in the history of artistic expression."

The "breakthrough" that the Al Faruqis speak of here is the overcoming of what seems to outsiders a debilitating limitation on Muslim artistic expression: the reluctance to represent natural forms realistically. This reluctance is not enjoined in the Qur'an itself. Historian Oleg Grabar suggests that the reluctance emerged in the century after the Prophet Muhammad's death in order to distinguish Muslim artistic expression from the emphatically representational style of the Byzantine Christians. But the key reason for the emergence is the internal need within Islam to forestall worship of the creation rather than of its Creator. Muslims began to take very much to heart the great Qur'anic statement of monotheism enshrined in the *adhan*'s *shahadah*: "I witness that *there is no god but God*." Giving this witness means, as we saw in Chapter 3b, that one can put absolutely nothing in the way of one's self-yielding to God: not money, not power, not prestige, nor any other trick or deception of the ego, including the deception of beautiful images of particular things. This is not a denial of the real beauty of those particular things. It is a guard against one's own too easily aroused tendency to idolize them.

The "breakthrough" the Al Faruqis allude to, then, is Muslim artists' invention of symbol systems that emphatically point beyond what is seen to what allows things to be seen — that is, to God. But since God cannot be seen ("No vision grasps God, but God grasps all vision, for God is the Most Subtle, the Most Knowing" — *Sura al-An'am* 6:103), the symbols themselves must both attract the eye and thwart it. Of course, all symbols can be said to work this way, both disclosing and foreclosing. Islamic symbols do so under the tremendous pressure of human yearning for God on one side and of God's eagerness for communication with us on the other. Islamic symbols glint and sparkle like diamonds pressed into being from the divine-human encounter.

This is why when the Al Faruqis speak of "infinite patterns," they are not talking about Muslim artists' desire to represent infinity itself. In the

---

1. Isma'il and Lois Lamya' Al Faruqi, *The Cultural Atlas of Islam* (New Jersey: Prentice Hall, 1986). Quotation from the book is on p. 163.

Qur'an's view, infinity, seen merely as the aggregate of individual created things, has no meaning in itself. Such an infinity begs the question of its origin and purpose. Infinity is instead symbolized by patterns suggesting the way in which the divine generosity brings individual things constantly into being. The Al Faruqis hold Muslim architecture to be the site where the symbolizing of infinity by repetitive patterns achieves its most sublime effect.

It achieves that effect, as I've said, in the horizontal as well as in the vertical dimension. And here personal experience rather than photography comes to my aid. I've seen the Mosque at Córdoba with my own eyes. Unlike the Dome of the Rock, which dominates the Jerusalem skyline, the Mosque at Córdoba is nestled almost invisibly within the old city center. What actually strikes the eye is the Catholic Cathedral which rises from the Mosque's midst. (The Cathedral was inserted there in the years after the *reconquista* by the royal family of Aragon.) The Mosque's ancient outer walls suggest the warehouse the structure was in part originally intended to be. And in January the Patio of Orange Trees, which Peggy and I crossed on our way to the Mosque's main entrance at the northern end, was drab and chilly.

The Mosque's unprepossessing exterior had lulled me into supposing that I was prepared for what I'd see inside. I'd already looked at photos of

View from inside the Córdoba Mosque.

the interior: photos of the rows on rows of double-arches stretching in all directions to support the roof, of the ornate *mihrab* or prayer-niche built into the southern wall, of the Cathedral's altar and other accouterments inserted into the southern section. I expected to be impressed, but not to be awestruck.

Yet once inside the structure, I found that I'd stepped into a deep, enchanted wood— like stands of pine near the family home in upstate New York where I grew up. I recalled how I felt when I entered such stands as a child. Though the trunks of the quiet trees would stand attentively erect, my eye was not drawn vertically to their crowns. Rather it was drawn horizontally along the receding corridors of trees until vision disappeared in the depths. At that point I would begin to hear the sound of my own breathing, the sound of my own heartbeat. It seemed to me that words were being said, but just beyond my range of hearing. A completely unaccustomed meditative mood would come over me, at once seductive and frightening. I could get lost in a place like this. Yet how attractive it would be to become lost in this way…

Decades later, in Córdoba, the meditative mood returned, though in a less confused, ambivalent form. I knew that it was a commonplace to envision as a vast grove of trees the Mosque's 365 double-arches atop 850 columns laid out in serene geometrical order across the tiled floor. Palms rather than pines are the trees usually evoked to describe the scene, and more fittingly. The alternating red brick and white limestone used in constructing the double-arches gives a warmer feeling than the cool greens and blues of pine forests, and palm groves surely would have come closer to the vision of Abd-ar-Rahman ("Servant of the Most Beneficent"), the Umayyad caliph of Andalusia who initiated the Mosque's construction and who reigned from 756-788 CE. There are hints that the caliph, missing his homeland in the East, insisted on orienting the Mosque at Córdoba in the same direction towards Mecca as the Umayyad mosque in Damascus, towards the south. (From Córdoba, Mecca lies to the west.) The caliph might have been just as susceptible to the reawakening of childhood wonder as I was, though he was in a better position than I to realize his dream architecturally, using visual elements familiar to him in his youth.

But for all the differences between groves of pines and groves of palms, silent words echoed in both spaces. The difference for me now, in the richly red-gold interior of the Mosque, was that these voices could become audible, if I listened carefully. The Mosque at Córdoba speaks the words of the Qur'an more clearly than pine trees do. For even though, according to the Qur'an, all things in nature, including pine trees, are *ayat* or signs of God's constantly creative presence, the *ayat* do not fully yield their meaning without the Qur'an to interpret them. Like any other mosque (the word means "place of prostration"), the Mosque at Córdoba provides the physical space for the Qur'an to resound, as well as visual guidance for its proper reception. Enabling wonder at God's generosity is a key function of that guidance.

Standing amid the "forest" of the Mosque's arches and columns, I recall that the Qur'an often uses trees as symbols. We've already probed the meanings of one of those symbols, from the "The Light Verse" in Chapter 1a. The symbol in that instance was drawn from an olive tree, a "blessed tree neither of the West nor of the East...," a tree symbolizing (among other things) the universality of God's fruitful invitation to humankind. In *Sura Ibrahim* 14:24-26 the symbol shifts to include the extremes of human response to such an invitation:

> Aren't you aware how God sets forth the likeness of a life-giving word?
> It is firmly rooted like a good tree,
> its branches reaching toward the sky,
> yielding its fruit at all times by the permission of its Cherisher and Sustain-
> er... while the likeness of a corrupt word
> is like a rotten tree, rooted up upon the earth,
> nothing lasting in it.

Here in Córdoba I'd discovered in the rows on rows of columns and double-arches a whole forest of life-giving words stretching horizontally as if towards infinity on all sides. Guided by *Sura Ibrahim* 14:24-26, I could see these symbols in a double light. I could see the columns and arches as signs of God's endless creative generosity spreading out in all directions. But I could also see them as signs of Muslims' fruitful artistic response to that generosity, first in wonder, but then in praise and thanksgiving. And further: I could see the artistic response as modeling and encouraging a similar response on the part of believers, so that the entire *ummah* or worshipping community assembled there in the Mosque could more easily become those fruitful trees extending their arms towards heaven.

The Al Faruqis are right. Muslim architecture, represented by the Dome of the Rock and the Mosque at Córdoba, but also by the Grand Mosque in Damascus, by the Taj Mahal, and by many other less-well-known structures, provides the best source of artistic effects evoking wonder at God's creative generosity. Yet wonder can express itself in smaller-scale forms as well. Many of these smaller-scale expressions are contemporary.

One of these contemporary sources is the painting of Egyptian-born, now England-based Ahmad Moustafa. Dr. Moustafa's website (www.fenoon. com) offers painting after painting in which Qur'anic calligraphy is used as the basis for on-going exploration of the principles of God's creativity. The basis for this exploration is Dr. Moustafa's rediscovery of the exact proportions and numbers that produce the visual harmony of Arabic script. These proportions and numbers themselves constitute the laws which govern God's creative action, according to earlier Muslim philosophical investigation into the works of Pythagoras and Euclid. Arabic script becomes in Dr. Moustafa's hands a visual form capable of hinting at the supreme orderliness of God who, as the Quran states (*Sura al-Qamar* 54:49), "creates everything in due measure and proportion."

Dr. Moustafa's canvases bring to life what might seem to those not familiar with the roots of Muslim artistic expression an overly abstract way of honoring God's creativity. But as we've seen, the aim of that expression is not to render the fruit of that creativity, that is, creation itself. The aim is directly to arouse wonder at the One who brings that fruit into being, not once and for all time, but continually, second after second. As the Al-

Ahmad Moustafa, *Landscape in Perfect Order and Proportion*, inspired by Qur'an *sura al-qamar* 54:49. Oil and water color on special 100% cotton paper, 135cm x 85cm.

Faruqis argue, numerical and geometrical symmetry is a key element in achieving that aim. Dr. Moustafa incorporates this element in his "Landscape in Due Measure and Proportion," a painting inspired by the Qur'anic verse above ("God creates everything in due measure and proportion"). An intense oblique light casts deep shadows on several complicated geometrical forms covered with calligraphy. The forms rest on a ground or floor patterned with symmetrical star shapes. The beauty of the painting owes much to Dr. Moustafa's superb handling of calligraphy, one of the highest forms of Muslim art, with a tradition so rich that I'll need to devote the entire next chapter to it. But the painting's beauty owes much as well to the tension between intense light and intense shade, between straight geometrical lines and curved calligraphic ones, as well as between the painting's realism and its un-earthliness. If this is a "landscape," it is a landscape seen only by the inner eye. I cannot speak for others, so I'll say here only that as viewer of this and other paintings by Dr. Moustafa I feel as if a veil has been lifted from a corner of the divine creative process. What I see engages me not as a spectator but as an invited participant in a mysteriously gracious energy that brings me and all creation into being and sustains us there in wonder.

I get a similar feeling from the black and white photography of Reem Al Faisal, who defines herself "as a Muslim artist, sprung from my native Saudi culture and history."[2] Reem Al Faisal too, like Dr. Moustafa, favors strong contrasts between light and shade, straight and curved lines, realism and un-earthliness. She too appeals through her chosen symbols to the viewer's inner eye, in order to encourage awareness of and awe before God's ongoing creative beneficence. Reem Al Faisal's chosen symbols are not derived from numbers or letters, however, but from austere juxtapositions of black and white. Her photograph of a mosque interior featured on the front cover of her book *Diwan Al Noor* (meaning "An Anthology of Images of Light") is typical of her work. Light streams from two arched windows high on a mosque wall, projecting or creating images of the window openings on the mosque floor below, while pillars gather to either side of the bright white shafts of light. Light in fact becomes the solid material here, more solid than the pavement of the floor or the side pillars. The creator of shapes becomes not the window openings but light itself. Darkness doesn't obscure what is not illuminated. Darkness is formlessness, waiting light's creating touch.

The touch that brings darkness into form brings form also out of the darkness of the human heart. Reem Al Faisal clarifies the moral direction of her art in her Forward to *Diwan Al Noor*:

> In my art I am seeking to show signs of the Divine in nature and in man. For me light is one of the many manifestations of God, which He casts in our pathways through life to remind us of His constant presence in ourselves and every place. Every photograph is a pattern of light and shade. For me, my photography is a way to praise God's glory in the universe.[3]

Reem Al-Feisal doesn't quote the Light Verse in this account. Perhaps modesty restrained her. She would never claim that a photograph like any of those in *Diwan Al Noor* actually *illustrates* that verse. Yet since God says in the Light Verse that "God speaks to humankind in symbols," then from humankind's response can emerge symbols of our own that are brought into being

---

2. Reem Al Feisal, *Diwan Al Noor* (Manama, Bahrain: Miracle Publishing, 1994), 92.

3. Al Feisal, *Diwan Al Noor*, 92.

Reem Al Faisal, mosque interior, *Diwan Al Noor* (Manama, Bahrain: Miracle Publishing, 1994) 92. Black and white photograph.

by the touch of the divine light, just as the mosque's shapes and stones are brought into being by the streaming light in Reem Al Faisal's photograph.

Peter Sanders, a British convert to Islam, praises God through photography, just as Reem Al Faisal does. Sanders's methods and materials are different from Reem Al Faisal's, however. Color is Sanders's photographic medium, and celebratory realism his atmosphere. The sections on "Creation" and "Weddings" from Sanders's website at www.petersanders. co.uk reveal Sanders's eye for joyful color and vigorous spatial relationships in natural scenes and cultural events photographed from around the vast and variegated Muslim world. But the "Travel" section is the one that most clearly and impressively evokes wonder at God's creative munificence even though what we see appears far removed from the seemingly infinite symbolic multiplicity of trees or stars, or from the abstract symbolism of geometrical and calligraphic forms, or from the creative power of light. What we see instead are the faces of Muslims from twenty countries stretching from China to the U.S. by way of India, Iran, Africa, Spain, the U.K., and many others. Yet despite the photography's realism, the faces we see, as Sanders told me during a personal conversation, aren't portraits. Sanders emphasizes instead the great variety of those faces, as they engage us from their particular cultural locations. The faces seem to proliferate like stars in the night sky, even while preserving the light of individual identity. In this sense those human faces shine even more brightly than the stars themselves. Sanders' artistry reminds us that humankind is considered by God highest in all His creation.

Sanders's principle of organization isn't geometrical or numerical, as in Dr. Moustafa's art, or light centered, as in Reem Al Faisal's. It is existential. Sanders told me he photographed his subjects not because they were photogenic in any obvious way, but because they revealed to him the inner beauty of the person. This beauty is a manifestation, he said, of the spiritual beauty of Islam itself, which Sanders equates with *salaam*, the inner peace of a soul given over wholly to God. But this inner beauty is elusive, veiled. Trying to photograph it, Sanders said, "is like chasing a moment, trying to capture a beautiful bird in flight." The photographs express this elusiveness in their contrasts of color and subtle compositional tensions. Yet the experience of the photographs themselves is meditative, since the art form allows the elusiveness to be symbolized, as if it were a bird held briefly in our hands. By this means art allows us both to appreciate and share in the creative dynamic of the beauty revealed to us. The beauty of God's generosity, mediated through Sanders's photography, inspires in us not only wonder, but also the desire to manifest our own inner beauty in our own human faces.

Dr. Moustafa's and Reem Al Faisal's abstract methods of arousing wonder at God's creative generosity contrast with Peter Sanders's lively representational style. So it will be fitting to end with a contemporary artist who combines many elements of these seemingly opposite approaches. That artist is India-born Salma Arastu.

Like Dr. Moustafa, Salma Arastu derives her art from the geometrical and numerical properties of Islamic calligraphy. And like Dr. Moustafa she uses her skill as a painter to give calligraphic forms vibrantly colorful expres-

Peter Sanders, *Tic Toc to the Rhythm of Life*, from the artist's China series.

sion. Yet unlike Dr. Moustafa, Salma Arastu's use of the calligraphic line brings to vision a human world, not an abstract numerical one. Her use of the calligraphic line allows us to see a link between her art and Peter Sanders's. Arastu hasn't confined herself to calligraphic painting. She has painted joyful communities of human faces emerging from calligraphic lines. She reverences the divine hand tracing its finger across the dust and lo, humanity springs forth praising its creator. Sanders uses photographic imagery for a similar purpose. In both Arastu's paintings and Sanders's photography we see visual analogues to Córdoba's "forest" of columns, each one "firmly rooted like a good tree,/ its branches reaching toward the sky, /yielding its fruit at all times by the permission of its Cherisher and Sustainer... ."

An interviewer asked Arastu what attracted her to calligraphy. Her answer:

> I lived in Iran and Kuwait for a while and I was totally amazed by the beauty of the calligraphy. I started copying the figure and just followed the strokes— they are very continuous and lyrical. That's how my figures became more lyrical, almost movement-like. Through the single stroke of a continuous line I want to bring all kinds of people in the world together.[4]

Bringing "all kinds of people in the world together"— that would be Sand-

4. Mehmet Dede, "The Flow of Humanity" at American Society for Muslim Advancement website: www.asmasociety.org/culture/visual_arastu.html

Peter Sanders, *Tic Toc to the Rhythm of Life*, from the artist's China series.

ers's goal as well. It would also be Dr. Moustafa's and Reem Al Faisal's goal, though Dr. Moustafa's love of geometric and calligraphic symbols and Reem Al Faisal's fascination with the creative power of light might seem less connected to human experience than Sanders's and Arastu's play with human face and form. We can say, perhaps, that Sanders and Arastu work more closely in the artistic tradition of the Mosque at Córdoba. They connect us with the horizontal dimension of God's creative generosity. They seek symbols of the human response to that generosity, symbols like those of the "good trees" of *Sura Ibrahim*. Dr. Moustafa and Reem Al Faisal by contrast, focusing our attention upwards as if we stood again beneath the Dome's cupola, seeks symbols in the geometric patterns and in the play of light that structure the generosity. But all four of these artists, whether working in representational or abstract forms, whether emphasizing the horizontal dimension of God's generosity or the vertical, are responding as one to the wake-up call of the *adhan*'s first utterance, *Allahu akbar*, "God is beyond all measure of greatness." All three are attempting in their various ways to "bring all kinds of people together" in wonder at God's Beneficence and Mercy.

"There it is! The sky-hook! The Lakers are up by two with three seconds to play!"

The name Kareem Abdul-Jabbar no longer strikes fear in my heart. Not that I've become a Lakers fan, but because the name now denotes for me —

with the word Abdul ("servant") restored to it — not the basketball player, but artists like the architects of the Dome and the Mosque, like Dr. Moustafa, like Reem Al Faisal, like Peter Sanders, like Salma Arastu, and many others. All are Generous Servants of the Restorer. The scale and nature of their generosity cannot be compared with God's, of course. Yet their tireless invention of symbols to awaken each new generation's capacity for wonder has a joyful lavishness about it. The lavishness heartens us and makes us want to respond generously too, in whatever way we can, in praise of the God who brings us into being each second and sustains us there.

Salma Arastu, *Tribal Joy*, from the artist's "Flow of Humanity" series.

Chapter 3d. Islamic Calligraphy as Invitation to Worship: "Music for the eyes"

I became aware of the Qur'an's visual beauty almost from the beginning of my visits to our Islamic Center. Examples of Qur'anic calligraphy drew my eye everywhere in the building: in framed reproductions on the Center's office walls, in painted areas on the walls of the *masjid* or prayer area where Siddiq and I would sit for my weekly lessons in *tartil* chant, in embossed gold letters arranged above the *mihrab* or niche from which the imam would direct *salat* or daily prayer.

I was already aware that the word "calligraphy" means "beautiful writing." I'd long been attracted to calligraphy in the fine brushwork of Chinese calligraphers, for example, or in some of the examples I'd seen of Christian monastic calligraphy in medieval Bibles and Psalters. Beautiful as these Christian works were, however, they didn't have a religious significance for me, not now, not in the twentieth and twenty-first centuries. Calligraphy as a product of and especially as a stimulus to worship seemed to belong to a remote, unrecoverable past.

But the Islamic calligraphy that attracted and held my attention at the Islamic Center seemed different. I assumed that, like Chinese and Christian monastic calligraphy, it grew out of an ancient tradition. Yet its relevance to the ongoing spiritual lives of my Muslim friends was unmistakable. Not that anyone at the Center commented on the calligraphy or discussed it, not at least in my presence. The calligraphy seemed rather to envelop the worship space and the worshippers within it, lightening and lifting spirits. It seemed to direct worshippers' attention to their purpose for having entered the building in the first place.

How calligraphy might actually direct worshipful attention was a mystery beyond my reach, at least initially. I couldn't sound out let alone decipher any of the calligraphic scripts. I could barely pronounce the words in the simply-lettered copy of the Qur'an my teacher Siddiq had given me. Yet even in my ignorance I loved to look at the flowing lines of calligraphic letters. I admired the way each calligraphic example, especially the more intricate ones, seemed composed and harmonized by a balance of elements (which included not just the letters but vowel marks and epigraphs and sometimes regal emblems like medallions and roundels). No single element of a calligraphic work seemed to dominate the others. (Indeed I learned later on that Muslim calligraphers strove to avoid creating a focal point within their compositions.) These visual examples expressed great energy. Yet the energy was somehow of a centered, focused kind. The energy seemed self-contained without at all feeling pent-up or under pressure. Islamic calligraphy, before I could pronounce or understand a word of it, seemed deeply serene. Islamic calligraphy, I felt, invited me into a state of contemplation.

Gradually, as my capacity to connect the alphabet with sound and meaning increased, some of the dimensions of that place began to become clear. My hand was perhaps my greatest teacher. This teaching began when I decided to copy out phrases from the text of my Qur'an. At first, I did this copying just to have the phrases handy on index cards for memorization. But then little by little I found I was enjoying the copying itself. I liked the way my hand felt as it formed the letters, moving from right to left, swooping up for vertical letters, gliding down and sometimes looping up and around for others, and then afterwards supplying the various marks indicating vowels. My hand taught me that the smooth movement of the pen and the varying thickness of the line affect the shaping of the letters, giving them that fluid contour that suggests the growth and exfoliation of vines and other curving structures. "Arabesque" took on a new meaning for me as my hand grew accustomed to linking the individual letterforms into words and sentences.

Linking letterforms into words is not easy to do in Arabic, it turns out. The shape of a particular Arabic letter changes depending on the letter that comes before and after it (unlike in English cursive script, where the letters keep their shape regardless of neighboring letters). I fancied that the letters behaved that way for a reason. They did so, I thought, because they were sensitive to each other, aware of each other's presence. They seemed alive. I could now appreciate the way that the anonymous calligrapher who had formed the letters in my Qur'an (a copy electronically reproduced from the calligraphed original) varied the thickness of his line to accentuate the life and liveliness of each of these interacting letter-words (or letter-worlds). I marveled at the apparent ease with which the letters had been formed. My own efforts seemed hopelessly clumsy by comparison — a necessary moment of humility for anyone attempting to assess true artistry.

During this process of familiarization I noticed that not all calligraphy was the same. The various examples of calligraphy which I formerly lumped together actually represented several styles of calligraphic script, each with its own history, character, and attraction. Each style combined rigor and freedom in a way known best to those who practiced the discipline, just as performances of classical music are best appreciated by those with the greatest musical training. I definitely stood on the outside of such a world of painstaking dedication. This world included not only the execution of the composition itself but also, and preliminarily, the painstaking preparation of the composition's physical elements: from reed pens and inks to the paper itself.

Yet even as an outsider I could admire great Qur'anic calligraphy in something more than a superficial way. The clear, straightforward style (called *naskh*) employed in my Qur'an text was immediately pleasing to me. Other styles took more time to appreciate. At first I puzzled over the elaborate *thuluth* lettering of my Qur'an's title, *al-qur'an ul-karim* ("The Generous Qur'an"), embossed on the book's cover. The problem wasn't just that the Arabic letters now tended to slope as the hand moved from right to left, but that they seemed also to weave in and out of each other. I understood now that this apparent confusion was in fact highly organized. For in *thuluth* calligraphy the consonants are no longer required to march in a rigid line along their horizontal axis. Instead, they are given leave to hover around that axis. But not randomly. The letters distribute themselves within a space organized by the overall design of the interweaving letters. Vowel markings that in *naskh* script are securely and reliably attached above consonant anchors now float more freely, like silhouettes of soaring birds. Yet these soaring figures never fly off altogether. They remain bound by subtle ties to their consonant perches. The effect on the beholder of these differences in script is dramatic. *Naskh* script turns the beholder into a reader. It moves the reader firmly and smoothly along from the beginning of a verse to the end. The reader tends to "hear" the line as if in *tartil* chant. *Thuluth* script abstracts the memory of that forward motion and translates it into a more purely visual realm. There, meaning no longer develops in temporal sequence but lies deeply within the present moment of contemplation, as if it were the visual equivalent of *tajwid* chant. The reader of *naskh* script becomes, when approaching *thuluth*, something more than a reader. She becomes an observer of verbal beauty visualized, made timelessly present to the eye.

Yet, for all the intrinsic beauty of calligraphic scripts, their function — like the function of chant, either in *tartil* or *tajwid* — is to draw attention not to themselves but to the greater beauty of the divine utterance inspiring them. The nature of this utterance escapes our human categories. Certainly the utterance was manifested to the Prophet Muhammad as a voice, for he himself was, according to tradition, illiterate, and could not have written the utterance down. Besides, oral poetry was by far the most developed and authoritative artistic form among the Arabs at that time. That is why the very first word manifested to the Prophet, the word *'iqra*, the initial word of what is now *Sura al-'Alaq*, is preferably translated "Recite!" (*'Iqra* is same word from which we get *qur'an*, the "reciting.")

But *'iqra* can also be translated "Read!" The fourth line of *sura al-'alaq* supports this translation:

> Read in the name of your cherisher and sustainer who creates
> Who creates humankind from a leech-like clot of blood
> Read in the name of your cherisher and sustainer, the Most Generous
>   [=*akram*, the intensive form of the adjective "karim" (or "kareem")]
> Who instructs with a pen

Instructs humankind in what it does not know
For indeed humankind goes beyond bounds
Thinking themselves their own masters,
But to God is their return… (*Sura al-'Alaq* 96: 1-7)

The word for "pen" in line four is the same word used by calligraphers to refer to their own precisely sharpened tool for inscribing the sacred words. The visual act of reading leads to the visual response of writing. Calligraphers take their inspiration from God's divine example. God's use of the divine pen encourages calligraphers' use of their own pen, fashioned from a simple reed.

So how should we understand '*iqra*? As meaning "recite"? or "read"? Which does Islam privilege, the testimony of the ear or the testimony of the eye?

Ultimately, Islam privileges both. While for reasons already stated, the ear in Muslim tradition is the first of humankind's means of apprehending God's word, the eye follows the ear in short order. Hastening this development historically was the need the Muslim community felt, after the Prophet's death, to correct divergent oral versions of the "Reciting" and to stabilize the text. Having the Qur'an in written form achieved those goals. The written text also made the Qur'an easier to study. Yet as the Qur'an was the word of God, its written expression needed to enhance worship as well. So already by the end of the seventh century (that is, within the lifetimes of those who might have met the Prophet as children) beautiful, highly stylized calligraphic inscriptions adorn the upper walls of the Dome of the Rock. In these ways calligraphy has played a key role in the encouragement and expression of faith almost from Islam's inception, and continues to do the same through the present day. Ear and eye are supremely conducive to the one thing necessary, worshipful attention. No competition exists between *tajwid* artists and calligraphers in Muslim tradition because both recognize their arts as contributing complementary responses to the divine communication. In fact, Muslim calligraphers often describe their visual work in terms of sound, but of sound reverberating within the spirit and imagination, not the ear. They evoke metaphors of sound in order to break the hold of an all-too-easy fixation on the visual elements of their art.

A visit to the website of the famed contemporary American calligraphic master, Mohamed Zakariya, confirms this distinction.[5] (Zakariya is the designer of the U.S. Postal Service's "Eid" stamp commemorating the holy month of Ramadan.) An assiduous student of and practitioner in the Ottoman calligraphic tradition, Zakariya speaks in precise, learned detail about his art's history, theory, and practice. Yet his language never becomes pedantic. That is because calligraphy for him, as for all its greatest prac-

5. www.zakariya.net/home.html

titioners, is not an end in itself, but an offering of beauty to the God who loves beauty, indeed as "a kind of worship, a religious event that prepares one for prayer."[6] And in evoking this beauty, Zakariya readily employs the language of song. What Qur'anic calligraphy does, Zakariya states, is "celebrate the sounds and meanings of the sacred text and preserve its accuracy." Zakariya cites approvingly an old saying that Arabic calligraphy is "music for the eyes." And Zakariya quotes with great appreciation the renowned Turkish scholar Mahmud Yazir's coining of the phrase "breath-like flow" (from the book *The Beauty of the Pen*) to characterize examples of calligraphic excellence.

Celebration of sound, breath, and music — these are among the metaphors with which calligraphers point to the influence of their art within the deepest region of our being. In that region calligraphy can create, as Zakariya puts it, "a visual harmony that resonates within the spirit." Calligraphy, like *tajwid* recitation, invites the worshipper towards that harmony. It can do so because it sees that reality as beautiful, and finds beautiful means and metaphors to answer to the beauty it sees.

All of Zakariya's calligraphic works that I'm familiar with extend this invitation. Take as an example his rendering of *Sura at-Tauba* 9:128, in which Zakariya highlights the phrase: "Ardently anxious is he for you." This calligraphic composition is inscribed with reed pen selected and sharpened by Zakariya's own hand, using ink of his own mixing and on paper of his own making:

> Now has come among you a messenger from among you;
> he grieves for what you are suffering;
> ardently anxious is he for you,
> for to the believers is he most kind and merciful.

The wonder of this composition lies in the balanced tension between contrasting elements. One such tension results from the contrasting scales of the lettering Zakariya employs. Zakariya's bold expansion and highlighting of only two words of the original Arabic verse, *harisun aleikum* (translated above as "ardently anxious [is he] for you") allows him to create the structural axes of the entire composition. Against this stabilizing effect of the large-scale letters run the words of the rest of the verse, in tiny letters, in a leftward-leaning style called *muhaqqaq*. Another tension results from within the two expanded words themselves. The vertical axis, developed from the Arabic letter for the letter "l" in *aleikum*, anchors the composition on the page. In tension against it are the other large black letters. The curving forms of these large letters contrast with the vertical thrust of the "l" and soften it, transforming its abrupt power into a more resilient, a more

---

6. Mohamed Zakariya, "Music for the Eyes" at www.zakariya.net/resources/music.html

Mohamed Zakariya, *Ardently Anxious*, Qur'an *sura at-tauba* 9:128. Ink, gouache and gold on paper prepared by the artist, 25¾" x 21¼".

pliable energy.

These balanced tensions underscore balanced tensions within the verse's meaning. God speaks tenderly here to his people, reminding them of the great gift from God they enjoy in the Prophet himself. God speaks of the Prophet in the most positive way, using words of him, at the end of the verse, that are also included among God's own names: the Most Kind (*ar-ra'uf*) and Merciful (*ar-Raheem*). The intention here is not to confuse God with God's creature, but to suggest the extraordinary status the Prophet enjoys in God's sight, and to reinforce the value of the Prophet's presence among the Prophet's people during their time of need.

The words Zakariya chooses to single out, though, are words that explicitly describe the human dimension of the Prophet's concern for his community: "ardently anxious is he for you." I suggest that the full meaning of Zakariya's composition begins to unfold for us to the extent that we allow the phrase to echo within us as "music for the eyes." A tension emerges within us, I think, in tune with the structural tensions already noted. God in God's unapproachable glory is speaking through the Prophet, but also directly to us, even in the midst of our fears and failings. And God reminds us that despite the immeasurable distance between God and us, there are yet channels between heaven and earth — like that vertically striking "l" of the "aleikum" in Zakariya's composition and its softening by the other surrounding letters — that allow fruitful communication, even the communication of a parent's anxiety. The Prophet himself is the channel and embodiment of that anxiety, almost as if the Prophet were living calligraphy. "Ardently anxious is he for you"— as if Zakariya's composition were saying: If God *would* become human, this is how God would be with you, right now, in whatever current form your distress and confusion are taking.

Mohamed Zakariya represents the best of what might be called the traditional practice of Islamic calligraphy, a practice that constantly seeks to use time-honored methods and materials to renew and refresh time-honored styles and approaches. Other Muslim artists have, however, sought to expand the range of the tradition and have found the need to employ different means to do so. This development has accelerated during the last few decades, and at the present moment is in a state of creative ferment as calligraphic elements are increasingly used to express reactions to current social and political realities. Many of those realities are tragic. Yet as widely diverse as present-day uses of Islamic calligraphy are, they always recall calligraphy's primary aims: first, to stimulate worshipful attention to God's mercy and, second, to encourage constant remembrance of the instruction already quoted from *Sura al-'Alaq*, that "to God you shall all return."

Sheila S. Blair's *Islamic Calligraphy*, a fine, comprehensive history of calligraphy in Muslim lands, opens our eyes to Islamic calligraphy's most recent developments.[7] In her last chapter, "The Many Faces of Islamic Calligraphy in Modern Times," Blair gives examples of the way calligraphy has recently been branching into different media, especially into painting and calligraphic sculpture. She also points out how calligraphy is increasingly being used for political purposes, by shaping responses, for example,

7. Sheila S. Blair *Islamic Calligraphy* (Edinburgh: Edinburgh University Press, 2008).

to the situation of the Palestinians or of women in Afghanistan. In many if not most of these instances the political cannot be easily separated from the personal, as Muslim artists use elements of the calligraphic tradition to express the joys and struggles of seeking beauty in situations and places never dreamt by the classic calligraphers of Persia and Turkey.

Suggestive as Blair's book is, however, it but scratches the surface of the vast amount of contemporary artistic activity inspired by the ancient art of Qur'anic calligraphy. The British Museum's 2006 show, "Word into Art: Artists of the Modern Middle East," gave much fuller access to this cornucopia. But the show did more than make available a vast amount of excellent contemporary calligraphic work that would otherwise have remained obscure. It also directed the viewer's attention to the difficult if not agonizing contemporary issues that are moving Muslim artists to seek new ways of responding to the question of how to live their faith in a violent world. For example, one section of the show, "Identity, History, Politics," displayed work containing poetry, calligraphic fragments, sometimes barely legible Arabic letters and scrawls, to portray struggles for meaning in the midst of tragedy and dislocation — the lot of many Muslims in the lands and the period covered by "Word into Art."

Even a show as comprehensive as the British Museum's "Word into Art" cannot include the fullness of those working brilliantly in the calligraphic tradition. I'll end by mentioning two contemporary artists who, though not included in the show, are making outstanding contributions.

One of these is Libya-born, now England based Ali Omar Ermes. Like Ahmad Moustafa, whose work we met in Chapter 3c, Ermes is not strictly speaking a calligrapher, since he prefers the relative freedom of oil painting to the strict procedures governing the use of the reed pen and ink in the calligraphic tradition. Yet Ermes's play with the shapes of calligraphic letters within the visual field of his canvases and his interweaving within and around those shapes of carefully selected Arabic poetry show his profound respect for that tradition. At the same time his setting of calligraphic elements against abstract, textured backgrounds connects him broadly with Western painterly traditions. Ermes's aim in uniting specifically Islamic elements with elements outside this tradition is to suggest the positive universal effect that the arts of Islam can still exert through the calligraphic word. "My vision," says Ermes on his website, is to help viewers "recognize the power of Islamic thought to re-ignite our modern imagination in its individual and universal sense" so that our imagination can embrace all of Islam's characteristics, "enjoy its fruits and refer to it as a major resource of hope and optimism for a better future for all humanity."[8]

The calligraphic work of Mohammed Ali aka "Aerosol Arabic" appeals, just as Ermes's work does, to our universal responsibility to heal our broken

---

8. http://www.aliomarermes.co.uk/profile/thevision.cfm

Mohammed Ali, *To God We Belong*, Qur'an *sura al-baqarah* 2:156
painted on a wall in the Bronx.

world, though Ali's favored tool is neither a reed pen nor a paintbrush but a can of aerosol spray-paint. Growing up in Birmingham, Ali caught from his peers an enthusiasm for graffiti art applied with aerosol paint cans. Then when he rediscovered Islam in his early 20's, he saw a connection between his beloved graffiti art and calligraphy. "As a graffiti artist," Ali explains, "I already had an obsession with the written word. So, it was fascinating to discover how Islamic art was focused primarily on the written word. But instead of man's word, it is the word of God, written in intricate, elegant, and fluid styles....I became drawn to Islam. This was my solace. It gave me meaning, and Islam was now a big part of my life."[9]

Ali's website (www.aerosolarabic.com) gives a vivid sense of the brilliance of his calligraphic artistry. But for my purposes Ali's most significant work is found on the outside wall of the building in the Bronx he spray-painted to honor the eight immigrant children from Mali killed in a Bronx apartment fire in March, 2007. The Arts Council England sponsored Ali's visit to the Bronx, and produced a video showing Ali bringing members of the grieving families together with people from the local community into the actual production of the artwork. The completed wall bears the Qur'anic

---

9. Abu Ali Bafaquih, "Islamically Sprayed," *Islamic Horizons* Sept/Oct 2007: 64-5.

Aerosol calligrapher Mohammed Ali helps a family member of the Mali children apply spray paint to *To God We Belong*. April 7, 2007.

verse: "[Blessings on those who, when calamity befalls them, say,] 'To God we belong, and to Him we will return'" (*Sura al-Baqarah* 2:156). Ali paints the phrase "'To God we belong...'" in calligraphic Arabic letters, and the rest in English, along with the names of the dead children. The most moving tribute to beauty's capacity to reach us even in our deepest grief is the response of family members of the dead children. Their weeping faces as they watch Ali at work testify to the power of Ali's art. But they aren't the only ones touched. The video also shows the solemn reactions of passers-by who are stopped in their tracks by the artwork in progress. Ali then invites these onlookers, along with family members, to help him in completing the project. Members of both groups add strokes of aerosol paint to the overall design under Ali's direction. In this way the finished work acquires a communal meaning, and an otherwise barren sweep of brick is transformed into a place of remembrance, of solidarity, and even of worship of the God to whom "we will all return."

Something contemporary British calligrapher Soraya Syed told me about her art takes on new light as I think about Ali's achievement, not only in the Bronx, but also in other communal calligraphy he has inspired. "The Qur'an plays a direct role in my creativity," she said. And then she added:

Furthermore, in practicing this sacred art, my aim and the hope is that the distance between Allah's and one's own creativity is minimal. There is a Hadith Qudsi [a statement by God transmitted not in God's own words but in the Prophet Muhammad's and so not inserted into the Qur'an] that God says about His servants: "When I love him, I am the hearing with which he hears, his seeing with which he sees, his hand with which he strikes, and his foot with which he walks."

I don't know if any of those adding a stroke of aerosol spray-paint to the wall in the Bronx were conscious of themselves as God's instruments, but it's not impossible. The calligraphic tradition, still vital, invites such human collaboration in the divine communication. And beyond that, beauty never ceases to attract us, even in our deepest grief, and makes us long to be beauty's ears, and eyes, and hands, and feet.

Chapter 3e. Playfulness and Immediacy: "And now, God, you're scratching my head!"

"Come alive to the prayer." This verse of the *adhan* summons each Muslim to *salat*, to assembly with the other faithful before God. The summons is directed not just to the body. It calls the entire person into life, into fullness of being.

Yet the body plays a key role during *salat* in engaging the entire person. *Sujud*, prostration, and *qiyam*, standing, are the physical manifestations of that engagement. Dr. Shafiq once explained the process to me this way: "When you place your forehead on the carpet, you are putting yourself at the very feet of God, you are bowing down right before him. Nothing stands between you and him, no distance, no priest, no intercessor —nothing. You are expressing directly to God your *islam*, your total self-giving to God. You are embodying what it means to say *la ilaha illallah*, 'there is no god but God.' But then, when you stand up, you are expressing your God-given dignity before him, as God's *khalifa*, trustee, and the receiver of God's *ruh* or spirit."

Despite the clarity of Dr. Shafiq's explanation, I still wondered what the inner connection might be between the two poles of self-giving and of dignified self-assertion. They seemed such totally different states of being.

A way to understand the relation between *sujud* and *qiyam* finally opened for me after I'd come upon some writings by the great medieval mystic philosopher Ibn 'Arabi. In his famous compendium, *The Meccan Illuminations* (*Al-Futu'ha't al-Makkiyya*), Ibn 'Arabi had defined the believer's essential relation to God as a relation to *al-jamil*, to God as the Beautiful One. But since all adjectives applied to God have an active sense, *al-jamil* describes what God does; God is Beautiful by creating our capacity for responding to Him beautifully. God does this for humankind by inviting it to know Him in a dynamic movement between two states of soul, a movement between fear and intimacy. And this is because God's Beauty manifests itself to humankind in two forms, as Majesty (Ibn 'Arabi calls it "the Majesty of Beauty") and as Beauty (which he calls "the Beauty of Beauty"). We bow in awe before one, draw close in joy to the second. Yet, as the *shaykh-al-akbar*, the Great Sage, goes on to say, these responses have their own inner dynamic: Fear must be balanced by intimacy in the approach to the Majesty of Beauty, and intimacy by fear in the approach to the Beauty of Beauty.

Dense as Ibn 'Arabi's analysis was, it encouraged me to trace *salat*'s inner unity more confidently. Even if, during *sujud*, humankind acknowledges its utter dependence as it lies at the feet of God in the Majesty of his Beauty, the acknowledgement does not crush humankind. It rather allows humankind to rise in *qiyam* to its rightful stature. Likewise, when standing before God in the Beauty of his Beauty, humankind has no motive for pride, since God's Beauty pierces it to the heart and makes it fall to its knees in surrender. What then struck me about *salat* is the way it ritualizes a perpetual relational exchange between creator and created. At one moment of that exchange, the two find themselves related asymmetrically, when humanity presses its forehead at the feet of the Majesty of Beauty. But prostration is not a fixed position. It is passed through, traversed, on humanity's way to the opposite moment of standing before the Beauty of Beauty, where humanity receives its dignity in exchange for its *sujud* or self-yielding. The basic asymmetry between creator and created does not disappear. But the relation between them becomes flexible. What makes the flexibility possible is the flexibility of beauty itself in its manifestation to the believer.

A key question for us in this chapter, however, is: How does the flexibility of beauty play out in relation to the Muslim artist?

There is a famous *hadith qudsi* that gives us a clue. The *hadith* allows us to imagine God as playfully courting human reciprocity, even as giving humankind the first move in the creator-creature relationship:

> I am as my servant thinks I am. I am with him if he makes mention of me. If he makes mention of me to himself, I make mention of him to myself. And if he makes mention of me in an assembly, I make mention of him in an assembly even greater. And if he approaches me by a hand's span, I approach him by an arm's length. And if he approaches me by one arm's length, I approach him by six. And if he approaches me walking, I approach him at a run.

The face of God, stern on many occasions, softens here. God, in response to human initiative, becomes lovingly, even (if one may dare say it) playfully engaged. God turns the vast difference in scale between Himself and His creature into symbols of His own welcome. A hand's span for us is an arm's length for God, our walk towards God is God's run towards us. This is God as *al-tawwab*, the One Turning joyfully to us at the least sign of our turning to God.

Sufi poets have been turning towards God for centuries. Their poetry is the record, even the occasion of this experience of turning. Their verses mirror God's loving welcome, and they too, like God, are mindful of their loved one's dignity — or difference. The poets' mindfulness has a different source than God's, of course. It lies not in mercy but in consciousness of God as *al-jalal*, the Majestic. Yet this consciousness does not frighten them. It rather heightens their desire and their joy even while stimulating a sense of their own absurdity within this asymmetric courtship dance. They long for God in laughter and tears.

Here is Rumi (1207-1273 CE), speaking directly to God:

> When I press my hand to my chest,
> it is your chest.

And now you're scratching my head!

Sometimes you put me in the herd
with your other camels.

Sometimes you place me at the front of your troops
as the commander. Sometimes you wet me
with your mouth like you do your seal ring
just before you plant your power.

Sometimes you round me
into a simple door knocker....

There's nothing to believe.
Only when I quit believing in *myself*
Did I come into this beauty....

There is no way to describe you.
Say the end of this so strongly
that I will ride up overm
my own commotion.[10]

A century later another great Sufi poet, Hafez, again expresses the joyful folly of the lover constantly thwarted by his creaturely weakness. (Hafez characteristically addresses himself in the third person in the final line of his poems.)

...As long as I circle the edge, like a compass, a disconnected point,
the vagaries of time will not stop blocking my path to the centre.

Sure, with perseverance, I could get my hands on sugar;
but the broken promise of Time hurries me on.

Let me sleep, I said, I'll see the image of the Friend in slumber;
but Hafez keeps me up all night with his groaning.[11]

Sufi poets do not speak from simple torment any more than they do from simple triumph. They shuttle between the extremes. For on the one hand God as *al-wadud*, the Loving, never disappoints the human lover. On the other, God never yields Himself fully to him or her. Rumi's "commotion" and Hafez's "groaning" are potentially tragic reactions to God's profound and ever-elusive difference. Yet tragedy is impossible. The commotion and

---

10. From *The Essential Rumi*, translated by Coleman Barks with John Moyne (San Francisco: HarperSanFrancisco, 1995), 269-70.

11. Hafez, "Beneath the Veil," in *The Tangled Braid*, translated by Jeffrey Einboden and John Slater (Louisville: Fons Vitae, 2010).

groaning are no sooner felt than they are tempered by signs of God's intimacy. Sufis have found, and still find, that poetry is the best way to express such a dynamic oscillation between distance and approach in their pursuit of the divine lover. And in the case of Rumi and of the Mevlevi Order of Whirling Dervishes inspired by him, they have found that dance expresses this dynamic as well.

I haven't been able to attend performances of the Whirling Dervishes of Konya. (Konya is the city in present-day Turkey where Rumi, a jurist by profession, wrote his poetry and where disciples in ever-increasing numbers sought him out.) The group's website (www.whirlingdervishes.org/) shows what the dance looks like and how it is understood.

The dance, called *Sema*, sets the dancers' bodies rotating in sympathy with the universal rotation of atoms around their nuclei and planets around their suns. Inspired by the Prophet Muhammad's own *m'iraj* (his rise through the heavens to the Throne of God and subsequent descent), the dance follows a highly stylized pattern in which the whirling dancers enact a spiritual ascent to heaven. But just at the point of their highest proximity to *al-wahid*, the One, the dance brings the dancers down to earth again. In this way they act out God's command to the Prophet and his followers that enlightened souls serve their fellow creatures, not their own happiness.

Rumi scholar Annemarie Schimmel speaks of how, for Rumi, all created things, from bees to angels, "stamp their feet" in a universal dance of praise.[12] Yet the stamping never becomes orgiastic or indulgently self-forgetful. Tempered passion is perhaps the best source of humor. Surprise and playfulness are this humor's manifestations, and they are always at the beck and call of the one who turns to *al-tawwab*, the One Turning.

I sensed the same humor one summer as Peggy and I and our Sufi friend, the interfaith minister Jamal Rahman, entered the cool interior of the Museum of International Folk Art in Santa Fe, New Mexico, to see a traveling exhibit called "The Sufi Arts of Senegal." The visual effect was bewildering. Soberly classical Islamic images somehow blended with contemporary African and international styles and artifacts. The bright colors of glass paintings depicting local saints and their feats, the swirling portraiture of Pepisto Boy's wall murals recalling the work of Diego Rivera and José Orozco, the intricate Qur'anic calligraphy dotting long prayer-papers resembling Chinese scrolls, the arresting, fine-arts quality paintings and assemblages of artists Moussa Tine, Chalys Leye, and others — all competed for attention. What was the meaning of this phantasmagoria? What thread led through it? What was "Sufi" about it?

Jamal came to my rescue by pointing out the key image amid the visual dazzle: a white-shrouded figure squinting as if from a blaze of sun in his

12. Annemarie Schimmel, *Rumi's World: The Life and Work of the Great Sufi Poet* (Boston & London: Shambhala Publications, Inc., 2001), 201.

eyes, face turned towards the viewer yet half-concealed by a swath of cloth. Versions of this figure, in just this pose, were visible everywhere: imbedded in glass paintings, elaborated in wall murals, dissolved into calligraphic forms, emanating ghost-like from a mixed-media collage by artist Samba Laye, printed as posters competing with Coca-Cola signs among arrays of hubcaps and engine blocks. The figure was that of the Mauride (Sengalese Sufi) Saint, Amadou Bamba, revered among Sengalese Muslims not only for defying Senegal's French occupiers, but also for his ever potent spiritual *baraka* or blessing. The omnipresent renditions of his image did more than honor him. They acted almost sacramentally to arouse the fervor and piety of his many followers and to strengthen their faith in God amid continuing toil and hardship.

Powerful as these separate images of Amadou Bamba were, they made most sense to me within a small enclosed area of the museum decorated to resemble a Mauride devotee's private home worship space. Bamba's white-turbaned figure in posters, photographs, and amulets dominated the space, while every other surface, including floor and ceiling, was filled by a wide variety of images and objects assisting the devotee's receptivity to the saint's *baraka*. The ceiling had been painted with paradisial motifs (palm branches, clouds, pools of water); colorful patterned prayer rugs and pillows had been laid on the floor; a boom-box had been placed on a stand that also held CDs of Mauride music and *tajwid* Qur'an recitation, accouterments for making tea, miniatures of the Ka'bah, prayer beads, and clocks that sounded the *adhan*; a spinning disco light had been mounted high up in a corner projecting all 99 Beautiful Names. The entire room felt like a Sufi poem, both celebrating the near presence of God while at the same time humorously laughing at its own vertiginous profusion of spiritual images and artifacts.

What were Bamba's devotees thinking when they decorated such rooms? According to the exhibit catalogue, devotees are expressing a desire to evoke two of the Beautiful Names for God: *al-zahir* and *al-batin*, the Manifest and the Hidden. For Mauride devotees, the colorful riot of images festooning their worship spaces serves the secret or source of their longing. None of the assembled images can express that secret. They even tend to veil it. But even as the images do that, they open the heart of the one who sits both surrounded and liberated in such spaces, forgetting self and remembering God. For Maurides, God's intimacy encourages a proliferating of imagery in the quest of the One who is beyond all imaging.

Expansively creative imagery in quest of the One who is beyond all imaging: this characterizes the work of many contemporary North American artists as well. Kazim Ali, poet and Professor of Creative Writing at Oberlin College, is one of these. Grounded firmly in Islam, Ali is comfortable spinning his poetic imagination through the imagery of other faith traditions too, as all spin their ways through God's marvelously unfathomable universe. "I exist only two cosmic minutes after you,/ an echo of your life's whispering," Ali begins his poem "Dear Father, Dear Sound."[13] Echoes and whisperings recur throughout Ali's poetry; this is how we hear a hint of God if we hear Him at all. Ali knows that any approach to God has to be elusive, because God's approach to us is always elusive, as is suggested by the Qur'anic verse: "Human vision does not grasp Him, but He grasps human vision, for He is the Most Subtle, the Most Knowing" (*Sura al An'am* 6:103).

To create a poetic equivalent for our probing, open-ended, ever-surprising and unfinished relation to God, Ali has developed the technique of the isolated image-couplet. Here it is in his poem "Afternoon Prayer," which also exhibits Ali's characteristic delight in word-play:

God, a curt question or a curtain
the call to prayer fading away.
May I request evening or more rain?
Doing laundry, getting new tires —
May I invest smartly, catch a later train?
Snow fills the margins, sunset across the river.
As we rush north, everything is pulled back,
God, a day's work, the echoing tracks —[14]

The opening word-play of "curt question or a curtain" images God as either teasing us from behind a curtain or entering our lives as a cosmic question-mark. Questioning is indeed core to Ali's cosmic vision; in fact, as in the line that follows — "May I request evening or more rain?" — much of his poetry is in the form of an unanswered question. The startling surprise of this particular question, following the space after "the call to prayer fading away," is also typical; in the gap between his couplet stanzas, Ali opens up a space of unbounded questioning, so that we never know where we'll land as the next stanza starts. Similarly with the stanza that follows: "May I invest smartly, catch a later train?" The rhyme of "train" with "rain" hints at a link between them, but we're left to draw the link or to leave it hanging, as the poet plays with our mind's expectations. Trains, we should note, turn up frequently in Ali's poetry; they are his primary means of transit through his gloriously (sometimes impishly) unfathomable cosmos. And those "echoing tracks" at the poem's end: they might be train tracks, or God's tracks, or any other reverberation of tracking that the poet deliberately leaves open by ending his poem with the inconclusive punctuation of a dash.

Another contemporary North-American Muslim artist with a delight in playfulness is Pakistani-born now New York-based Asma Shikoh. Her

---

13. In *The Fortieth Day* (Rochester, NY: BOA Editions, 2008).
14. In *The Fortieth Day*.

series of acrylic self-portraits entitled "Liberated" depict, in words from her website www.asmashikoh.com, the "visual interplay of popular icons and the *hijab* (the head scarf adorned by Muslim women), highlighting the role of individual practices in the shaping of a unique national identity. It reflects my belief in the self-empowering identity of American Muslim women." The interplay Shikoh speaks of is bold, brilliant, and humorous. In "The Story Teller" and "The Activist," she poses as a triumphant Marvel Comics Super-Heroine in vividly red and green *hijab* and flowing *jilbab* respectively. In "A Group of 8 Sketches," the outline of her *hijab* becomes a screen for projected cultural images drawn from computer icons, from photographs of New York skyscrapers, from painted illustrations of children's faces, and from other contemporary non-Muslim sources. The firmness of Shikoh's faith permits this easygoing play between her own Muslim identity and North-American cultural forms and preconceptions. As Shikoh said to me in a personal correspondence:

> Religion and our daily lives, this world, our immediate environment, are all part of me, and the Prophet never shunned any one over the other... so accepting all together is very easy and holds no confusion for me.

Shikoh's eclecticism reminds us that turning to God, whether in painting, dance, or in densely imagistic Mauride prayer spaces, can have a centripetal effect. All creation — including cultural elements from outside Islamic tradition — tends to be pulled by the force of God's attraction into the vortex of the dance. Rumi's poetry is famous for abounding with objects and ideas bursting in not directly from the Qur'an but from his own cultural milieu: reed flutes, wine jugs, lions, bears, and broomsticks, as well as stories of fabled Kings, Queens, and Wizards from Rome to China.

Eclecticism, immediacy, and playfulness — these qualities characterize the art of many contemporary Muslim artists who, like Asma Shikoh, are learning to combine the artistic traditions of their homelands with those of the West. They combine the traditions in different ways and with different emphases, of course, but all with the aim of startling us out of the stifling, stereotypical images we have of ourselves and of others and in that way to free us to glimpse our deeper human unity.

This boundary-breaking capacity of contemporary Muslim art is evident in the work of the two Pakistani-born Muslim artists with whom I'll end this chapter: Naif Al-Mutawa, the creator and co-writer of the comic book series *The 99*, and rock star Salman Ahmad. Al-Mutawa and Ahmad have the advantage of working in popular media that attract a far larger audience than the fine arts do, and an audience consisting mainly of young people.

Al-Mutawa's superheroes mirror *The 99* is target audience of Muslim youth. The superheroes are a multicultural group of young Muslim men and

Asma Ahmed Shikoh, *The Activist*. Acrylics on board, 22"x48".

women united by a dedication to overcome social injustice. Each of the 99 superheroes comes from a different country where Muslims live, and each brings to this combat a power embodied in his or her connection to one of the qualities of the ìBeautiful Names.î So the Saudi character Jabbar (*al-jabbar*) acts as the Powerful, and the Emirate character Noora (*an-nur*) acts as the Light, for she can see the light and darkness in everyone.

The marketing of *The 99*, promoted as "the world's first superhero team based on Islamic culture," is just as energetic as its visual and story-telling style. Employing illustrators from Marvel Comics and other mainstream comics publications, *The 99* also shares the Marvel Comics website. Al-Mutawa is not apologetic about this corporate relationship. Just the opposite. His assertion is that Muslim youth worldwide — *The 99*'s primary audience — need the reinforcement of positive, life-enhancing Islamic values that *The 99* provides in order to counteract the negative, destructive image of Islam produced and carried out by extremists. Muslim youth also need to see that Muslim culture embodies universal values of cooperation and care for the marginalized shared by the other world religious traditions. Ultimately, *The 99*ís audience is youth everywhere. That is why the Marvel Comics connection is key for Dr. Al-Mutawa, to make sure his universal message reaches a universal audience.

Rock star Salman Ahmad's achievement exemplifies how deeply and widely the arts can influence and even direct our universal longing for peace and reconciliation. In his early years, Ahmad himself had to reconcile an apparent personal and cultural contradiction of his own: between a love of God instilled in him by his India-born Sufi grandfather and a passion for the electric guitar. The reconciliation finally occurred when, as lead guitarist of Junoon, Pakistan's top rock band, he risked his career and his life to promote peace and sustainable development between India and Pakistan. While touring India, in May 1998, he and his band protested against the nuclear arms race between the two countries. Junoon was immediately banned from Pakistani television and radio. Band members received death threats. But they remained faithful to their vision and to the power of their art to convey it, and the next year were given an award by UNESCO for "outstanding achievements in music and peace." The group has put their creativity in the service of environmental issues as well. "The worst thing you can do as a songwriter," says Ahmad, "is to be didactic or try to be preachy, but we have tried through the music to make people more aware of their environment." In 2004 Ahmad was appointed as a United Nations Goodwill Ambassador on HIV/AIDS. "'Goodwill Ambassador' is a big, glorified term," Ahmad remarks modestly, "but I am just a footsoldier. The role of people in my position is to keep shining a light on the problem and to try to get as many people on board to coordinate and cooperate as possible.… I don't know if there's a measure of how many of [our listeners] resonate as passionately as I do, but they do listen. And it's the power of intention. If you are doing something from the heart it touches people — and if it touches only one person it will be worth it."[15]

Ahmadís artistic mission, like Al-Mutawaís and the missions of the other artists weíve looked at in this chapter, echoes the idea Rumi expressed in a poem quoted earlier: ìOnly when I quit believing in myself / did I come into this beautyÖî Ahmad encourages his audience to ìquit believingî in supposedly religious sanctions of violence and ugliness and to believe instead in truly religious sanctions of conscience and beauty. The means Ahmad uses to express that beauty, the electric guitar, is not traditional for Islam, but I donít think Rumi or Hafez would have scorned it. For Godís intimacy liberated the Sufi poets to search the world for symbols that might express something at least of the joyfully playful energy of the divine-human dance, a dance to which, once we catch the tune of it, all the rest of us, no matter how humble our starting point, are always free to join.

Daisy Khan, the Executive Director of the New York-based American Society for Muslim Advancement (ASMA), made a comment to me recently that has helped me put contemporary Muslim artistic developments in perspective. "There's a contrast," she told me, "between traditional Muslim artistic expression, focused on worship, and contemporary expression, which is more focused on healing on the personal and communal level, and on identity and social issues."

I'll have more to say in Chapter 5c about how Daisy and her husband, Imam Feisal Rauf, have been employing contemporary Muslim arts as vehicles for healing our collective social wounds. Suffice it to underline here a discovery that the most imaginative contemporary Muslim artists are making: that their art is neither stifled nor betrayed by Western methods or approaches but actually invigorated by them. Joyful freedom of expression in response to God's intimacy is the antidote of fear— fear of self, fear of Other. The world becomes larger, becomes whole, in response to a God who meets us freely within our own most private freedom to respond.

15. http://www.unep.org/OurPlanet/imgversn/154/ahmad.html

Chapter 3f. Longing for Transcendence: "The fountain in my midst is like the soul of the believer"

Our friend Yasmin — introduced in Chapter One — has many talents. One of them is for dress design and decoration. Until Yasmin took on the mission of establishing a parochial school at Rochester's Islamic Center, she taught chemistry at a local college while also running a small dress-making business. Peggy bought several outfits there. Loose in cut and modest in design, the outfits are distinctive for their subtle use of colored fabric and especially for their hand-painted motifs. Many of the motifs suggest arabesques — flowering designs reminiscent of calligraphy. Peggy looks wonderful in them (a husband can be expected to say no less!) and often wears them when she goes out to dinner or leads a retreat. Yasmin's dresses combine an artist's touch with comfortable attractiveness.

Yet these dresses, attractive as they are, looked like poor togs indeed alongside the clothing Yasmin designed and wore during a Ramadan celebration I attended not long ago. I cannot forget how beautifully Yasmin had matched the fabrics for the four main parts of her outfit, the *hijab* (or head scarf), the *qameez* (the loose-fitting tunic), the *shalwar* (the flowing ankle-length skirt), and the *jilbab* (the full-length gown worn over both *qameez* and *shalwar*). Each part of the whole was a slightly different shade of cream, and I'd note a subtle interaction among the fabrics whenever Yasmin moved or whenever even a slight breeze stirred an edge or hem. Adding to the subtle effect was the way in which the floral motifs Yasmin had painted on the fabrics opened or closed themselves to view as she moved or as a breeze blew.

"So this is what she hopes to wear in the Garden," I said to myself.

I wouldn't have had that thought if I hadn't seen Yasmin's outfit when and where I did. On neutral ground, I would almost certainly have given the clothing a much narrower interpretation. I would have assumed that its real purpose was to call attention to and enhance the wearer's own beauty. My gender and cultural background would have enforced such a reading.

Even if I'd gotten past a reaction of that sort, I would still have understood the beauty of Yasmin's clothing in a restricted way. I would have been thinking primarily about her artistry in handling certain cultural conventions. Since Yasmin is from Bangladesh, I would have been trying to guess the extent to which her creativity had enhanced those conventions. I would have been puzzling in just the same way about the garments worn by the other women present, especially the women from Somalia, with their swirling, vividly colorful *jilbabs*. The flair and brilliance of Somali dress contrasted with the subtle sobriety of Yasmin's apparel.

But seeing these garments during a Ramadan celebration, where the local community (along with local Muslim communities everywhere) gathers to honor the revelation of the Qur'an to Muhammad, I gave instead a wider and truer meaning to the garments' beauty, and especially to the garments Yasmin wore. Knowing her artistic gift and firm religious commitment, I saw her dress as the response to God's invitation to the Garden. Placing her artistic talents at the disposal of such a response was, I knew, Yasmin's warmest intention. I knew also that the Qur'an sanctions such an intention. "Who is there who will forbid the beauty that God has brought forth for God's creatures?..." (*Sura al-'Araf* 7:32). Beautiful clothing is not in itself a snare and a delusion but a gift to be worn in thanksgiving to God and in anticipation of the "fullness of being" to which the *adhan*, the Call to Prayer, invites all Muslims.

Because it is seen as such a gift, beautiful clothing such as Yasmin's blurs the common Western distinction between craft and art. The utilitarian function of Yasmin's Ramadan garments is hardly to be distinguished from its function as a celebratory thanksgiving to the source of all Beauty. I was struck by this unity of craft and art when I came across at a later date the work of Saudi-born Huda Totonji. Recognized as a master calligrapher, Dr. Totonji is also highly skilled in other media. But it is her photography that I want to call attention to, especially the photographs in her "Calligraphy Projections Prayer Series: Photography and Arabic Handwriting." In the example from the Series reproduced here, a female subject wearing hijab and jilbab faces the camera against a black background, head bowed, while prayers in Arabic are projected upon the woman's quiet, meditative form.

This photograph, like Yasmin's garments, is an act of thanksgiving flowing from the creation of a visual symbol of the soul's purification and emergence into the Light of God. As Dr. Totonji wrote to me:

> The light source coming on the calligraphic work indicates an opening into the heavens. The process of purification of the soul is expressed in the illuminated handwritten prayers. As a result of the experience articulated, the worshipper is reborn. Elevation and sincere faith illuminate from the soul with a candle lighting the devotee's new path. The use of the *chiaroscuro* effect in these photographic series was inspired by Michelangelo Merisi da Caravaggio's use of evident light source. It further adds to the visual and spiritual meaning of the work that combines text and image.

The result is not at all meant as a work to be admired at a distance but rather as an inspiration to be followed, both by the viewer and the artist herself. As Dr. Totonji puts it, speaking of the purpose of Muslim art in general:

> The intention of the Muslim artist is a spiritual one that focuses on the beautification of the environment that surrounds him or her to come closer to God through his or her artwork.

Whether we call it craft or art, the unveiling of the purified soul suggested

Huda Totonji, from "Calligraphy Projections Prayer Series".
Color photograph.

symbolically in Yasmin's tailored garments and Dr. Totonji's photography is a process fully completed only in the life to come.

For artists like Yasmin and Dr. Totonji, the Adhan's final phrase, "Come alive to fullness of being," is at once an artistic mandate and goal. Artists are to make the way to that goal visible and desirable and arrival at it attainable. But what exactly is this goal? "Fullness of being" sounds fine but fuzzy. What exactly does the phrase point to?

One of my favorite characteristics of the Arabic language is its tendency to keep alive the basic, concrete meanings of its word-roots. The word from the Adhan translated as "fullness of being," for example, comes from an Arabic word whose root meaning is "split" or "cleave," with particular reference to breaking the earth or plowing the ground for planting. That might seem a pretty mundane kind of meaning, worlds away from the notion of "fullness of being." But in Arabia's desert environment, the fertility of the ground cannot be taken for granted. Pre-Islamic nomadic tribes fought to the death over rights to green areas around oases where animals could be pastured and crops cultivated. To be able to plow the ground for planting was perhaps the greatest of all blessings, since from it so many other blessings flowed. Included among them was rest from toil and the cultivation of social life and of the arts, especially poetry, the quintessential art-form of nomadic peoples.

The Qur'an doesn't disparage such blessings. It insists instead that they be universalized — by prohibiting tribal competition for resources. No one is to be excluded from the oasis except those who refuse to abide by the new rules, God's rules: rules that mandate behavior promoting the common good. "Fullness of being" cannot be the reward for a lucky or powerful few or for a single tribe. It must be in reach of all.

Yet the Qur'an also insists that "fullness of being" cannot be achieved in this life. It can come to fruition only in the life to come. All the concrete blessings flowing from a refuge in the desert where food is plentiful become symbolic of the award that awaits the *muttaqqun*, the God-conscious, in the Hereafter. Having served God and God's creation faithfully during their earthly lives, they enter the final oasis of heaven, called *al-jannah,* "garden," in Arabic. So when Muslims hear the *mu'adhdhan* chant "Come alive to fullness of being," they hear the whole range of the Qur'an's revolutionary ethical appeal and they taste the Qur'anic imagery that makes that appeal beautiful.

Imagery of the Garden is scattered all through the Qur'an, sometimes in abbreviated form, like a song's refrain, sometimes in extended verse pictures. Two *suras* in particular, *Sura ar-Rahman* (The Merciful) and *Sura al-Waqi'a* (What Will Come to Pass*)*, stand out for the richness and complexity of their Garden imagery, so much so that Muslim artists tend to be especially fond of them both. (Artist Asma Shikoh calls *Sura ar-Rahman* a "beautiful inspiration.") Here is a glimpse of the Garden in *Sura al-Waqi'a*:

What of those who have attained to righteousness?
They will be among lote-trees heavy with fruit,
under acacias with tiered flowers
in extended shade
and water ever-flowing
and fruits in abundance
always in season
always permitted,
and with them their spouses
raised high among the blessed
for we will bring them into renewed being
raising them in youth and virginity
loving, perfectly compatible
in age and righteousness,
many from of old,
many from recent times... (*Sura al-Waqi'a* 56:27-40)

No vain talk will they hear there, no mischief,
But only the words "salaam, salaam." (*Sura al-Waqi'a* 56:25-26)

The Garden's lushness answers the dream of desert-dwellers, with its fruits and waters and shade in never-failing abundance. But the Garden's tactile pleasures are not ends in themselves. They provide the setting for what the Qur'an calls *jaza'*, "reward," the fruition of our human nature. Unlike the fruition of other living things, however, human fruition is attained, not by a natural, instinctual process, but by a yielding of the will that requires humankind's assent. Requires but does not force. Yet to refuse assent is to refuse the Garden as well. Humankind's "reward" for refusal is the Garden's anti-type, *al-jahannama* (Gehenna). *Al-jahannama* answers to desert-dwellers' worst nightmare: becoming perpetually lost in the sand-dunes at a perpetual noon of blazing fire and heat. References to *al-jannah* usually come paired with references to *al-jahannama*. The two, the Garden and Gehenna, serve as constant reminders of the serious choice that confronts us every moment of our lives.

While the Qur'an insists that the choice between the Garden and Gehenna belongs to the individual and to the individual alone (the Qur'an sternly prohibits any help from intercessors), the individual's choice itself is manifested communally. Those opting for Gehenna will find that their idolatrous obsessions will isolate them from their fellows during their lifetimes. Their obsessions will pit them against each other and harden their hearts towards the poor. They will suffer their commensurate "reward" in Gehenna by suffering alone. In fact, their suffering is the fiery consciousness of their eternal isolation. Those opting for the Garden will fulfill their communal obligations during their lifetimes, especially those laid down by the "Five Pillars": witness, daily prayer, fasting, alms-giving, and pilgrimage. They will enjoy the Garden in community.

So much nonsense has been written lately about the Garden's rewards that we should spend a moment looking at what really goes on there. Contrary to some reports, the Garden is not in any way the site of orgiastic riot. It's true that the reward is pictured from the male point of view — the "spouses" in the passage from *Sura al-Waqi'a* quoted above are clearly female. And it's true also that these female spouses have been resurrected in human flesh at a perpetual peak of beauty. But the passage also makes clear that both members of the spousal pair, male and female, are perfectly matched not only in what a hadith calls their "glorious body of the resurrection" (at their prime of physical beauty at the age of 33), but also in their righteousness — because their righteousness has brought them into the Garden in the first place. Perfect compatibility on all levels between one man and one woman is the reward for both. There is no hint here of male-only sexual gratification. What's felt instead is an analogy between each pair of spouses and the perfect pairing of the original human pair, Adam and Eve, in paradise. But the spouses in the Garden are unlike Adam and Eve in that they have been freed from the forgetfulness that brought about Adam and Eve's exile.

Another difference from Adam and Eve is that the spouses in the Qur'anic Garden are not alone. They are placed at a banquet table (the perennial image of human communion at its finest) with other pairs as perfect as themselves. Their enjoyment never cloys nor wearies. It constantly gratifies. When they converse, with each other primarily, but also with others as fulfilled as themselves, they speak neither "vain talk" (no triviality, no boasting), nor "mischief" (no back-biting, no plotting). They delight instead in uttering *"salaam, salaam,"* that is, words reflective of the couples' inner peace and goodwill. The couples in the Garden engaged in this way suggest human community as God intends it to be.

The Qur'anic imagery of the Garden reconfirms the imagery of the Garden in Genesis and reawakens the dulled human desire to be welcomed into it. Muslims, inspired by verses like those in *Sura al-Waqi'a*, were eager to find hints of the Garden even in this present life. So when Muslims overcame the Sassanid (Persian) empire in the decade after the Prophet Muhammad's death, Muslims were instantly charmed by the beauty of the enclosed gardens they found there and rapidly transformed them into living images of *al-jannah*, the Garden of gardens. Called *chahar-bagh* (literally, "four-gardens"), these gardens feature a fountain or pool at the center of a space divided into four quarters and planted with a variety of shade-producing shrubs or trees, along with flowers and sometimes even vegetables. Usually channels of water mark off the quarters. The symbolism of the number four is important. The number four is an ancient symbol of natural wholeness. It encompasses the four cardinal directions, the four elements, and the four seasons. Biblically, the number four conjures the four rivers of Paradise. In hadith we hear of the four celestial rivers, of milk, water, honey, and wine, that the Prophet Muhammad saw on his *mi'raj*, his Ascent through the heavens to the Throne of God. And in the Qur'an itself, *Sura ar-Rahman* depicts the Garden as divided into four parts, each corresponding to different degrees of blessedness. Sufi exegesis takes the symbolism even further. The *chahar-bagh* becomes a map of the four inner qualities of spirit, essence, heart, and soul. Philosopher Frithjof Schuon remarks, "It is important to emphasize that the fourfold form of the Islamic garden is not just a whim of design but a reflection of a higher reality."[16]

The *chahar-bagh* remains to this day one of the key artistic expressions of Muslims' ultimate hope, and it does so in its simplest as well as in its most elaborate forms, whether as bits of greenery within the modest enclosures of private homes throughout the Muslim world, or as complex horticultural designs in Qattar and other Gulf states. Simple or elaborate as the *chahar-bagh* design might be in particular cases, however, the design is always focused around one universal element: water. For though the passage from *Sura al-Waqi'a* above mentions water only once, in the phrase "and water ever-flowing," the epithet most closely associated with the Garden each time the Qur'an mentions it (more than 120 times!) is "beneath which waters flow."

The environmental reasons why flowing water would be so treasured are clear. But the Qur'an also makes an explicit connection between water and God's mercy: "And among God's signs God shows you the lightning, fearful to the ignorant, hope-filled to the wise, for God then sends down the rains to nourish the earth after its death. There is a parable here for a discerning people" (*Sura al-Rum* 30:24). The beauty of water expressing God's mercy is mirrored in the beauty of the human soul receiving it. That is the point of an inscription in the *chahar-bagh* of the Alhambra in Spain: "The fountain in my midst is like the soul of the believer, immersed in the remembrance of God."

I was not, however, able to locate that inscription during Peggy's and my visit to the Alhambra a few years ago. Of course, I had no opportunity to hunt for it. I was otherwise occupied.

We were not there alone. We had tagged along with our son, daughter-in-law, and our two granddaughters: Jordan, age two and a half at that time, and Phoebe, just turned one. So that their parents, with Phoebe in a stroller, might enjoy the Alhambra's beauty in peace, Peggy and I took charge of the lively, athletic Jordan. Our self-sacrificing gesture did not at first seem to cost us much. We all approached the rather drab outer walls of the Alhambra as a relatively calm, well-organized family group. (The Alhambra, from the outside, looks like just another part of the hilltop fortification where it

---

16. Quoted by Emma Clark, "Underneath Which Rivers Flow," in William C. Chittick, ed. *The Inner Journey: Views from the Islamic Tradition* (Sandpoint, ID: Morning Light Press, 2007), 83.

is situated.) But what followed once Peggy, Jordan, and I passed inside is a blur. Something in the spirit of the interior set Jordan off. Down the stately corridors she raced at top speed while we older folks panted behind, fearful that she would disappear behind an arch or into a dark side room or else fall into a fountain or an irrigated stream. Peggy and I snatched an occasional glance at delicately carved stone calligraphy on a wall here, and caught our breath in the cool shade of lush foliage there, but we were otherwise in a state of panic. I doubt either of us could have described ourselves as "immersed in the remembrance of God."

But that was not the Alhambra's fault. The spirit of the place might yield itself immediately to toddlers; there is indeed a playfulness implicit in Qur'anic descriptions of the Garden. But for grown-ups, the Alhambra's spirit works at a much slower pace. For us, the spirit of the place needs to penetrate the heart, and that usually takes time.

Afterwards, seated with our family at a little restaurant outside, Phoebe and Jordan remembering God in their own way with ice-cream cones, I did have time to reflect on what I had glimpsed in my whirlwind passage through this most beautiful of settings of the *chahar-bagh*. It was in that reflection, a reflection still continuing, that the beauty of the Alhambra began to unfold for me.

Actually, the Alhambra's beauty had begun to unfold for me long before I visited it, during the time in the late 1980's when Peggy and I lived in Santa Fe, New Mexico. We rented sight-unseen a three-room casita near the center of town. Our front door faced on a dusty, dead-end street with an ancient pick-up truck settling into the dry grass where the street ended. Nothing here but drabness, like the unremarkable approach to the Alhambra. Yet the back wall of our tiny house served also as a wall surrounding our landlord's courtyard garden. Through small windows in our kitchen and bathroom, we could look out on the garden and appreciate its cool, irrigated greenery, its colorful climbing plants, its pleasant, shady walks. Songbirds twittered in the branches and sipped at a tiny pool of running water.

This was not strictly speaking a *chahar-bagh*, of course. But our landlord's house, like most houses in Santa Fe, preserved the Moorish influence the *conquistadores* had carried with them to New Spain centuries before. As a child of the North-east, I was not used to courtyard gardens. Gardens in my experience were either a source of food or an object for display. Houses were objects of display as well, and opened to the front. Houses that put a barrier up to the outside world and that focused inward were novelties. But I could see the point of such a design in Santa Fe's desert surroundings, and I quickly became charmed by the idea of enclosure, especially after we'd had the opportunity to escape the hot desert sun within courtyard walls, whether at our landlord's invitation or at the homes of Santa Fe friends.

Even while sprinting through the Alhambra I could tell that I had arrived at the source of what had delighted my senses years before in Santa Fe. But I also began to realize that this source offered more than gratification of the senses. And I see now what that "more" is: the gratification of the human spirit. The Alhambra does not offer gratification in the usual ways — in triumph or in a sense of prideful accomplishment. Rather, gratification is offered in inner equilibrium, in psychological poise. Every detail of the Alhambra's construction, whether in stone or in water, promotes the psyche's softening and gentling. As Rumi puts it, speaking of examples of the *chahar-bagh* in his hometown of Konya and environs, "The real gardens and flowers are within, they are in people's hearts, not outside."[17] Yet the gentling does not end in psychological stability alone. That stability becomes the calm inward surface upon which God's spirit can be reflected without distortion. The Alhambra's elusive inscription — "The fountain in my midst is like the soul of the believer, immersed in the remembrance of God" — says it best. The Alhambra, with its ubiquitous waters and still pools and flowing fountains, its *chahar-bagh* gardens, its shade, its translucent interiors, its stone calligraphy hanging overhead like dense foliage, seeks to be internalized, not to be gaped at. The Alhambra is not so much an architectural show-piece as the invitation to an inward state of quiet. The Alhambra's drab exterior symbolizes the inward direction of its appeal.

But among Muslim arts, it's not just the art of the Alhambra or the *chahar-bagh* that functions this way, to bring humankind into an inner sanctum where we are given a foretaste of the Garden. What we often call "crafts" or "minor arts" function this way too. Carpet-weaving is one of these; so is the production of textiles, tiles, and glasswork. In Islam, these "minor" arts are actually "major." Each takes basic elements of the human household environment and transforms them into symbols of their place within the Garden. These symbols often incorporate floral and geometrical designs and patterns suggestive of the Garden's fecundity and everlastingness. Yet because the objects bearing these symbols — objects such as carpets, textiles, tiling, glassware — are everyday objects of household use, they play an intimate, concrete role in the unfolding of daily life. These are symbols that are prayed upon, sipped from, walked upon.

And worn. Of all such arts, apparel-making is perhaps most honored. As Seyyed Hossein Nasr puts it, "nothing is as close to the human soul as the human body. And Islamic dress, for both men and women, emphasizes their spiritual character."[18] Yasmin's Ramadan finery comes to mind. Each hour of life should find us touching or touched by a concrete sign of the

17. Quoted by Emma Clark, "Underneath Which Rivers Flow," in Chittick, ed., *The Inner Journey*, 83.

18. Seyyed Hossein Nasr, "Islamic Art" in *Islam and the West*, The Modern Scholar Series (Prince Frederick, Maryland: Recorded Books, 2004).

Garden.

For souls at peace, the touching and the being touched flow easily from the spirit's center. And so I end with a contemporary artist, Uzma A. Mirza, whose calligraphy brings us from the Qur'anic word to the Garden and back again in a circulating stream of imagery. Many of the forms and themes of Islamic art we've touched on throughout these sections are passed through in her work. Take her watercolor painting, "Green Notes: A Goodly Tree" (featured on the official 2008 Islamic Society of North America calendar). A musical staff, formed from water-drops and green growth, arcs from the bottom left of the painting to the upper right corner. On it, five of the Beautiful Names "are flowing like resplendent notes," as the calendar description puts it. Then, arcing in the opposite direction, from right to left, and balancing the flow of notes like eddies in a stream, are strands of liquid calligraphy "speaking of the Goodly Tree as a sign of the Good Muslim: Good human." The verses are from *Sura Ibrahim* 14:24-25, ones we've seen earlier, in Chapter 3c. They served us then to anchor the imagery of the Córdoba mosque's "forest" of supporting columns. Here, in Mirza's painting, they anchor our glimpse into the heart of the "Good Muslim: Good Human." It is a heart alive with creative vigor. At the top of the painting, a line of the staff becomes a branch and sprouts pinwheeling green leaflets.

Uzma Mirza, *Green Notes: A Goodly Tree*, Qur'an *sura ibrahim* 14:24, 25 & five Names and Attributes of God in Arabic composed on a harmonic staff. Watercolor on paper, 30" x 22".

On a branch sprouting out of the bottom line of the staff, a realistic songbird perches firmly, beak tilted back to receive a seed — or is the seed a water droplet? Or a musical note? Or a calligraphic dot?

While on one level "Green Notes: A Goodly Tree" symbolizes human creative vigor, on another it symbolizes God's own creativity. God stimulates and sanctions the artist's echo and response. God's "life-giving word is firmly rooted like a good tree, its branches reaching toward the sky, yielding its fruit at all times by the permission of its Cherisher and Sustainer...." (*Sura Ibrahim* 14:24). The artist is like the songbird in Mirza's painting. It feeds on the divine fruit, then trills it out joyously in playfulness with form. We are drawn to this playfulness. We dream of the Garden where fullness of being, including fullness of the imagination, is the order of the day.

But we also strive to enter into that fullness even here, even now, as artists of daily life. Mirza is explicit about the ethical goal of her work:

> Through the pens in art (as watercolor, ink, and mixed media as well as the sublime in Nature's signs and natural phenomenon), the sound and meaning of the Divine attributes become a vessel and a nourishment or a reminder for the balance of our hearts, our selves, our communities, and hence the striving for a balanced world.[19]

A wonderful quotation to end with, as it sums up the purpose of all Islamic art. It will lead us later, as well, into into the topic of Part III: an exploration of the living-out of that purpose, in behavior as beautiful as the artworks that help inspire it.

---

19. http://www..thepenandtheinkpot.org/02.html

CHAPTER 4: ART INFORMED BY CHRISTIAN FAITH

Chapter 4a. "Beauty is always ready to give more."

One lush summer afternoon in the mid 1990s, I took a book and a pen and pad of paper out into the hammock hanging on our upstairs back porch under a canopy of leafy tree branches. The book, called *Burning Bright: An Anthology of Sacred Poetry*, was a collection of poems from the three Abrahamic traditions, selected and arranged according to the motifs of the rhythm of a day: morning, noon, night.[1] I'd been sent the book by a literary journal asking me to review it. Hence the pen and paper — to take notes as I read through the poems.

But something happened as I lay there in the lightly swaying hammock, browsing through the book and making notes for my review. My arms, with the book in one hand and my notepad in the other, soon lowered to my lap; my eyes gazed upward at the leafy branches, as my mind rested with a phrase from the poem I'd just been reading. I don't recall now what the phrase was, but I remember how it kept repeating itself softly in my mind like a mantra. I felt suspended in the poem, suspended in the hammock. Suspended as if between heaven and earth. The mantra of the poem's line began to act in me like a prayer, opening my spirit to God's presence. I realized that for the first time ever (except for the Psalms in the Bible), I was praying with and through a poem.

For decades I had read and studied poetry. After all, my doctorate had been in literature. But I'd previously read in order to analyze, as I had intended to do that day in the hammock in order to write the review. Was it the hammock's swaying suspension, its relaxing of my bodily and mental tautness, that released me into poetry's expansive, prayerful space?

The question is unanswerable. But I do know that this afternoon in the hammock changed my relation to poetry forever. Having once experienced poetry's opening of my spirit — its unexpected creation of a space where I could expand into the grace of the living and ever-present God — I threw my whole being into embracing poetry's welcoming invitation. From that time on, I dedicated my work to sharing poetry's invitation with others: through retreats, workshops, and writing books on how to enter and grow in poetry's openness.

---

1. Patricia Hampl, ed., *Burning Bright: An Anthology of Sacred Poetry*, (New York: Ballantine, 1995).

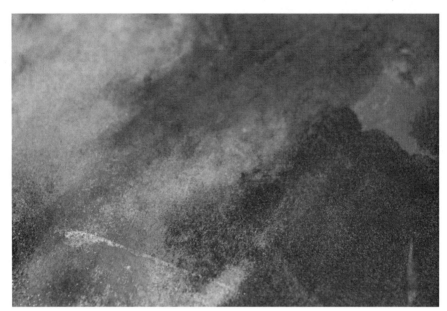

Makoto Fujimura, *Countenance Three 2008*. In this Nihonga painting, colors move from shimmering golds at upper left to deep sky blues in middle to richly textured greens at bottom right. (See back cover for full-color partial reproduction.)

Soon I was finding the same invitation offered in other art forms as well. When I gaze now, for instance, at any of the abstract paintings by the contemporary Japanese-American artist Makoto Fujimura, I'm drawn into what he calls their "grace arena." As Fujimura explained to an interviewer: "The pigments I use have a semi-transparent layering effect that traps light in the space created between the pigments and between layers of gold or silver foil. This creates a 'grace arena' in which light which is caught creates space. It is neither the Renaissance system of creating pictorial depth through perspective nor is it the Modernist emphasis on the surface space."[2] Fujimura's layering technique follows the thousand year old Japanese painting tradition called Nihonga. But after his conversion from agnosticism to Christianity, in the midst of his rising artistic career, Fujimura found that the Nihonga materials and the ambivalent space they create were taking on new symbolic value for him. The ambiguous space became a field for "the grace that exists between the immanent reality of earth and the transcendent reality of heaven."[3] "I want my works," he wrote elsewhere, "to create a worship space inviting the viewers to God's throne, where an encounter with the living, but invisible, God is

---

2. Interview with James Romaine: "Art as Prayer," www.makotofujimura.com/essays/faith_and_art1.html

3. Makoto Fujimura, "River Grace," *Image* journal #22 (Winter/Spring 1999): 30.

made accessible."[4] And the Nihonga materials themselves took on biblical symbolism in his mind. The silver foil came to represent our human weakness and betrayal of God, since for thirty pieces of silver Jesus' own disciple Judas betrayed him, as the Gospels recount. The gold foil, on the other hand, represents God's glorious triumph, the golden city established by God at the end of time, according to the New Testament's Book of Revelation.

Furthermore, for Fujimura all the precious minerals from which his pigments are made carry the symbolic weight of God's extravagant gifts to us. In the Bible, he notes, precious stones are embedded in the walls of Solomon's temple and in the garments of the high priest.[5] God abundantly gives us these gems and the talents to create beautiful objects from them, so that we in return will use these gifts of treasure and talent to celebrate his glory. Fujimura's paintings are costly to create, so he has thought a lot about whether this expense is justifiable. He has come to feel deeply that it is — as long as the art is glorifying not the artist himself but God. In an essay "The Extravagance of God," he writes: "the extravagance can only be justified if the worth of the object of adoration is greater than the cost of extravagance. The glory of the substance poured out can only reflect the glory of the one to whom it is being poured upon. And if the object of glory is not worthy, then the act would be foolish and wasteful."[6]

But his favorite way of explaining the artist's call to create extravagantly for God is to recount the personal impact on him of the Gospel episode of the woman who anointed Jesus' feet with costly perfume. The story is told in Mark's Gospel (14:3-9) and Matthew's (26:6-13), where the woman is unnamed, as well as in John 12:1-8, where the woman is identified as the Mary whose brother Lazarus has just been brought back to life by Jesus. In an interview that Fujimura published online as "Art as Prayer," he was asked how Mary models for him the role of the artist:

> *Fujimura*: I am referring to the account in John 12 where Mary comes to the place where Jesus was staying and poured out her perfume. Here, she is the sister of Martha and Lazarus, whom Christ raised from the dead. In this state of complete and utter amazement, her heart was full of thankfulness. She was overwhelmed with emotion and she didn't know what to do. Then she realized that the only thing that she had valuable enough with which to somehow respond to this amazing miracle was this perfume, which was worth about a year's wages. She anointed Jesus with a perfume aroma that He went to the Cross with. That was the only thing He wore on His body on the Cross. She seems to me to be the

---

4. "Ten Commandments for Artists" on his website at www.makotofujimura.com/essays/10_commandments1.html

5. Fujimura, "River Grace," 31.

6. www.makotofujimura.com/essays/extravagance_of_god.html

quintessential artist because she responded with this intuition rather than calculation.

Interviewer: If Mary was the quintessential artist, then Judas was the quintessential art critic. His response to that scene was outrage and to condemn it as wasteful. I don't want to go too far with this comparison but there are many people, both Christian and non-Christian, who view the visual arts as something 'extra' at best or a total waste at worst, but not essential in any way. Is there a model in the story of Mary about the value of art?

Fujimura: Certainly. What Jesus said to her, and those around Him as well including Judas, was "she has done a beautiful thing and wherever the Gospel is preached what she has done will be remembered." That is an amazing commendation for someone like me who tends to work from the heart, who tends to work with precious and costly materials. I remember that the extravagance of Christ's love for me prompted an extravagant response. Eventually, I came to connect what I do as an artist with Mary's devotional act. Maybe that is the one act we can look to as the centerpiece for a paradigm of creativity.[7]

"She has done a beautiful thing." Actually, Jesus speaks these words not in John's account but in Mark's and Matthew's; Fujimura is merging the Gospel accounts here. But that is not important. What is key is his sense of extravagant giving as the model for artistic work and as the essence of beauty itself.

Also intriguing is the resonance of the original Greek word for "beautiful" in this passage. The Greek word used by both Mark and Matthew is *kalon*, which has a marvelous range of meaning. Literally it does mean "beautiful," but throughout the original Greek New Testament this beauty can apply to physical appearance or to moral behavior: that is, *kalon* can mean "lovely" or "free from defects"; but it can also mean "praiseworthy," "morally good," "desirable," "blameless." So this very passage is sometimes translated, aptly enough, "She has performed a good service for me."

Art's beauty as extravagant gift, as good service poured out in gratitude, as invitation into a "grace arena": Fujimura's experiential conviction of this role for art's beauty is given theoretical grounding by Christian theologian Susan A. Ross, in a small gem of a book called *For the Beauty of the Earth*.[8] Ross's key term — which enfolds all that Fujimura is expressing in his paintings and essays — is *generosity*. "A central dimension of genuine beauty," she writes, "is the quality of generosity." In fact, generosity is "intrinsic" to beauty. "Real beauty does not exclude; rather, it invites. Real

7. Interview with James Romaine: "Art as Prayer," www.makotofujimura.com/essays/faith_and_art1.html

8. Susan A. Ross, *For the Beauty of the Earth* (New York: Paulist Press, 2006). The quotations that follow are from pp.14 and 30.

beauty does not 'count up,' but rather flings its gifts to anyone who asks." (Recall Fujimura saying that the woman who anointed Jesus with costly perfume was responding not with "calculation" — not "counting up" — but with wild extravagance.)

Ross is interested in the effect that beauty has on the person who experiences it, whether the beauty is of nature or of the fine arts (or, as we'll see in Part III, of human behavior). "Real beauty invites exploration and depth; it does not shut the door prematurely to the questioner. Beauty is always ready to give more. When we encounter a beautiful work of art, we find ourselves unable to exhaust fully the beauty that it offers." This is why, I'd say, we find ourselves unable to move away from a certain sculpture or painting in a museum. Or why, reading poetry in the hammock, I found the poem opening its door and drawing my whole being into itself, holding me suspended in its expansive mystery. This expansive mystery into which beauty welcomes us would be explained by Ross as God's very self: "the God whose love is so immense that this God is with us in our very flesh" as Jesus Christ.

Musician and theologian Jeremy S. Begbie finds musical metaphors apt for this notion of beauty's inexhaustibility. Classical Western art, from Greek civilization through the Renaissance and the Enlightenment, had defined beauty in terms of proportion, and harmony: a beauty that was fixed, contained, balanced, measurable. But today, Begbie writes, "a theological account of created beauty will be *wary of closed harmonies.*"[9] Our sense of beauty as Christians must be grounded in the triune God — that is, in the infinitely creative love circulating among the three persons of the Trinity. So, then, "as far as divine beauty is concerned, if the 'measure' of beauty is outgoing love for the sake of the other, it will not be long before we are forced to come to terms with *excess* or *uncontainability*, the intratrinitarian life being one of a ceaseless overflow of self-giving. There is still proportion and integrity, but it is the proportion and integrity of abundant love."

Begbie has Bach's music mainly in mind here. In the "apparent limitless abundance of development" of Bach's *Goldberg Variations*, for instance, Begbie hears "an evocation of infinity… the infinity of proliferating novelty, the ever new and ever more elaborate richness and bounty generated by the Holy Spirit as creation shares in the excess of God's own abundant differentiated infinity."[10] But Begbie finds this evocation of God's gratuitous abundance also in the famous poem "Pied Beauty" by the nineteenth century British poet Gerard Manley Hopkins. The "pied" of the poem's title means "variegated," and the poem celebrates God's apparently inexhaustible creativity in producing what Begbie calls "a diversity of particulars."

9. Jeremy S. Begbie, "Created Beauty: The Witness of J.S. Bach" in *The Beauty of God*, ed. Daniel J. Treier et al, (Downers Grove, IL: InterVarsity Press, 2007), 29.
10. Begbie, "Created Beauty," 38-9.

The poem begins:

> Glory be to God for dappled things —
> For skies of couple-colour as a brinded cow;
> For rose-moles all in stipple upon trout that swim;
> Fresh-firecoal chestnut-falls; finches' wings...

And the list of creation's stunningly variegated variety continues, until the poem closes with:

> He fathers-forth whose beauty is past change:
> > Praise him.

God's overflowing generativity: it elicits in artists the desire to respond in kind. Hopkins's exuberant play with language is the poet's return gift to God for the exuberance of divine creation itself. So is Bach's proliferation of variations on a theme and Fujimura's creation with paper and pigments of a mysteriously inviting light-filled space. And our own response as viewers or listeners or readers of this art? Our spirits expand with art's expansiveness. We are, with beauty's intrinsic generosity, always ready to give more.

Chapter 4b. Playfulness and Surprise: "Defamiliarizing the familiar"

Every August the journal *Image*, whose subtitle is *Art, Faith, Mystery*, sponsors a weeklong gathering called the Glen Workshop, in recent years at Saint John's College in Santa Fe. Artists working in a range of genres but all grounded in Christian faith come together to practice their craft and to share their experiences and visions as Christian artists. The sharing takes place in workshops and lectures and performances but also in a special way at meals. Most of the 200 or so participants stay in the dorms and eat at the college cafeteria. Mealtime conversation turns into spontaneous seminars on crafting novels of spiritual journey, composing music for worship, bringing the arts to impoverished communities.

During the 2007 Glen Workshop, when George and I were in the early stages of this book, I took advantage of the mealtime camaraderie to ask some of the faculty about ideas that George and I had been percolating. What elements of their Christian faith most informed their creative work? Was "beauty" a term important to their own creative vision? Did they think that beauty is a characteristic of great art — and that beauty in general serves the good of the world? And how about theologian Susan Ross's assertion that "a central dimension of genuine beauty is the quality of generosity": how did this notion of beauty's intrinsic generosity strike them?

Everyone to whom I showed Ross's quotation smiled expansively and agreed with a nod: *yes, this is a key insight, that generosity is at the heart of beauty and of art*. Sculptor Ginger Henry Geyer, who was on the faculty that year, was typical in responding instantly "I like this idea of generosity." But Ginger went on in an intriguing direction: "I think you should add *playfulness* into the concept of beauty. And this would soften people's image of Islam as hard and violent."

Geyer's own art *is* decidedly playful, but it's a playfulness in the service of serious issues. With theological training and a droll wit, she produces art that simultaneously tickles our fancy and pokes at our preconceptions. She wants to tease and delight us out of our complacencies, to prod us awake from our somnolence. The medium she has chosen is a surprise treat in itself: a unique mix of porcelain, painting and story.

Take her glazed porcelain piece *Fighting Fire with Fire* (1999). It is a two-foot high bright orange fire hydrant. On one side she has painted an adaptation of a famous 16th century German altarpiece by Matthias Grünewald, depicting the resurrected Christ exuding flaming power. On the other side is an image of Hephaestus, the blacksmith and god of fire in ancient Greek mythology, painted in the style of classical Greek vases. Geyer explains on her website how *Fight Fire with Fire* came about:

> If you saw a burning bush, would you call 911? A fire hydrant asked

Ginger Henry Geyer, *Fighting Fire with Fire*, 1999.
Glazed porcelain with acrylic, 24" x 11" x 11 1/2".

me this question one day as my dog paused to pay her tribute. While waiting, I noticed two things about the orange hydrant's design: it had a cruciform shape, and it was fluted like a classical Greek column. These two hints were enough to begin the construction of a three-part porcelain sculpture. It seemed to have something to do with that great call to inclusivism: *"For in the one Spirit we were all baptized into one body— Jews or Greeks, slaves or free—and we were all made to drink of one Spirit."* (1 Corinthians 12:13).[11]

For Jesus, of course, was a Jew. And this "First Letter to the Corinthians"

---

11. http://gingergeyer.com/art_stories/stories/fighting_fire.html

from the New Testament was written by his apostle Paul to a Greek community. Geyer's musings continue:

> What image in art history might represent God as fire? The cruciform shape of the hydrant called for a Crucifixion. But somehow that didn't click. A Resurrection was needed. Most images of the Resurrection show Christ standing on the tomb, arms at his side or one raised to hold a banner. But there was this one, this wild and fiery Resurrection from Grunewald's Isenheim Altarpiece. A Christ with open arms, it perfectly fit the wide side of the fire hydrant.

So she borrowed Grunewald's resurrected Christ and painted a copy of it on her porcelain hydrant. For the classical Greek allusion on the hydrant's other side, "I found a Greek vase image of Hephaestus the divine blacksmith. This skinny little character is pounding away at his smithy, probably humming 'If I had a hammer'. He fit the front valve of the fire hydrant just fine. Hephaestus was a kind god in the Greek pantheon... He created all sorts of things out of metal and represents the ideal artist...."

Geyer considers the process of developing her sculptures to be part of the art work itself. And so she goes on:

> I worked on the piece while at a retreat, and individuals asked skeptical questions, such as, 'What the heck does a fire hydrant have to do with art?' and 'Is this about water or fire?' Who knows about art, but both mythology and scripture are filled with the paradoxical symbols of water and fire. There's the burning bush [from which God called Moses to lead his people out of bondage in Egypt (Exodus 3:2)] and then there's this one: *"For the Lord your God is a devouring fire, a jealous God."* (Deuteronomy 4:24). There's Noah's flood and then there's, *"Let anyone who is thirsty come to me, and let the one who believes in me drink...out of the believer's heart shall flow rivers of living water.'"* (John 7: 37-38). Lest our evangelism gets too 'hell-fire and damnation' oriented, we must ask ourselves: What fires are we putting out? Dare we hose down the fire of passion? The Resurrection does not put out the fire, it fuels it; at the same time it provides us with living water."

I've quoted at length Geyer's own words because they represent so well her uniquely disarming combination of down-home unpretentiousness and genuinely exploratory probing of biblical symbolism and theological questions. The passages she quotes here from the Bible all came to her *during* the process of creating *Fighting Fire with Fire*. That is, she did not begin her creative process with a Scripture passage in mind that she wanted to illustrate; that would be to impose dogma on her art, and no true artist (Christian or otherwise) works in that direction. To start with dogma and then illustrate it "artistically" is to produce pious cliché. Rather, truly Christian art engages Scripture and articles of faith as they happen to bubble up into the artist's consciousness, and the bubbling usually takes the form of a big splashing question mark. Hmm, the artist wonders, is *this* the spiritual meaning that my art work is leading me towards? Our experience as viewers of the finished work is then comparable: instead of being presented with a literal and hence dull representation of all-too-familiar beliefs, we're startled into finding the truths of our faith coming at us afresh, splashing us awake into a new alertness about what they might mean for our lives.

It's our daily lives, with their ordinary objects and routine activities, that Geyer takes as the material for her art. As she explains on her website, "I comb my middle-class American world for sacramental objects — such as fire hydrants, toys, make-up mirrors and sleeping bags — and invest them with scripture and art history. This rooting around in tradition fires my passion. If the work succeeds in defamiliarizing the familiar, the incongruities in it may collide and expose divine mystery."

Other things collide and crash in revelatory ways as Geyer works. Consistent with her sense that she can create only by letting go of preconceived outcomes, only by giving up control so that the work can surprise her as it develops, she has chosen to work in a notoriously uncontrollable medium: porcelain. She explains porcelain's peculiar challenges in an article in the journal *Image*: "A piece will warp, crack, and shrink up to ten per cent — and usually in the final firing after most of the work has been done." So "I have learned that perfectionism is not what carries the meaning in my art. The direct link between the spiritual and technical processes here is in the transformation by fire.... I feel defeated whenever I open the kiln to find severe flaws. Sometimes the piece is not redeemable, but often the flaws function as revelation.... Art-making is similar to working with the poor in that we will burn out if we cannot let go of a precisely desired outcome. For a year and a half, I directed a small program of art-making for homeless people. It didn't take long to understand the difference between charity and justice, or to find deep joy. But doing so required giving up the desire for good or quantifiable results and learning that the value is simply in the hospitality."[12]

Hospitality in the production of art means being able to welcome whatever surprises come along in the creative process, because only in this way can the artist be alert to God's truth, however unexpectedly it might appear. At that lunchtime chat with Ginger Geyer at the Glen Workshop, I asked if the playful openness in her art might be called a kind of beauty. She paused and crinkled her brow. "'Beauty' is tough for me; it's not how I see my work. And it was a negative when I was in school. But if you think of it as the beauty of *truth* — that's fine."

And, yes, I do think of it as the beauty of truth. I'm helped in understanding this notion of art's "truth" by the way that multi-media artist Steve Scott talks about it in his contribution to a collection of essays by Christian

---

12. Ginger Geyer, "Calling: Art and Signage," *Image* #33 (Winter 2001): 93

artists called *It Was Good: Making Art to the Glory of God.*[13] Like Geyer, Scott is candid about the exploratory and even bumbling nature of his creative process. "I am learning about 'truth' even as I am revising, editing, deleting, abandoning and restarting. For me, it is part of the journey I have been called into by the ultimately Truthful One.... I believe there is 'truth' in the process of searching for the right sound — even enhancing it with the right kind of echo!" For artists consciously working out of their Christian faith, Scott insists, "the limitations, idiosyncrasies and even flaws in our chosen medium — be it words, clay, paint, canvas, film, or sound — become essential ingredients in our vocabulary of 'expressed truth.'... For me, there is plenty of 'truth' that comes through the dead ends and the false starts."

"Often the flaws function as revelation," Geyer had said. Geyer's and Scott's comfortable embrace of their *mistakes* as a possible means to *revelation* might be mind-bending for us at first. But what a lesson it offers for the way we live our lives as people of faith in a world chock full of our own and others' mistakes and flaws.

American poet Mark Jarman is another contemporary artist whose work turns us topsy-turvy; and in Jarman's vision these head-over-heels surprises are actually core to Christian faith itself. Conscious that he is writing in a society and an epoch that is largely skeptical of religious claims, Jarman knows that he must startle his readers into attending to those claims at all. And even for his Christian readers, who presumably accept these claims, Jarman understands how sleepily numb we easily become to the astounding truths of our faith. Take the Resurrection. We celebrate it yearly with colored Easter eggs and chocolate bunnies for the children and white lilies in our churches and homes. Yet how many of us can comprehend what it means — for our individual lives and for the whole cosmos — that Jesus Christ was raised from the dead?

To help burst open our minds to this wonder, Jarman wrote the following untitled sonnet:

> Today is fresh, and yesterday is stale.
> Today is fast, and yesterday is slow.
> Today is yes, and yesterday is no.
> Today is news, and yesterday's a tale.
> The grave is empty. Last night it was full.
> The glorious means of death was once a shame.

---

13. Steve Scott, "No Time Like Now," in *It Was Good: Making Art to the Glory of God*, ed. Ned Bustard (Baltimore: Square Halo Books, 2006), 168-171.

Someone is God who had a common name
That you might give a child or animal.
It happens overnight. The world is changed.
The bottles in the cellar all decant.
The stars sign the new cosmos at a slant.
And everybody's plans are rearranged.
Today we meet our maker, in a flash
That turns the ash of yesterday to flesh.

Jarman placed this sonnet as the epilogue to his volume of poems published in 2000 called *Unholy Sonnets*.[14] He doesn't at all mean by this title that his poems are irreverent. Rather, he is playing off of the 17th century British poet John Donne's famous series called "Holy Sonnets." Donne wrote in a Christian culture that was confident about the reality of the holy, whereas in our contemporary secular Western culture the very concept of holiness is suspect. So Jarman chooses oblique, unexpected, not-obviously-holy (hence *un*holy) entrances into divine mystery, in order to startle us with divinity's power. As he explained in an interview in *Image* journal: "I knew I was writing religious poetry, devotional poetry, but I didn't want to exclude readers who might not believe as I did, and I didn't want to rely on the traditional language of religious belief. My aim, which is clear to me now though I can't say it was then, was to surprise a reader in the midst of a religious poem."[15]

The first surprise of this particular sonnet is how colloquial it is. The string of opposites in the opening four lines is beguilingly simple, almost like a children's rhyme, with its neat contrasts between *today*'s good qualities and *yesterday's* poor ones. Only with line five — "the grave is empty. Last night it was full" — does a Christian reader realize, with a start, that the *today* is the very day of Christ's resurrection. The grave in which Christ's body had been entombed is discovered on Sunday morning to be empty, because God has raised him from death; all the Gospels recount this core miracle on which Christian faith became founded. So in Jarman's poem the oppositions suddenly take on a greater import. The full grave become empty, the shameful death of crucifixion made glorious, the common name of Jesus become the very name of God: these startling reversals are the story of God's salvation of humankind.

The sonnet's remaining six lines stay with this salvific wonder, playfully helping us picture its implications for our own lives and for the whole cosmos. First Jarman — with in-your-face boldness — takes two clichés: "It happens overnight. The world is changed." But used here with reference to the Resurrection, they lose their clichéd character and take on, remarkably, the weight of earth-overturning literal truth. Next he offers two concrete, almost cartoon-like images of what happens when the earth *is* liter-

14. Ashland, Oregon: Story Line Press, 2000.
15. "A Conversation with Mark Jarman," *Image* #33 (Winter 2001): 67.

ally overturned: wine bottles stored in the cellar pop open and tip, pouring themselves out; and the stars slant at a new angle in the sky. Then another outright cliché: "everybody's plans are rearranged." Ordinarily this is a ho-hum phrase ("my child got sick so all my plans for the day had to be rear-ranged"), but in this context we hear it as the most startling truth of Christian faith: because Christ was raised from the dead, indeed everything we had ever considered solid and planned out is now forever rearranged around this central fact. What Ginger Geyer does with everyday objects, Mark Jarman does with everyday language: familiar idioms and familiar truths of faith are defamiliarized by setting them together unexpectedly, so that (as Geyer had said), "the incongruities may collide and expose divine mystery."

Exposing divine mystery is what Jarman goes on to do in the poem's final two lines. Again, we get two blatant idioms: "Today we meet our maker" (which for Christians is a slang way of referring to God's judging of all our deeds at our death) and "in a flash"— which usually just means "quickly, instantly" but here makes us picture a literal fiery flash at Christ's resurrection. In fact, it's a mind-blowing resurrection image comparable to Geyer's fire hydrant glowing with the power of the resurrected Christ, because in the poem's final line that flash acts transformingly on "ash." The final line bursts all our familiarity open: the flash "that turns the ash of yesterday to flesh." For the first time in the poem, the meaning isn't imme-diately clear. We can't quite make sense of the line, yet we're dazzled by its rapid-fire transformations of sound: *flash* to *ash* to *flesh*. Then we wonder: what can it mean that yesterday's ash becomes flesh in today's flash of meeting our maker?

What can it mean? Like Geyer, Jarman intends his art not to give us answers but to unsettle us with questions. The fun and challenge of good poetry like Jarman's is that it pushes us to explore new possibilities of connec-tion that we hadn't previously seen. So, for instance, as we ponder the puzzle of the closing line, we notice that it cycles us back up to the poem's very beginning: "yesterday" is where we began, and the poem's last word, "flesh," rhymes with the first line's "fresh." So we are drawn to wonder whether and how our own flesh might be made fresh by the Resurrection's "today."

"The poet who is working with religious subject matter has a big job," writes professor Jill Peláez Baumgaertner, a poet herself. That job is "noth-ing less than revitalizing the language so that it expresses truth, which it cannot do in hackneyed forms that are, essentially, dishonest: masking truth, glossing over it, never piercing to the core of an experience, never unmask-ing its paradoxes and ambiguities."[16] Revitalizing language, unmasking the paradoxes of our faith, and renewing hackneyed forms so that they glisten

---

16. Jill Peláez Baumgaertner, "'Silver Catching Midday Sun': Poetry and the Beauty of God," in *The Beauty of God*, ed., Daniel J. Treier et al (Downers Grove, IL: InterVarsity Press, 2007), 148.

with brilliance for us again: Jarman's whole poetic career has been devoted to this project. During the time he wrote "Today is fresh," he was intrigued by the sonnet form; he delighted in refreshing it with colloquial language that surprises us into re-awaking to the truths of our faith. More recently, inspired by the prose rhythms of the Bible, he has taken on the challenging form of the "prose poem."[17]

One of the best-loved passages in the Bible, for Christians, is the text known as the Beatitudes (a gem of a prose poem in itself): Jesus' exhortation, early in his ministry, to the curious crowd who has come to hear his teaching. Both Matthew's Gospel (5:1-11) and Luke's (6:17, 20-3) give us the Beatitudes, in slightly different versions. Jarman wrote the prose poem "On the island of the pure in heart" as a deliberate recasting of Matthew's version, which goes as follows:

> Blessed are the poor in spirit, for theirs is the kingdom of heaven.
> Blessed are those who mourn, for they will be comforted.
> Blessed are the meek, for they will inherit the earth.
> Blessed are those who hunger and thirst for righteousness, for they
> will be filled.
> Blessed are the merciful, for they will receive mercy.
> Blessed are the pure in heart, for they will see God.
> Blessed are the peacemakers, for they will be called children of God.
> Blessed are those who are persecuted for righteousness' sake, for
> theirs is the kingdom of heaven.
> Blessed are you when people revile you and persecute you and utter
>   all kind of evil against you falsely on my account. Rejoice and
>   be glad, for your reward is great in heaven, for in the same way
>   they persecuted the prophets who were before you.

What Jesus is teaching here is already a radical overturning of society's values and expectations. It's not the rich who will enter the kingdom of heaven, but the "poor in spirit." It's not the bold and powerful who will inherit the earth, but "the meek." It's not the war-makers who are God's children, but the "peacemakers." Christians know these lines by heart, but know them so well that perhaps we don't really hear their radical import. So in his prose poem "On the island of the pure in heart," Mark Jarman creatively pictures traveling to a string of islands where the Beatitudes are lived out, but with unpredictable, puzzling results. The poet doesn't engage the Beatitudes in order, nor does he consider all of them. But the poem's every line makes us stop stock still, pondering what on earth we had previously thought that this particular Beatitude meant.

---

17. "A Conversation with Mark Jarman," *Image* #33 (Winter 2001): 70

ON THE ISLAND OF THE PURE IN HEART

On the island of the pure in heart, we did not see God. But an influx of pink scallop shells, each the size of a fingertip, covered the sand.

On the island of the meek, a stench drove us back to the ship.

On the island of the poor in spirit, a glassy blankness came down like rain and asked a riddle that stumped us.

Riflemen among spraypainted rocks fired at us, on the island of the righteous. One rock said, "Byron, 18—."

On the island of the merciful, we obtained mercy.

On the island of the peacemakers, we depleted our numbers by hand-to-hand combat, until there were only two of us — a soul and a body.

Even as they urged us to depart, on the island of the persecuted, they begged us to stay.[18]

Jesus has told us, in one of the middle Beatitudes, "Blessed are the pure in heart, for they will see God." Maybe so, the poem implies; but if *we* visit the pure in heart, what do *we* see? Not God — but "an influx of pink scallop shells." The poem's unexpected image at first seems incongruous and irrelevant: what can this influx of pink scallop shells have to do with God? But when I stop to ponder the image (and it's a lovely one, really, image of delicate super-abundance, of God's generosity in creating such an influx of beauty), I wonder, well how *would* anyone "see God" in any case? Which takes me back with a fresh question to the biblical text: those "pure in heart" who Jesus promises "will see God": what exactly *will* they see? How *can* we "see God"? How might God appear to the pure in heart?

And so on, through the whole poem, which I don't have space here to follow along further. I urge you to do so, though, for the startling refreshment of mind and spirit that you'll experience. Jarman's gift as a poet is to shake us awake with his images. Or *swirl* us awake might be a better metaphor for our experience as his readers. For when his images are (as here) biblically connected, the poem turns the text and our previous assumptions about it upside down and inside out, swirling us around like a life-sized question mark in motion. To borrow Geyer's phrase again, Jarman's poems rouse us by "defamiliarizing the familiar."

Nearly a century ago, a Russian poet named Osip Mandelstam made a simi-

---

18. Mark Jarman, *Epistles*, (Louiseville, KY, Sarabande Books, 2007).

lar point in an essay on reading poetry. "What distinguishes poetry from automatic speech," he said — meaning by "automatic" speech our every-day talk or writing, used without thinking —"is that it rouses us and shakes us awake in the middle of a word. Then the word turns out to be far longer than we thought…"[19] Though Mandelstam's assertion applies to Jarman's and to all good poetry, it was Dante whose work Mandelstam had particu-larly in mind.

Dante Alighieri, who lived in 14th c. Italy, is considered the greatest Christian poet of all time. Although in this chapter on Art Informed by Christian Faith, I'm focusing primarily on contemporary artists, so that they can be brought into the current, crucial Muslim-Christian dialogue, it's important to ground them in the two-thousand-year tradition from which they come. Both Ginger Geyer and Mark Jarman, for instance, are quite consciously working out of — and playing creatively with — traditions of Christian art: Geyer in her borrowing of famous paintings of earlier periods and Jarman in his *Unholy Sonnets* playing off of Donne's *Holy Sonnets*. The problem with talking about "traditional Christian art," however, is that there is no such lump of a thing. Christian art has developed historically. New art forms and expressive conventions have developed for each epoch in interplay with changes in Christian spirituality — changes not so much in doctrine or core belief as in how cultures integrate them into their per-ceptions and people integrate them into their lives.

Dante's culture was the high Middle Ages, when Christianity was the unquestioned ruling religion of nearly all Europe. It was a Christianity that had become, in theology and in artistic representations, cosmic in scope. That is, God's saving plan for all humankind in Christ was envisioned as encompassing and indeed connecting every detail in heaven and earth. Intricate correlations matched points on the human body to certain virtues of human behavior, and on up and out to celestial beings like the angels, and through natural elements like plants and winds to the stars. Dante inher-ited this cosmological Christianity and made of it a magnificent three-book poem called *The Divine Comedy*. (He also inherited Christianity's ambiva-lence towards Islam. In *The Divine Comedy* he puts Saladin and Averroes at their ease in Limbo along with the pagan philosophers but subjects the Prophet Muhammad and his son-in-law Aly to gruesome torment in Hell.) Dante's bold originality was two-fold: he wrote his poem in the vernacular Italian language instead of in Latin (which for a thousand years had been the literary language of Christendom), and he made himself the central character, the pilgrim who progresses through this moralized cosmology and takes us along with him on his moral journey.

Dante the character begins *The Divine Comedy* with the sudden and

19. "Conversation about Dante," 1933-4, in *Osip Mandelstam: Selected Essays*, translated by Sidney Monas (Austin: University of Texas Press, 1977), 13

alarming realization that he has lost his way in life. He has somehow strayed from the virtuous path, has become too entwined in worldliness and ambition, and is desperate to find his way back to a life that accords with God's will. To his rescue appears the renowned pre-Christian Roman poet Virgil, who instructs Dante that in order to leave behind his life of error, he must go by a painful and circuitous route — through the regions of the dead. First he must descend through Hell (where his and all other human sin abides eternally), then ascend through Purgatory (where the dead renounce and are purged of their sins), then finally ascend through Paradise (where the graced beings who are freed from sin rejoice forever in the dazzling light of God's grace). Virgil himself, who stands allegorically for "human reason," will be Dante's guide through the first two regions. But as a non-Christian he can go no further, so Dante's beloved Beatrice (symbol of God's love) will lead him through the final third of his journey.

It's quite a "dramatic concept," as Hollywood filmmakers would say: this journey of Dante as "everyman" through a cosmos constructed imaginatively with such moral clarity, while the eternal life of his very soul (damnation or glory) is at stake. Along his way, at each level of increasing sinfulness or, later, of increasing virtue, Dante meets people from his native Italy whom he has known personally or has heard of. He is continually astounded to find out who is where and why: someone he'd thought virtuous is deep in Hell; someone he'd thought sinful is nearly out of Purgatory. And we as readers are astounded and challenged right along with him; we find ourselves drawn in at each step to compare our own place in the pilgrimage with his. There could hardly be a work of art that "defamiliarizes the familiar" more comprehensively than *The Divine Comedy*: every facet of our familiar life, from the most personal erotic details to public political maneuverings for power, is discovered anew in a startling place that forces us to re-assess every familiar value and behavior that we'd taken for granted.

Dante's *Divine Comedy* is universally acclaimed as a "beautiful" work. But in what does its beauty consist? There is the beauty of its sound in the original Italian: phrases that flow in and out of one another in a tour de force rhyme scheme called *terza rima*. In this complex poetic form of three-line stanzas, lines one and three of each verse rhyme, while line two is then rhymed by lines one and three of the following stanza, so that the whole poem pulses forward while doubling back on itself at the same time in an interlocking drama of sound and sense.

But mere formal elegance alone doesn't account for the beauty of this work. The interlocking, forward-thrusting lines carry us through an interlocked, forward-thrusting moral universe which — though entirely imaginary — compels us by its clear moral truth. It is the beauty of seeing the entire cosmos ordered according to an imagined but utterly convincing divine plan, with every detail of personal or political life known to the core by God's omniscience and given its place in the cosmic plan of God's saving gift for us in Christ. Here without doubt is beauty for the good of the world, art that envisions how we humans should behave. There can be no greater instance of creativity as moral power.

And, remarkably, despite the fact that no one today believes in the literal truth of Dante's medieval cosmology, *The Divine Comedy* continues to speak compellingly to readers. And to poets as well: many major contemporary poets try their hand at rendering Dante's verse into their own current vernacular. They're challenged not only by the complex *terza rima* poetic form but just as much, I suspect, by the poem's moral vision. Today's secular world, and even today's Christianity, has lost that medieval confidence in a divinely ordered meaning to our universe. We keep reading and re-writing and re-reading Dante's masterpiece in order to be aroused by its challenge to live beautiful lives.

Chapter 4c. "Life pulsing with mystery"

At prayer one morning during the months that I was writing this book, the revelatory image came to me of Jesus "messy with muck."

Here's how it happened. After breakfast each day, George and I say Morning Prayer together, then sit silently for twenty minutes simply hoping to be aware of God's presence. For the past quarter century of practicing this silent prayer of awareness, I've tried to follow the Christian contemplative prayer tradition called "apophatic," which means "without images": that is, I try to let myself be emptied of all that is not God so that God's being can fill me, if only for these brief moments. But on this particular morning something different happened. Maybe it was because my therapist had been urging me to become comfortable with my inner messiness. Or maybe that wasn't the reason; how God comes to us is always essentially mystery. How God came that morning was in an image: a clear, startling image from the marvelous 22-sonnet poem called "Love's Bitten Tongue," written by the American poet Vassar Miller, who died in 1998. The poem traces Jesus' life as it is intertwined with the poet's own spiritual journey, and this scene in the poem's final sonnet draws on the account in John's Gospel of Jesus' first appearance on earth after his death and burial. This appearance, which proves that he has been resurrected from the dead, is to his friend and follower Mary Magdalene, and in the Gospel she mistakes him for the burial grounds' gardener until he speaks her name. Vassar Miller imagines the wondrous scene in these lines addressed to Jesus:

> Being pierced open by Your whisper, 'Mary...'
> The woman gapes at Your gardener's clothes
> Messy with muck and juices of bud and berry... [20]

The image of the newly risen Christ still "messy with muck" overwhelmed me with gratitude that morning. Here in his first appearance as his Risen Self, Christ is still deep into the earthy stuff of our human condition. And I thought: yes, he shares our human condition in all things but sin, which means he shares our psychological messiness and muck. So in his muddy "gardener's clothes" he is alive as the Risen Life and Love of my very messiness. Of the messiness of us all as we try to live our best in this messy world.

To encapsulate this grateful sense of Christ alive with us in all our daily doings, Christian spirituality has developed the concept of "the sacredness of the ordinary." Because our very God took on human flesh in Jesus and lived an ordinary human life, all things of ordinary human life are now made sacred. Some of the artists we've met so far in this chapter have commented on the Incarnation's sacralization of the material stuff of life as

---

20. *If I Had Wheels or Love: Collected Poems of Vassar Miller* (Dallas: Southern Methodist University Press, 1991).

key to their faith and their art. "The Incarnation is most significant to me because it dignifies matter," sculptor Ginger Geyer said to me in our chat at the Glen workshop. And Makoto Fujimura writes (in his essay "Abstraction and the Christian Faith") that in his abstract paintings "I want to affirm and celebrate the physical.... As I live and breathe the culture of New York, as I am called to live to 'seek the shalom and prosperity of the city,' I must work incarnationally, and get my hands dirty."

For major works of art that were composed specifically in order to dramatize the sacredness of the ordinary — and our interconnectedness over time and space *in* this sacredness — I can't think of better examples than two recent and acclaimed novels, *Ursula, Under*, by Ingrid Hill, and *Gilead*, by Marilynne Robinson.

First published by Algonquin Books in 2004, *Ursula, Under* was such a success that Penguin Books put out a 2005 edition especially designed for book clubs. The story centers on two-year old Ursula Wong, a happily bouncy child of Finnish and Chinese-American descent, who falls into an abandoned mine shaft while on a picnic in Michigan's Upper Peninsula with her young parents, Jason and Annie. They've come to the spot to explore Annie's family heritage; her grandfather had been killed in a mining accident deep in a shaft around this place seventy-five years before. While we as readers are waiting in suspense during the rescue effort that is covered on national TV, while we are sharing in Jason and Annie's agony, Hill tells us the life stories of Ursula's ancestors, as far back as a third century B.C. Chinese alchemist named Qin Lao on Jason's side, and an eighth century deaf Finnish woman named Kyllikki on Annie's.

Each of these ancestral stories is a gem glistening with the wondrousness of the particular: the particularity of each ancestor's personal psychology and of the texture of daily life in each widely spaced time and place. And each story hangs especially on the marvel of conception of new life. The fragility and improbability of each hard-won conception, without which Ursula would not have come to be, leaves us astounded by the chain of miracles that brings each of us into existence at all.

Hill underscores the precious fragility of individual existence by creating several of her characters as disabled by a circumstance beyond their control. Annie was permanently crippled as a child when hit by the car of the crass, uncaring alcoholic Jinx Meulenburg; the Chinese alchemist's servant is mute and he himself nearly sterile; Kyllikki went deaf from a fever; and there are more. "I wanted to write about these individuals," Ingrid Hill said in her interview for Penguin Books, "in a way that would foreground their humanity... These are all people who are in one way or another broken, imperfect, and I hope it's clear that they are also priceless."[21] They sur-

---

21. http://us.penguingroup.com/static/rguides/us/ursula_under.html

round and reinforce Ursula's own pricelessness and fragility. As Hill puts it, "To argue the preciousness of any individual's life, Ursula is a great place to start because she is... both beautiful and blameless. But beauty comes in many forms, and yes, I believe it holds true for even the hardest cases."

By the "hardest cases," Hill is referring to Jinx, to whom she devotes a whole chapter, as she has for Ursula's various ancestors. Jinx embodies the de-valuation of life. Watching the rescue efforts on television she blurts out in disgust, "All of that goddamn money and energy . . . Wasted . . . on that goddamn half-breed trailer-trash kid." The character of Jynx, Hill has said, was her meditation on evil. Hill is convinced that somehow the sacredness of life shines through even the worst of our meanness. "Life itself is a mystery,"[22] Hill has Justin say to Annie, and Hill herself agrees. "The most intriguing things (people, events, trends) in life have a hidden order and simultaneously pulse with mystery: sometimes they give up their secrets to us and sometimes they don't."[23]

Though Ingrid Hill is a practicing Christian, she doesn't at all try to preach a specifically Christian sense of life's mystery in the novel. Most of the characters scarcely think in religious terms. Once Annie does in passing, while slicing scallions early in her marriage. (As with all the novel's characters, Hill presents Annie's thoughts in third person and in the present tense.)

> *This time of the afternoon*, she thinks, *reminds us each day that we're mortal: it says, the end's coming, repent, repent.* She marvels at how the sun keeps up its rounds and remembers a number of reasons she keeps on believing in God. She ponders the differences between white and green onions, in chemical terms. Why she cries when she slices the white ones and seems quite fine now.[24]

Only for Jason's mother, Mindi Ji, is Christian faith central to her character. On watch with the others during the final chapter's rescue attempt, in the tension Mindi Ji turns to the New Testament. She prays fervently for Ursula's safe recovery, of course; but because she is reading the Letter to the Hebrews, which speaks of "a cloud of witnesses" surrounding us all, she imagines this cloud of witnesses as all of Ursula's ancestors, whom we've come to know so intimately in the novel's course, "and the Chinese blood in her rises up and petitions the ancestors too, 'Dear ancestors, preserve this child. She is all you have to carry on your line.'" So even the novel's Christian representative enfolds in her faith the connectedness with every other faith and culture which is the book's core vision. In fact, speaking of *Ursula, Under* with another interviewer, Hill cites a Jewish source: "I often think of Martin Buber, the Austrian Jewish philosopher whose chief subject

---

22. Ingrid Hill, *Ursula, Under* (New York: Penguin Books, 2005), 66.
23. Interview at http://us.penguingroup.com/static/rguides/us/ursula_under.html
24. Hill, *Ursula*, 183.

was the nature of existence as *encounter*. He said, 'All real living is meeting.' That seems self-evident to me — that unless we connect on a genuine level with people and the natural world, we are not really living but just passing through. I like to *connect* wherever and whenever I can...."[25]

Marilynne Robinson's *Gilead*, which won the 2005 Pulitzer Prize for fiction, also dramatizes our human connectedness across generations.[26] In *Gilead*, however, unlike in *Ursula, Under*, the generations spanned are more confined in time and space. "Gilead" is the name of a fictional town in Iowa where the novel is set and where John Ames, the novel's first-person narrator, now in his seventies, has spent his life as a Protestant minister (in the Congregationalist denomination), just as his father and grandfather had done. To those three generations Robinson adds a fourth, represented both by Ames's seven-year-old son, to whom the meditative narrative is addressed, and by Ames's namesake, John Ames (Jack) Boughton, the adult son of his best friend. Ames's meditations are absorbed with both "sons": the mystery of innocence embodied by the seven-year-old and the mystery of evil embodied by the young man, Jack. For like Jinx in *Ursula, Under*, Jack Boughton is a person apparently devoid of goodness, one whose existence seems designed to destroy the well-being of others who are struggling to live decent lives. Reverend Ames's moral challenge is to find forgiveness in his own heart for Jack and by doing so to bring this errant second "son" back into connectedness with others. A similar challenge had faced Ames's own father and grandfather, who came into conflict over how Christians should respond to the injustice of slavery and to war.

Forgiveness, always hard won, and then sometimes only tentatively, is nevertheless an affirmation of human connectedness. And affirmation is the core of Rev. John Ames's being. What is immensely engaging about this character whom Marilynne Robinson has created with such tenderness is that in the midst of all this tumult of generational conflict, he can hold fast to a deeply life-affirming vision and sensibility. Everything in his narrative voice bespeaks the sacredness of each ordinary thing and of every person, even finally the bedeviled John Ames Boughton. Most often this sacredness is imaged as light. Ames uses the image when he describes the effect people have on him when they come to him in confession. "I am struck," he says, "by a kind of incandescence in them, the 'I' whose predicate can be 'love' or 'fear' or 'want,' and whose object can be 'someone' or 'nothing' and it won't really matter, because the loveliness is just in that presence, shaped around 'I' like a flame on a wick, emanating itself in grief and guilt and joy and whatever else."

25. Zinta Aistars, "The Smoking Poet: An Interview with Ingrid Hill, author of *Ursula, Under*," on a website now discontinued; quoted courtesy of Ingrid Hill.

26. Marilynne Robinson, *Gilead* (New York: Farrar, Straus, and Giroux, 2004). Quotations that follow are from pp. 44 and 55.

But his loveliest and most profoundly Christian use of light imagery is aroused in John Ames by the "shimmer" in seven-year old son's hair in the sunlight. The shimmer doesn't blind John to the boy's ordinariness. "You're just a nice-looking boy, a bit slight, well-scrubbed and well mannered." Yet the son's very ordinariness is the source of what makes him extraordinary.

> It's your existence I love you for, mainly. Existence seems to me now the most remarkable thing that could ever be imagined. I'm about to put on imperishability. In an instant, in the twinkling of an eye. [Ames is quoting 1 Corinthians 15:52]
>
> The twinkling of an eye. That is the most wonderful expression. I've thought from time to time it was the best thing in life, that little incandescence in people when the charm of a thing strikes them, or the humor of it. "The light of the eyes rejoiceth the heart." [Proverbs 15:30] That's a fact.

That shimmer in his son's hair illuminates for Ames the connection between embodied life in this world and the "imperishability" of the embodied life to come.

For Christians this is what is meant by an incarnational vision. As contemporary Christian painter Ed Knippers has put it:

> The human body is at the center of my artistic imagination because the body is an essential element in the Christian doctrines of Creation, Incarnation and Resurrection... Disembodiment therefore is not an option for the Christian.... and there is something about the physicality of a painting that reminds us that we can never escape our physicality.... The fact is, we are stuck with the body. Without the body, there is nobody there. We must deal with it. We must explore the mystery of its meaning.[27]

Poet and playwright Jeanne Murray Walker said something similar to me at another meal-chat at the Glen Workshop. I asked her "Are there 'moments' of the Christian narrative that especially inform your creative vision and practice? — the Transfiguration, the Cross, the Resurrection? Do any of these particularly move you as a Christian artist?" Jeanne's immediate response was "The Transfiguration speaks to me. Transfiguration as transformation. When I see art I'm transformed by it. And when I write [poetry or plays], there's something that has transformed *me* that I want to pass on." I pushed a bit further: "Is there a Christian grounding for you in this sense of art as transformative?" And she was quite clear what that was: "It's Christian because of the Incarnation. Embodiment. Milton scholarship speaks of God's 'accommodation' to humankind. God is beyond us, so he has to accommodate his

---

27. Ed Knippers, "The Old, Old Story," in *It Was Good: Making Art to the Glory of God,* ed. Ned Bustard (Baltimore: Square Halo Books, 2006), 76.

infinity to our senses — this is the Incarnation. I've been a believer (not that there haven't been doubts too) since I was six, so this is part of me."

It's certainly part of her poetry. With a view that embraces at once the cosmic and the common, Walker's poems picture the ordinary stuff of life transformed by mysterious contact with a transcendent, transfiguring force. Often — as for Marilynne Robinson's narrator — this force is imaged as sparkling light, as stars or as fire. In "The Stars of Last Resort" Walker imagines starlight trapped inside a humble autumn melon.[28] In "To Mr. Auden in a time of war," which ponders light's eternal battle against darkness, she imagines her own creative power as light pictured in the marvelous image of pizza dough:

> In this dark time, I want to make light bigger,
> to throw it in the air like a pizza chef,
> to stick my fists in, stretching it
> till I can get both arms into radiance to the elbow
> spinning it above us.[29]

And in a playfully exuberant poem called "Poetry," she finds in Christ's transfiguring light the very source and blessing of poetry's irreplaceable value. The poem unabashedly confesses her giddy adoration of a particular book of new poetry by an unnamed poet. With delighted extravagance, she declares that it's a book "I love/ so much I'd like to eat it." Wildly, she purges her office in order to make space for the honored book, tossing out a lifetime of accumulated stuff which seems worthless in comparison. But in the poem's final stanza she comes to one object she must keep:

> Only the illumination of Saint John stays.
> In my study's scooped-out heart
> I wait beside the book, which glows
> with light borrowed from some distant star.
> I look at Saint John's face. He gazes from
> his throne, his eyes blazing with love
> and understanding. Tongues of flame
> play over him, sent from the Source
> who is both arsonist and fireman,
> and in his right hand, he holds a book.[30]

The "Source" is Christ himself: "both arsonist and fireman" exactly as in Ginger Geyer's sculpture *Fighting Fire with Fire*. Here in Jeanne Murray Walker's poem his role is to catch Saint John up in the fiery blaze of heaven which blesses the transfiguring power of the book — and by implication of all art.

The cherished book "glows/ with light borrowed from some distant

---

28. In *Image* journal #53 (Spring, 2007).
29. In *The Christian Century*, Feb. 6, 2007.
30. In *The Christian Century*, Dec. 26, 2006.

star." In the tradition of Christian art, the blazing light of stars shining on earth is emblematic of Christ as the light who penetrates earth's darkness transformatively. "I am the light of the world," Jesus proclaims in John's Gospel; and we noted in Chapter 2b that Christ walks through that Gospel — and through the entire history of Christian thought and experience — as the light shining in the world's darkness, which the darkness (whether of evil, suffering, or death) cannot overcome. All of the Christian arts have tried in their various media to represent this transfiguring light of Christ alive in the world. But the art form for which this representation comes most naturally — because light is its very medium — is photography.

In fact, this is precisely what excites contemporary photographer Krystyna Sanderson about her medium. "As a photographer I find the process of working with light and darkness extraordinary," she writes in an essay, "A Sense of God's Presence."[31] "I find light wrestling with darkness to be a powerful metaphor of the spiritual struggle between good and evil, between God's will and all that opposes God." To capture the sense of light transforming darkness, she goes to places like the Cloisters in New York City: a reconstructed complex of medieval monasteries that serves now as museum and meditation space. While photographing here for her series *Places of Light*, "my experience of the presence of God through the light was as concrete to me as the physical world of arcades and columns made out of stones.... The power of light 'burns' into the stone the same way the power of the light of Christ burns into the darkness of humankind."

Sanderson was personally transformed by working with the penetrating light of her artistic medium — so much so that it was through her artistic process that she was drawn (as painter Makoto Fujimura also was) to a conversion to Christianity. It happened through Sanderson's early series called *Masks*, which creates close-up photo portraits of faces of people who would not ordinarily be seen as attractive. At first she had been drawn "to the beauty and mystery of the people I photographed." But gradually what began exciting her was their *inner* beauty, the beauty of their spirits. Finally, after her Christian conversion, these "faces of people of all ages, sexes and races — in some cases because of lack of hair it became impossible to tell their gender — became archetypal and iconic, exemplifying Paul's words in Galatians that 'there is no longer male or female, for all are one in Christ Jesus.'.... I saw the faces I had photographed as revealing the image of God in which all people are made."[32]

The ordinary transformed by God's light, "life pulsing with mystery" (as Ingrid Hill put it): this is Krystyna Sanderson's vision, whatever her photographic subject. Her series *Solitude: Light and Stillness* captures women

31. Bustard, ed., *It Was Good*, 220.

32. "A Sense of God's Presence," in Bustard, ed., *It Was Good*, 211-224. Quotations from Sanderson that follow are all from this essay.

Krystyna Sanderson, *Places of Light #9*, black and white photograph 11" x 14".

in the stillness of meditation, while light (say from a window, which for Sanderson represents eternity) penetrates their inner spirits. "As a photographer, but also strongly identifying with the photographed subjects, I see not only light streaming through the window in the dark interiors, but also light streaming into my heart and soul, and am able to experience the contentment of being me, the stillness and peace that can only come from God, and the joy of beholding God's beauty." And even in the darkest of darkness, Sanderson can see and project hope through her art: her series *Light at Ground Zero* finds, she writes, images of "the light of God's radical grace, mercy and love" next door to Ground Zero at Saint Paul's chapel, which served as respite and hospitality space for rescue workers after 9/11.

Photography is the art of light and darkness. Christian photography is the art of capturing God's light transforming the darkness of our lives. In "A Sense of God's Presence," Sanderson enumerates the kinds of spiritual darkness that we contend with: "the darkness of fear, the darkness of poverty, the darkness of self-hate, the darkness of hating another, the darkness of addiction, the darkness of self-centeredness, the darkness of loneliness." She concludes: "to be in darkness is to be without hope, to be desperate, to give up. But there is nothing more joyous than light when one is in darkness. Light means hope."

Krystyna Sanderson, Jeanne Murray Walker, Marilynne Robinson, Ingrid Hill: these are artists who awaken us — by inventively different ways — to the beauty of God's transformative light in our lives. The moments of the Gospel narrative that most deeply ground and animate their creativity are Jesus' Incarnation and his Transfiguration.

But there are other Christian artists whose creativity is most grounded in the Passion: in the Jesus of the Cross. They focus on our brokenness, and some — as we'll see in the next chapter — are able to find a redeeming beauty even here.

Chapter 4d. "Broken Beauty"

In Chapter 4 so far, we've considered how art informed by Christian faith can enact God's generosity; how it can tease and delight us into recognizing anew the truths of our faith; how it can open us to the sacredness of life's ordinary moments. Art acting in these ways calls and recalls us to the good in ourselves, to our goodness as creatures made in God's image. But what about when we are bad? What does Christian art do with our ugly behavior, our evil tendencies: our personal wrong-doing and the dreadful horrors that we collectively inflict on one another?

As we saw in Chapter 2c, the core Christian image that collects our ugliness and transforms it is the Crucifixion. Christ suffering on the Cross is a victim of human evil; as victim he shares in the suffering inflicted on all victims; yet as God who will pass through this dreadful death to a resurrected life, he carries with him the promise of glorious new life for us all. The Crucifixion, then, naturally plays a large part in the history of Christian art. This book isn't the place to trace this whole history, and there are many fine studies which do. Where I want to start is with the thirteenth century figure of Saint Francis of Assisi (1181-1226), because Francis modeled a radical way of following Jesus which has influenced Christian devotion and art ever since.

Saint Francis is one of Christianity's most beloved figures. He embraced the Gospel message of poverty and brotherly love with such passion and charm that soon he had many followers of his own. For Francis, to be a Christian meant imitating the life of Jesus quite literally, and so he gave up all possessions and joyfully traveled around giving comfort to the sick and outcast. So close was Francis's identification with the humanity of Jesus that he received as his "reward" the very wounds of Christ in his own body: bleeding holes in his hands and feet where Jesus had been nailed to the Cross.

Art historian Timothy Verdon, in an essay called "Broken Beauty, Shattered Heart," explains the significance of Francis's miraculous wounds for Christian devotion and art. Francis received God's law, Verdon writes, "not on tablets of stone or wood but graven into his own flesh by the finger of the living God. The new law — Christ's law of a love so great it can accept death for others — is written in human flesh! It was novel and irrefutable proof of the worthiness of the flesh, of its eternal value, of the dignity of human beings who are soul but also *body*."[33]

European visual art representing the Crucifixion quickly absorbed the Franciscan spirit, so that — in the famous Crucifixion fresco of fourteenth century Italian painter Giotto, for instance — Christ's body looks like a real

---

33. Timothy Verdon, "Broken Beauty, Shattered Heart," in *A Broken Beauty*, ed. Theodore L. Prescott (Grand Rapids, MI: Eerdmans, 2005), 29.

human body of flesh and blood. Whereas in previous centuries, Christ's body on the Cross had been depicted with symbolic iconography (because the idea of the divine Christ enduring suffering was unacceptable), now his body was portrayed naturalistically, suffering as any human being's tortured body would.[34] And it was not only representations of Christ which were transformed by Franciscan spirituality. All humanity, every human body, was now affirmed in its infinite value, as Verdon notes. Out of this astounding new affirmation of the flesh developed the European movement known as Christian humanism, producing the great Renaissance art which relishes the body's beauty: the works of Leonardo de Vinci, Michelangelo, and many others. In the Renaissance tradition, Verdon observes, "humanity is pictured in relationship — with others, with oneself, and with God."[35]

Christian humanism continued to underlie representations of the body in Western art until, in the eighteenth century, Christianity itself came to be questioned. Challenges to Christian belief began with what is called the Enlightenment, which celebrated as the source of all truth the "light" of human reason unaided by divine revelation. This challenge to Christian faith grew during the nineteenth century's Romantic movement, which placed in the solitary human person — the person *out* of relationship with others or with God — all the glory which religious faith attributes to God. By the start of the twentieth century, God was being declared "dead" in fashionable circles, and religious faith (which for Europe meant Christian faith) was being dismissed as superfluous. The individual human person could do just fine, it was declared, on his own.

But as the twentieth century advanced, the isolated human person didn't do so well. Two world wars, brutal totalitarian dictatorships, genocides, and a disastrous economic depression combined to shake people's confidence in humanity. I'm aware of brushing cultural history with a broad stroke here, sweeping across immensely complex movements of collective psychology, and — furthermore — confining myself to Western civilization. It is fair to say, however, that by mid-century, a despairing sense of alienation had become the dominant Western outlook; the popular French philosophy existentialism even offered a kind of perverse celebration of the alienated individual. Art forms responded by expressing this breakdown of communal meaning in their particular media: music broke apart traditional harmonics; fiction fractured narrative sequence and developed the device of the intentionally "unreliable" narrator; poetry spurned traditional meters and rhyme patterns. And the visual arts? They represented the human body as disfigured, dismembered, fragmented. Think of Pablo Picasso's cubist figures, for instance, all angular pieces stuck oddly together.

34. Richard Viladesau, *The Beauty of the Cross* (New York: Oxford University Press, 2006), 138-9.
35. Verdon, "Broken Beauty," 31.

In this collapse of coherent meaning, however, a few artists held fast to a Christian vision and recast it powerfully for their broken times. I'm going to focus on two — the British poet W. H. Auden (1907-1973) and the French painter Georges Rouault (1871-1958) — because between them they searingly saw through their era's brokenness to the human evil behind it but also further back and deep to God's healing mercy. Auden was the great twentieth century artist to castigate our self-willed isolation from one another and from God. Rouault was the great twentieth century artist to move us toward overcoming this isolation and reclaiming coherence in God's love.

During his long career, Auden was continually rethinking what it meant to be a Christian, and he came to see Christ's miraculous birth and sacrificial death as the two core moments of the Christian narrative, with "loving your neighbor" as the core of the Christian message. In Auden's view, we habitually — indeed, willfully — ignore the astounding gift of these moments and this message. This is our sinfulness, as Auden sees it: that we distract ourselves from the wonder of God made flesh; that we distract ourselves from the shameful death that we inflicted on God in Christ and continue to inflict on Him in every act of violence; and that we shut our eyes to the needs of our neighbor, who is created in God's image.

Wry indirectness and scathing wit are Auden's characteristic mode. So in his book-length poem *For the Time Being* (1941-2), subtitled *A Christmas Oratorio*, he plays with the notion that at Christmas we have "time" for everything in the world except attending to our true "being," which is our life in the Being of Christ born this day. Beset by insecurities about believing the Christmas story in a secular age that belittles it, we let ourselves get too busy with trivialities ("bills to be paid, machines to keep in repair") to give the miraculous birth the time of day, so to speak. When Christmas is over, we pack up the decorations with the uneasy awareness that "Once again/ As in previous years we have seen the actual Vision and failed/ To do more than entertain it as an agreeable/ Possibility, once again we have sent Him away."[36]

Similarly, we manage to pass Good Friday distracting ourselves from the Crucifixion which we Christians presumably commemorate on this day. Auden's seven-poem sequence *Horae Canonicae* (1949-54) holds a mirror to our Good Friday hypocrisy. On this day, Christ died to redeem our sins; such is our Christian belief. But we belie our belief because we can't bear actually to look at the means of redemption. What humankind did to Christ on the Cross is too horrible to face. So instead of facing it and acknowledging our complicity — for every act of our own violence against a fellow human being re-crucifies Christ — we let ourselves pretend a bewilderment. "We are surprised/ At the ease and speed of our deed/ And uneasy: It

36. W.H. Auden, *Collected Poems* (New York: Random House, 1976, 1991).

is barely three," which is the hour of Christ's crucifixion, according to the Gospel accounts. "Mid-afternoon, yet the blood/ Of our sacrifice is already/ Dry on the grass." We wonder uncomfortably what to do with the rest of the day, then decide to take a nap — that is, to sink into a collective amnesia. Meanwhile, the meaning of this event "Waits for our lives."

Do our lives catch up to the meaning which God offers us in Christ's self-sacrifice? In Auden's view, the answer is a devastating no. God offers us the beauty of our bond with one another in Christ. Yet every time we look away from someone's pain, we break this bond. Indifference is our crying sin; indifference mocks God's command to love our neighbor; indifference slaps God in the face. Such is Auden's condemnatory vision.

French painter Georges Rouault, nearly Auden's contemporary, shared Auden's dismay at our human propensity to cut ourselves off from God and from human community. Like Auden, Rouault holds a mirror to our self-imposed human brokenness. But in Rouault's paintings, something else is mirrored as well: the compassion of an infinitely merciful God. What Rouault manages to do in his art is to move us to *look* at others' pain with the eyes of divine compassion — to look at it and see it as our own.

Rouault is now justly considered the West's major twentieth century visual artist of the Christian spirit. Yet during his career, everything about his art was unfashionable. When the shimmery light of the Impressionists was in vogue, Rouault's paintings were dark, marked by heavy lines and large splotches of black. When popular paintings depicted lovely images of well-off people enjoying picnics, Rouault offered painful images of pensive clowns and defiant prostitutes. When European intellectual life was declaring God dead and religion an outmoded superstition, Rouault painted biblical themes, focusing especially on the figure and face of Christ suffering his Passion.

Rouault's recurrent subjects throughout his long creative career were people marginalized and mocked by society — gypsies, prostitutes, prisoners, clowns — and his Christs were of this company. Rouault crafted an artistic style that brings us under their skin, into their suffering, while at the same time honoring a mysterious sacredness transforming their pain.

I see it all as I page slowly through a book of color prints of Rouault's paintings. I pause often: over, say, the 1906 *Prostitute at Her Mirror*, glaring at herself in full recognition of the hopelessness of her brutal life, while the artist makes us see a hidden dignity in her acceptance itself. Or I'll pause over the 1917 *Old Clown*, whose dark eyes seem to penetrate his self-delusion and our own. And I always stop at the 1920 *Le Christ dans la banlieue* (*Christ in the Suburbs*). The painting depicts the street of a poor factory town — not at all what we think of today as suburbs. The scene is at once bleak and beautiful, grimy yet glowing with the moon's reflected

Georges Rouault, *Le Christ dans la banlieue* (*Christ in the Suburbs*).

light, symbol of divinity suffusing with hope even the darkest darkness of our lives. And there in the foreground embodying hope itself is the figure of Christ. We know him by the painting's title, and by the peace of his bodily posture, but otherwise he is one of us, accompanying the two smaller and more darkened figures down the road — as he accompanies us all.

When I look at a Rouault painting like this one, an immense hush surrounds me. I'm drawn into a meditative space where life's trivialities have vanished and what remains with forceful urgency are the basics of the human condition, simultaneously pathetic and glorious. The pathos lies in our smallness, our weakness, our futile efforts to mask our pretensions. The glory is God's gift of merciful love shining nonetheless deep into and through our beings.

Life's pathos struck Rouault in a vision which he described in a letter to a friend:

> Ever since the end of one lovely day when the first star to shine in the

sky clutched at my heart, I can't say why, unconsciously, I have derived from this instant an entire system of poetics. That gypsy wagon
standing on the side of the road, the emaciated old horse grazing on
the thin grass, the aging clown sitting beside his wagon mending his
bright, multicolored costume — this contrast between brilliant, scintillating things intended to amuse us, and this infinitely sad life, if one
looks at it a bit objectively... Then, I expanded it all. I saw clearly that
the 'clown' was myself, ourselves... almost all of us... that this rich,
spangled costume is given us by life, we're all of us clowns, more or
less, we all wear a 'spangled costume,' but if we are caught unawares,
the way I caught that old clown, tell me! Who would dare to claim that
he is not moved to his very depths by immeasurable pity.[37]

"The clown was myself, ourselves..." Rouault never lost this deep identification with the pathetic and slightly ridiculous in all of us. Yet he also never
ceased to see our simultaneous glory: that even in our brokenness we are
loved by God, and in this love made beautiful.

How does a painting convey this complex vision of beauty in brokenness? Rouault's characteristic style has been called "transfigurative realism" or "realism transcended." His friend the great Catholic philosopher
Jacques Maritain called it a realism not of material appearances but of "the
spiritual significance of what exists (and moves, and suffers, and loves,
and kills); it is realism permeated with the signs and dreams that are com-
mingled with the being of things."[38]

Rouault was able to see, as he once put it, "all beauty both visible and
hidden."[39] A practicing Catholic all his life, he painted out of his profound
absorption of the Christian vision of human wretchedness whose ugliness is
yet transformed in being mercifully redeemed by God's grace. Knowing his
own weakness and utter dependence on God gave him a humility which, I
would say, draws the viewer into his paintings as into the heart of a fellow
pilgrim struggling along the human journey. Rouault wrote of his work:

What I have done is nothing, don't make much of it. A cry in the night.
A sob that miscarried. A strangled laugh. Throughout the world, every
day, thousands of obscure, needy people who are worth more than I
am, die at their tasks. I am the silent friend of all those who labor in
the fields, I am the ivy of eternal wretchedness clinging to the leprous
wall behind which rebellious humanity hides its vices and its virtues
alike. Being a Christian in these hazardous times, I can believe only
in Christ on the Cross.[40]

37. Letter to Edouard Schuré, undated, in Pierre Courthion, *Georges Rouault*
(New York: H. N. Abrams, 1962), 86.

38. Jacques Maritain, *Georges Rouault* (New York: H.N. Abrams, 1952), 12.

39. Courthion, *Georges Rouault*, 246.

40. Rouault, in his letter-preface to Georges Charensol, *George Rouault,
l'homme et l'oeuvre* (Paris, 1926), quoted by Courthion, *Georges Rouault*, 202.

And so he painted Christ on the Cross over and over again throughout his career: Christ in his crucifixion, but also Christ in other moments of his Passion as recounted in the Gospels, especially his being mocked by the Roman soldiers. This moment of Christ being mocked can be seen as humankind's nadir, the deluded depth of our sinfulness: here is humanity mocking its own God. But what Rouault usually depicts is not so much our sinfulness as Christ's noble absorption of it. The paintings of *Christ Mocked* show a torso or head bowed with silent dignity under its humiliation. Similarly with Rouault's many *Crucifixion* paintings: outlined heavily in black, Christ absorbs all human suffering while transforming it into divine love.

Rouault's Christian vision stands out dramatically in the landscape of twentieth century Western visual art, dominated as it was by the sense of breakdown of human community that I mentioned earlier: the certainty that human life was devoid of transcendent meaning, that the fractured and isolated individual had to stand (or fall) alone in a hostile universe. A brokenness determinedly without beauty was the century's predominant artistic vision. The very concept of beauty was, in fact, belittled in the art world.

Out of this context, around the start of the twenty-first century, American painter and professor Bruce Herman developed the idea of gathering fellow Christian artists for an exhibition that would recover the representation of beauty that Christians understand as core to our human brokenness, core because Christ shares in our brokenness and hence makes it mysteriously whole. By 2006, Herman and his like-minded colleagues had produced the magnificent book *A Broken Beauty*[41] and had mounted the major exhibition of this name in California and Toronto.

The fifteen visual artists chosen for the exhibition share a vision that recovers the Renaissance Christian humanist affirmation of the human body, in itself and in its relationship with other people and with God. But they are not simply returning imitatively to Renaissance artistic styles; their materials and techniques are contemporary, as are the situations evoked in their art. It is very much in our current twenty-first century world that they see human suffering, ugliness, pain. And it is precisely in this human messiness that they see God, incarnated in Christ, giving it a meaning which we perhaps can't quite make out but which in faith we trust is there. As sculptor and professor Theodore Prescott puts it in his essay in the book *A Broken Beauty*, "Christians believe that God is not repelled by the ugliness of human life, and that belief necessarily reconfigures our own understanding of beauty and ugliness in terms of who people are and how we see

---

41. Theodore L Prescott, ed., *A Broken Beauty* (Grand Rapids, MI: Eerdmans, 2005).

Mary McCleary, *Ash Wednesday, Waller County*,
mixed media collage on paper.

them."[42]

Like Rouault, then, the artists of *A Broken Beauty* create their work out of the Christian vision of a human wretchedness redeemed mercifully if mysteriously by God's grace. And like Rouault, this vision draws them into a love of neighbor grounded in the certainty that every person is equally beloved of God. Prescott notes that in some instances, "the bodies depicted in *A Broken Beauty* are literally those of neighbors — family and friends. In other instances the bodies are metaphorically conceived. But all of the bodies speak of a desire for a human image that can carry the weight of complex meanings, where beauty is not a mask and brokenness is not the only reality. They are an artistic affirmation of the real presence" — of God's sacramental presence in every experience of our lives. "Surely," Prescott concludes, "the exhibition will have accomplished its purpose if it helps us

42. Theodore L. Prescott, "The Bodies Before Us," in *A Broken Beauty*, 23.

see the bodies before us as neighbors, not strangers."[43]

So it is a *moral* sense of beauty — rather than a merely aesthetic one — that informs the art of *A Broken Beauty*, as it did the poetry of Auden and the painting of Rouault.

---

43. Prescott, "The Bodies Before Us," 24.

Chapter 4e. Longing for Transcendence: "Beauty enchants and this enchantment comes from God."

Music was dear to my life long before religion was. I grew up in a household without any religious practice, where God was never mentioned, yet a household which treasured the arts. Most of my time outside of school during childhood and adolescence was spent at the Peabody Conservatory of Music in Baltimore, with lessons in piano, composition, and dance — all of which I loved, though I had no particular talent in any of these fields. My grandmother, who taught piano at Peabody, used to take me to the symphony concerts that my parents couldn't afford. I blissfully soaked the music in, knowing that I didn't really understand it but feeling nonetheless somehow wonderfully nurtured by it.

So since childhood I've thrived on listening to classical music, and in early adulthood Bach became a favorite. I was in graduate school at the time, getting my doctorate in literature, and I valued the intellect above all other human faculties. The brilliant intricacy of Bach's musical patterns was what delighted me about his work. But gradually, in my late twenties, another dimension of his music began to draw me. Listening often to a record that George and I owned of the *Mass in B Minor*, I started sensing in the second *Kyrie* section (the text means "Lord, have mercy") a longing which pulled at my heart. What was it a longing *for*? I didn't know, and yet the music unquestionably spoke for me, expressed something at the core of my being. And the *Gloria in excelsis*: such celebratory joy! "Glory to God in the highest," it sang out. Then came the first movement of the *Sanctus* ("Holy, holy, holy, Lord"), with its solemn grateful reverence, breaking out into the lighthearted praise of *Pleni sunt coeli* and the *Hosanna*. ("The heavens and earth are full of your glory; praise in the highest!") Finally, the contrition and yearning of the closing *Agnus Dei* ("Lamb of God, who takes away the sins of the world, have mercy on us") moved something in me that I'd never sensed before, as did the intense desire of the concluding *Dona nobis pacem* ("grant us peace"). I began wondering who or what this God might be who inspired such praise, gratitude, longing, contrition, but above all joy. I began vaguely wanting to share in a relationship to this God.

A decade later I was sharing in it at my baptism. Of course during that decade many other forces combined to draw me toward the Christian faith. But it was the great music of Bach's *Mass in B Minor* which first awoke my soul's longings and gave them a voice. The music's beauty spoke a truth that I found I could not live without. (Years later, reading the twentieth century philosopher Simone Weil, I was struck by her statement about Christianity: that anything which has produced so much beauty cannot be devoid of truth.)

I wonder if it was a similar pull which drew crowds by the millions — over twenty-seven million, in fact — to view Michelangelo's famous marble sculpture of the *Pietà* at the 1964-5 New York World's Fair. Of course the celebrity status of this renowned work of art was a big part of its attraction. And the extraordinary circumstance of its being permitted to be on display away from Saint Peter's Basilica at the Vatican, its home since Michelangelo completed it in 1499 or 1500 (scholars are unsure of the date). Endless crowds from around the world visit the sculpture there, as well. Silent, meditative, they gaze on the life-sized Jesus lying dead in his Mother's lap, the two figures carved from a single block of white Carrara marble. What in Michelangelo's statue makes it one of the most beloved works of Christian visual art?

There's the mastery of the art form itself. Out of the massive marble block (5 1/2 feet high and over 6 feet wide), Michelangelo has carved the Mother and Son in a conjoined pyramidal shape, with the apex as Mary's head bent over her Son, the base as the wide ripple of her abundant robes, and the sides formed by an intimate interplay of their two bodies. The line of the sculpture's right side is formed first by Mary's head, then her right shoulder and arm cradling her Son's head bent back in death, then his right arm hanging down with her right hand supporting his torso under his right armpit, then her right leg hidden under the flow of her robes supporting the weight of his back, with the marble folds of her robes continuing the pyramid's right side down to the base. The sculpture's left side begins again with Mary's head, then follows her left arm and hand held out with palm open toward the viewer as if in a gesture of both offering her Son and accepting the divine will of his death for our sakes. Her outstretched fingers visually meet his left knee, and the rest of the statue's left side follows Christ's dangling leg down to its foot suspended just above the base of Mary's robes. The message of the entire pyramidal shape is that these two figures form an inseparable whole in this profoundly sorrowful moment.

For it is the moment just after Christ has died and been taken down from the Cross. Michelangelo has put holes in Christ's hands and feet and a slight gash on the right side of his chest, to indicate that this is indeed Christ crucified. But otherwise we wouldn't know. In fact, this marble figure of a beautifully formed man pulses with life. Blood seems to be flowing in his raised veins, and his face is utterly peaceful, as if calmly asleep; there are no signs of the whipping and scourging that he was subjected to preceding his crucifixion, no signs on his face or limbs of the agony that a crucified body would have suffered. Michelangelo's intention in representing a dead yet vibrant Christ was to express the Christian-Neoplatonist belief which he shared with the Italian intellectuals of his time: the belief that spiritual reality resides in the material world, and that divinity manifests itself especially in the beauty of the human body. All the more so, then, for the very Son

Michelangelo, *Pietà*, in St. Peter's Basilica, The Vatican, Italy.
Marble, 5 1/2 feet x 6 feet.

of God himself: death could not rob him of life, and his peaceful beauty in death demonstrates the power of divine life within him.

This astonishingly tranquil beauty of Christ's body in Michelangelo's *Pietà* helps account, I'd say, for the work's widespread popularity. And the Son's peace is inseparable in this work from the Mother's. Mary's figure also exhibits an extraordinary calm that would come (in Michelangelo's view) from the deep spirituality of her nature, from the divine light that she embraced when she assented to bear God's Son in her womb.

In fact, in a daring conflation of the moments of Christ's death and birth, Michelangelo has sculpted the two figures so that Mary appears to be giving birth to her Son once again: her thighs are open (modestly, of course, under the folds of her flowing garment), and the Son is offered to us between them. But it is now the crucified adult Son, the Son who has given his life for our sakes.

The Pietà theme did not originate with Michelangelo, but what he did with it was strikingly original. The theme was first devised in the late thirteenth century Gothic culture of Germany and France, where a desire for emotional and intimate religious imagery had developed, mainly under the influence of the Franciscan spirituality that we met in the previous chapter. Medieval religious imagery had been formal and distant, because God and Christ were conceived on a cosmic scale. But after Saint Francis and movements following him envisioned a more intimate relation with Jesus, artists began creating poems and songs and visual works representing Jesus suffering on the Cross, works intended to elicit sorrowful gratitude for his self-sacrifice. The Pietà theme emerged from this context — despite the interesting fact that it is not at all grounded in Scripture. Nowhere in the Bible does Mary hold the body of her crucified Son. But religious longing of the era needed this image: the grieving Mother cradling her tortured Son. Their pain is the dominant message of the Gothic representations of this new image, usually in crude wooden sculptures. Jesus and Mary are both horribly disfigured: Jesus by his wounds and Mary by grief.

Michelangelo took this Pietà image and doubly transformed it. He sculpted his figures into glisteningly beautiful marble forms evoking a profound and vibrant peace, as we've already noted. This itself was already strikingly original. Yet even further, he manages in the postures of his two figures to evoke through them another image of Mary and Jesus that was popular in fifteenth century Italian art: the young Mother presenting to the world the newborn Babe on her lap. In the hundreds of Renaissance art works on this theme, the Madonna sits enthroned in her luscious robes. In his *Pietà*, Michelangelo has sculpted Mary in this pose and clothing. And, further reinforcing the evocation of Madonna-and-Child, he has made for the Mary of his *Pietà* a clearly youthful face, so that here at her grown Son's death she remains the age that she was at his birth.

The complex of emotions aroused in the viewer by Michelangelo's subtle conflation of images is what I suggest as a third reason for why this work is so widely beloved. Grieving Mother and Dead Son evoke our sorrow; yet viewing the incarnational splendor of these bodies — their spiritual energy caught and conveyed by polished stone seemingly become flesh — we feel awe at the divine power which brings death to life. The visual echoes of Mother and Child elicit our wondrous gratitude that God chose to take on the vulnerability of our human condition. And the background resonance with an image of actual birthing recalls Mary's assent to open her body to God's mystery, eliciting our thankful praise of her and also our hope that we too might open ourselves to be God's vessels.

No one could put in a nutshell all that a great work like Michelangelo's *Pietà* achieves, all that it evokes, recalls, calls us to. Its beauty recalls our deepest longings for restoration of whatever has been lost in our lives; its beauty invites us to hope; its beauty acts — we might say — as God's way of attracting us to transcendence. Philosophy professor Bruce Ellis Benson, in an essay cleverly titled "Call Forwarding," observes that beauty's very nature is to call out to us, to forward to us God's primal call to follow Him who is beauty itself and all beauty's source.[44] How, though, does beauty manage to attract us to God? Benson finds his answer in the same Neo-Platonic philosophy that inspired Michelangelo, and specifically in the sort of word-play that ancient Greek thought delighted in. The Greek words for "to call" (*kalein*) and "to enchant" (*kelein*) are etymologically akin. For Neo-Platonism, this kinship suggests that beauty's way of calling us to God is by enchanting us, while of course this very enchantment has God as its source. "So beauty enchants," Benson concludes; "and this enchantment comes from God."

Did beauty enchant the millions of viewers who filed past Michelangelo's *Pietà* at the 1964-5 New York World's Fair? The question, though intriguing, is impossible to answer, since such an inward, spiritual force cannot be measured. I must confess that I myself missed the call of the *Pietà*'s spiritual power when I joined the throngs filing by the sculpture at the Fair. But the lack was in me, I now believe, not in Michelangelo.

It was the summer of 1964 when I went to the World's Fair with my first husband and his family, who lived nearby. So I would have been twenty years old. My memory of the day is vague, mostly the visceral recollection of standing in long lines outside in the dust, thirsty under an uncomfortably hot sun. One of those lines would have been for the *Pietà*. I vaguely remember the relief of finally reaching the cooler inside of the exhibition area; I vaguely remember a surrounding darkness, the brightness of the highlighted statue, and lots of flickering blue lights. (Hung around

44. Bruce Ellis Benson, "Call Forwarding," in *The Beauty of God*, ed. Daniel J. Treier et al, (Downers Grove, IL: InterVarsity Press, 2007), 70-83.

the statue were strings of simulated blue votive candles, which struck me as kitsch.) I remember willing myself into a sense of awe, yet aware that mine was an awe steeped in ignorance. With no religious upbringing and at that point almost no knowledge of Christianity, I had no context for what I was seeing. My husband and in-laws were Jewish and seemed as out of touch with the sculpture's meaning as I. From a college Art History course, I could appreciate the achievement of sculpting marble into swirls of drapery folds and life-like human form. But without any religious context for what I was seeing — without even a basic familiarity with the story being told — I could not connect with the art work's call to transcendence. So Michelangelo's *Pietà* did not affect me as Bach's *B Minor Mass* did less than a decade later.

Maybe I just wasn't ready. But my experience serves as a caution to me about assuming that beauty works on us in some magical way. No, beauty's "enchantment" is not automatic. Nor would Benson argue that it is. On the contrary, he insists that once we are called by God through beauty, our reception of the call lies in our response. Only if we are open to beauty's call can we then forward the call along to others — by joining in the beauty that is already in process as God's enterprise on earth.

I do believe that we all — all humans, by our very nature — long to join in this enterprise. People still at an unformed stage of life (as I was in 1964), as well as people thoughtfully committed to agnosticism or atheism, wouldn't put that longing in religious terms. But they might be comfortable with how poet Mark Jarman, in an essay on the purpose of metaphor in poetry, talks about our need for wholeness.[45] Noting the necessary fragmentation of human life, how we are aware of living in bits and pieces, Jarman observes that we all sense that this fragmentation is not our true self, not our desired destiny. We long, he writes, "to recognize a unified self, a restored relation." All metaphor, he continues, draws together two disparate things, so that "in making a metaphor we are enacting that impulse toward unity or reunification, to the restored relation." But in this mortal life, we know that all is transience, that any restored relation is at risk of again falling apart. "One of the beauties of metaphor is its promise of putting a fragmented self back together. One of its dynamic and exciting issues is the way that promise isn't quite kept."

What animates Jarman about metaphor — and metaphor, I'd submit, can operate in all art forms, though it is most evident in poetry — is this continual tension between the promise of restoration to a wholeness and the inevitable failure of the promise. Great art often recognizes that we are not quite as are meant to be, that we fall short of our longing for unity with one another and with the divine source of our being. In Christian terms, this art

45. Mark Jarman, "To Make the Final Unity: Metaphor's Matter and Spirit," *The Southern Review* (Spring, 2007).

recognizes that we are fallen creatures living in a fallen world. But art can also — and this is Jarman's point about metaphor — give us a glimpse of the wholeness and call us into that restored relation.

I think my favorite work of art that dramatizes this tension between the fulfillment and the failure of the promise of restored wholeness is the 1986 Danish film, *Babette's Feast*. (My second choice would probably be Mozart's opera *The Marriage of Figaro*.)

Director and screenplay writer Gabriel Axel based *Babette's Feast* on the short story of that name by Danish author Isak Dinesen, and Axel stays fairly faithful to the text and tone of Dinesen's tale. Ever since the movie won the 1986 Academy Award for Best Foreign Film, people have argued over the relative merits of film and written story. While I treasure what Dinesen was able to do with the prose of her tale, I'm in the camp that finds the film wonderfully richer still — precisely because Axel's visual medium conveys the story's spirit and layers of texture better than prose alone can. So in my comments that follow, it is the film that I'm speaking of.

In fact, the film's opening credit sequence already tells half the story in its background images, nearly drained of color. A stark, gray coastline, from which the camera pans back over the gray rooftops of a tiny rustic village surrounded by dried out brown grass; then quick cut to a close-up of rows of identical dried gray-white fish hung upside down on rough-hewn horizontal wooden planks. A fish is an ancient symbol for Christ, but the Christianity lived in this remote, drab corner of mid-nineteenth century Denmark is — we will soon learn — dried out. The Dean (minister) of the local sect has taught his small flock of followers a strictly ascetic Christianity which scorns the pleasures of this world. He counsels them to await instead the joys of the next life, the heavenly Jerusalem of their favorite hymn: "Jerusalem, my heart's true home... You keep us clothed and fed; never would you give a stone to the child who asks for bread." The Dean's two daughters, Martine and Philippa, middle aged and dressed identically in brown cloaks over long gray dresses as they enter camera range in the film's next shot, have remained unmarried in order to devote themselves to good works. And that's what they are doing, in a spirit of peaceful contentment, in this first sequence of our meeting them: carrying their baskets from house to house, bringing food and comfort to the infirm.

Threats to the sisters' peaceful contentment had, however, entered in their youthful days, and the film now flashes back to the upsetting episodes of "two gentlemen from the great world outside." Both men are distinctly colorful, each in his own way. The young officer Loewenhielm, in bright blue uniform, is a rake; his father exiles him to his aunt's mansion near the Dean's village for three months of reflection on his follies. Riding by the village, Loewenhielm sets eyes on the lovely young Martine and instantly falls in love with her. In the household's piety, he finds what appears to him a purer, simpler life that beckons him. But it is not to be; suddenly he feels invisible in this setting and knows that a life for him there would be "impossible." With regretful farewells to the heart-stricken but silently restrained Martine, he flees.

Next the French opera star Achille Papin arrives on the Danish coast, seeking (he believes in his self-delusion) its stark quiet in order to ponder the futility of his life of fame. But when he hears the beautiful, young Philippa singing in the church choir, his scorn of fame drops away as he is gripped excitedly by a vision of her destiny as the diva he will make of her. She'll have Paris at her feet! He is astute enough, though, to couch his offer of singing lessons to Philippa's father in more acceptable terms: "she will sing like an angel; that's important when one sings God's praises." Papin's whole being is colorful, with the vivacity of a man of the stage. And as he encourages Philippa to sing with him a seductive Mozart duet between two lovers, color comes to her face as well. But it's the color of blushing, and she tells her father she wants no more singing lessens. Papin departs, defeated.

The colorfulness of the secular world's glamour (whether of the military or the stage) now banished from the village, the film returns to the present time of its opening scenes, fifteen years later. The Dean has died. In stormy darkness, the Frenchwoman Babette is hurled into the sisters' lives. Fleeing the political turmoil in France which has killed her husband and son, she bears a letter from the flamboyant Papin begging the good sisters to take her in. "Babette can cook," he laconically says. But he waxes eloquent on Philippa's great talent, sadly lost (he bemoans) to the world. He has grieved this loss all these years, he writes, but is consoled by the faith that "in Paradise I shall hear your voice again. There you will be the great artist that God intended you to be. Ah! how you will enchant the angels."

Of course the good sisters do take Babette in as their cook. In a gently comic sequence they show her how to slice and boil the palid dried fish, then how to make their staple thick (and decidedly unappealing) brown soup called ale-bread. Babette is a conscientious servant, learning the local customs and soon even reducing the sisters' food budget by her apparently miraculous way of bargaining down prices with the shopkeepers.

The film then jumps forward some dozen years, focusing first on what has happened to the Dean's little flock since his death. Gray-haired and aging, they've become increasingly querulous among themselves in their founder's absence. Lifelong resentments rankle; with ugly, hardened faces and unforgiving hearts they exchange bitter recriminations. The good sisters are discouraged and helpless before this dissolution of brotherly love around their tea table; only when Babette (wearing a pendant Cross over her apron for the first time in the film) enters with tea and chastises them like children are they momentarily silenced.

The plot moves quickly now to get to the grand event of the film's title: *Babette's Feast*. The sisters announce that in honor of the upcoming hundredth anniversary of their father's birth, they wish to celebrate in a special way with the flock. Babette receives news that the French lottery ticket she has renewed each year has finally been picked; she has won ten thousand francs. With this new-found wealth, she begs the sisters to let her prepare a special meal — a real French meal — for their father's birthday party. Unwillingly (not wanting to cause her any trouble or expense), they assent.

So all is in place for the marvelous sequence of scenes leading up to and presenting Babette's feast; the sequence will comprise fully half of the film's total length. Babette's face glows with pleasure as she secures her exotic ingredients from France: a huge live turtle for the soup; a cage of chirping quails; a whole case of varied French wines; and more. With the grandeur of a liturgical procession, she leads the carts carrying her supplies from the coast, where they've arrived by boat, into the village.

And when the great evening arrives, the camera focuses all its attention on Babette's astounding culinary feats as she prepares dish after magnificent dish of delicacies in the tiny kitchen. The film's color brightens with close-ups of her pink hands flying in their artistry as she shapes each beautiful creation and lovingly places it on a gleaming silver platter. Among the guests, we've learned, will be General Loewenhielm himself, who happens to be visiting his aged aunt, one of the Dean's disciples. "So we shall be twelve for dinner, not eleven," Martine reports to Babette.

And now we are treated to the Feast. *Babette's Feast*. The grim-faced disciples in their drab clothing file in around the elegantly set table, which glistens with cut glassware and ornate silver candleholders. Having been warned by the sisters that the dinner is likely to be so seductively pleasurable as to be perhaps from the devil, they've taken a vow not to speak a word about the food during the meal. What follows through the entire feast is a comic triumph, both in comedy's ordinary sense as funny in its incongruities and also in its higher sense as divinely motivated restoration of relations. Because what we see happening in the course of the Feast is that — in the words of Bruce Ellis Benson quoted earlier — "beauty enchants, and this enchantment comes from God."

Enchantment does come over the dour flock as Babette's luscious food and superb wines slowly have their effect. Never before has the flock been permitted to indulge in the sensuous beauties of this world. Now they savor this utterly new experience — reluctantly at first, since they've sworn not to enjoy the meal. But beauty's power overcomes their pious scruples; each disciple's resistances gradually give way. These faces that throughout the film have been sober and grim begin re-shaping into smiles that are clearly breaking forth from within: from a joy never before experienced, a joy that seems to take each disciple by surprise. We watch their transformation: the hard edges of their expressions softening; their gray faces turning pink with the flush of glorious food and wine.

This is the dear, drab flock which had always assumed that beauty and joy were reserved for Paradise, for the Jerusalem that would be their home after this dark life had passed away. But now they are experiencing Paradise right here in the present. In their flush of receiving this gratuitous gift, members of the flock find themselves — toward the Feast's end — whispering to one another words of reconciliation of their old, festering disputes. The climactic visual image of their enchantment by the beauty that Babette has created for them comes as they leave the Feast to go out into the cold night: spontaneously joining hands, smiling broadly now, they form a circle dance around the village well, as they quietly sing a hymn that "eternity is nigh… so that our true home we shall find." But they've just found it — a literal taste of it — here and now. This is the film's loving irony: The Dean's disciples have experienced, for the first time in their lives, a foretaste of the bliss that eternity (in their doctrine) promises them; yet they don't quite comprehend the grace that they've received.

Grace is not too strong a word; for religious — and specifically Christian — imagery has been subtly interlaced all through the Feast and its preparation scenes. We've already noted the Cross that Babette first wears when chastising the flock for their quarreling; during her joyfully ardent creation of the Feast itself she continues wearing her Cross, a silently visual message that her artistry is self-sacrifice for the sake of the flock's reconciliation. We've noted, too, the liturgical nature of Babette's procession of goods for the Feast. And we've already heard of Martine's announcement that there will be twelve disciples at table, like the twelve disciples at the Last Supper. Then there is the abundance of flowing wine (a key Christian symbol for Jesus' pouring out his life for the sake of our unity with one another in God), and a mumbled comment by one of the brothers at dinner about the "wedding at Cana" (the feast, recounted in John's Gospel, where Jesus miraculously turned water into wine for the wedding guests' enjoyment). Also during dinner, the General — who from his large experience of the finer things of life is the only guest to appreciate consciously the unsurpassable quality of the banquet they are being served — recognizes the meal's prize dish as the creation of an extraordinary woman who was chef of the renowned Cafe Anglais in Paris. "She had the ability," the General says to the mystified diners around the table, "to transform a dinner into a love affair… which made no distinction between bodily and spiritual appetite."

These are all hints of who Babette is and what her Feast is accomplishing. In the film's final scene, we receive the full revelation. The guests having departed into their magical dance of unity around the well, Martine and

Philippa come into the kitchen to thank Babette for the wonderful meal. In response, Babette confides two crucial facts about herself, which burst for us (though not for the sisters, who don't quite comprehend the implications) into recognition of her true identity. First she quietly says, "At one time I was the head chef at the Cafe Anglais." This means nothing to them, but to us who have heard the General's remarks, it is a revelation that Babette has had a famed creative life. Then she tells the sisters that she has spent her entire lottery fortune on this single meal and so has no funds left for returning to Paris; she will remain in their humble home as their servant. And in this extravagant act of self-giving, we see her for certain as what we might have already guessed: as a figure of Christ, who came among us to serve, to give the entire gift of himself — his divine being — in order to draw us to into the joy of divine life. When the sisters object that now Babette will be poor, she responds passionately, "An artist is never poor. At the Cafe Anglais I was able to make them happy— when I gave of my very best."

Artist and figure of Christ: Babette is revealed as both. And so in her person, Christ and the artist merge — as the creator of beauty whose purpose is to make people happy, to heal their sad brokenness and make them whole. We have seen this happen; we've seen divine grace work through Babette's art to bring joy and reconciliation to the discontented, querulous flock. We've seen how the beauty she creates in her Feast enchants them with a taste of Paradise on earth; and this taste transforms them, even if only for the evening of this meal. "Beauty enchants and the enchantment comes from God." In Babette we see this statement come to life.

What's lovely about the film is that it won't just leave us here, with this fulfillment of restored relation. Remember Mark Jarman's comment, cited earlier, that while metaphor — and potentially all art, I suggested — shows us the promise of wholeness, it also admits the inevitable failure of the promise. In *Babette's Feast* we are given, in the film's final lines, both the fulfillment of the promise and its failure. Moved by Babette's great sacrifice of giving all that she had for their sakes, Philippa seeks to console her with words that well up from her own heart. (She seems only vaguely conscious that she's quoting Papin's very words about herself in his letter so many years ago.) "But this is not the end, Babette," she says with deep feeling. "In Paradise you will be the great artist that God meant you to be!" Then stepping forward to embrace Babette, Philippa utters the film's final line: "Ah, how you will enchant the angels!" We see the sweet irony. Babette knows she is already the great artist that God means her to be. She has brought Paradise to earth for an evening through her art. Those she has enchanted are this dear, drab flock whom her art has transformed — for the time of its spell — into angels.

Yet another level of irony is also operating in Martine's words. There's a deeper sense in which Martine is right: "this is not the end." As marvelous as Babette's Feast has been, it is merely a metaphor of the Heavenly Feast awaiting us all. This is the Christian truth that Martine intuits, though she puts it in the words of the worldly Papin.

Finally, we are aware as the film ends that we too have been enchanted by art's beauty: the beauty of the entire film itself. And so we are left with exactly the resonance sensed by Martine and, just previously, by the disciples dancing around the well: we feel that such beauty experienced here on earth must come from a higher source. Great art points beyond itself. Art's beauty is God's way of attracting us to the transcendent life that we can experience on earth in passing moments but which awaits us for certain in heaven, in Paradise.

In an interview in *Image* journal, Catholic Christian novelist Ron Hansen speaks about the art of writing as a "sacrament." He defines sacrament in the classic Christian way, as "a visible sign of an invisible grace." Hansen goes on to say that sacraments are "symbols of something that God is actually doing to us." Christian churches that celebrate sacraments (such as baptism, marriage, and primarily the Eucharist) see God truly present in these acts. "Sacraments all function as ways of telling stories about God's relationship to us," Hansen says, adding "And that's what I think writing is doing as well."[46]

What I'd add to Hansen's comments is that I think all the arts are doing this as well — or *can* do it if that's their intention. Certainly *Babette's Feast* tells a story about God's relationship to us, as does Michelangelo's *Pietà*. And I would extend Hansen's concept of sacrament further to the beauty produced by the other arts as we've touched on them throughout this chapter on Art Informed by Christian Faith. Beauty's extravagant generosity — which we saw exemplified in Chapter 4a primarily by the "grace arena" of Makoto Fujimura's paintings, but also by the music of Bach — is surely a dimension of the invisible grace of which art is a visible (or in the case of music, an audible) sign. In Chapter 4b we saw how art can draw us to God by playfully surprising us, by defamiliarizing the familiar in order to shake us awake to God's action in our lives. The examples there, of Ginger Geyer's porcelain sculpture, of Mark Jarman's poetry, and of Dante's *Divine Comedy*, are all visible signs of invisible grace — delightful or even shocking visible signs of the surprises that God has in store for us. Chapter 4c's theme of the sacredness and transformative power of the ordinary things of daily life is right at the heart of the concept of sacrament. The novels of Ingrid Hill and Marilynne Robinson, the poetry of Jeanne Murray Walker, the photography of Krystyna Sanderson: all these are unquestionably ways of telling stories about God's graced relation with us. Even the material of Chapter 4d, on our human penchant for evil, in its darkness brings us

46. "A Conversation with Ron Hansen," *Image* #57 (Spring, 2008): 66.

into God's light. Auden's poetry and Rouault's paintings, as well as the contemporary visual artists of "broken beauty," all tell the story of God's accompanying us in our suffering, even in our ugliness.

In fact, Chapter 4d quoted sculptor and professor Theodore Prescott asserting that even art depicting human ugliness can be redeemed by its embrace of God's real presence — God's sacramental presence — in our midst. Such art "will have accomplished its purpose," he wrote, "if it helps us see the bodies before us as neighbors, not strangers." In this statement is a confidence that art can transform our ways of seeing and being in the world; that art can help us see strangers and perhaps even enemies as neighbors; that art can act as a moral force in our lives. But all this will be our topic in Part III.

Dialogue: A Muslim and a Christian compare their arts

Christian: Whew, we've been engaging such a lot of art. So many art forms, so many art works, inspired by each of our faiths. Such an overflowing of creativity, all to the glory of God. I hesitate even to begin our dialogue, fearing that we'll oversimplify the wealth and range of all this artistry. Where do you think we should start?

Muslim: How about starting with the Light, as we did in our previous Dialogue? With the "Light upon Light" of the Qur'an's Light Verse? God imaged as Light for both our faiths.

Christian: Yes, the Light upon Light! In fact, though he wasn't mentioned in the previous chapters, a contemporary Palestinian Christian artist named Kamal Boullata has painted a silkscreen actually entitled *Nur 'ala nur* ("Light upon Light"). Though a Christian, he was inspired by the Qur'an for this painting. It was chosen for the British Museum's 2006 *Word into Art* exhibition featuring contemporary calligraphic art from the Middle East. In much of Boullata's work, he told the exhibit organizers, "I have been alternatively using verses from Christian as well as Muslim sources where the word 'light' occurs. Having been raised in a Jerusalem Christian Arab family I felt free to borrow words from the Holy Qur'an or from the Sufis as well as from the Gospel of Saint John and from Church liturgy where the word appears. Light has been central to my work and it still is."

Muslim: Light has indeed been central to much of the art work that we've heard about in the previous chapters. Immediately I picture the Dome of the Rock, its dazzling interior surface described as drawing the spectator up towards the Source of all light. Or the high artistry of the *tajwid* style of reciting the Qur'an: the reciter, we were told, draws himself and his listeners towards the light of heaven and earth, that is, toward Allah, God.

Christian: These recollections from the chapter discussing Muslim art intrigue me. They intrigue me because I'm sensing in Christian art both a parallel and — well, not exactly a contradiction, but a different dimension or focus for the way art reflects the Light of all lights. First the parallel. An acclaimed twentieth century Christian writer of fiction, Flannery O'Connor, once said "My faith is not what I write about or what I paint about but it is the light by which I see."[1] Her comment now strikes me — now that I'm in dialogue with you about these matters — as every bit Islamic as it is Christian.

Muslim: Yes, yes, and yes. We heard these very sentiments expressed at the close of the discussion of the *adhan*: that for Muslims, "Beauty is God's and God's alone, offered to humankind not as an idea to be contemplated but as a light to be followed."

Christian: Following the divine light. Yes, I think most artists inspired by Christian faith would concur that this is what they aim for in their creative process. Yet here's where I also sense a major difference from Muslim art. The divine light for Muslim artists seems essentially *transcendent*... the Light they are drawn *towards*. And although this is the case for some Christian art, too — we heard, for instance, about Dante's *Paradiso*, with its vision of God as transcendent heavenly light — most of the Christian artists that we've just been hearing about find God's light mainly in the ordinary stuff of everyday life. Their divine light is *incarnational*; there's no escaping that term when talking about Christian art. I'm recalling the discussion of the novel *Gilead*, where the sacredness of every thing and every person was most often imaged as light. Or the poem where Jeanne Murray Walker pictures starlight trapped inside a simple melon.

Muslim: So how would you say that "incarnational" light is different from "transcendent" light?

Christian: I can only speculate... who can 'know' such things? We are talking about God, after all. But when I recall what has been said about light in both our religions, and about the art that derives from that light, at least then I can say a couple things. One is that "your" transcendent light is equally transcendent for me, though the difference is that for me this very light walked the earth as Jesus Christ — and still walks the earth as the Risen Christ.

Muslim: So the transcendent light that walks the earth as Christ also walks in those who share in that light... and it is this vibrantly present — even tangible — light that Christian artists strive to depict?

Christian: Well said! Whereas for Muslim artists — let me see how I do with this — for them this light remains transcendent, reaching down into the created world to illuminate it and shining everywhere in the created world as long as the light is not blocked by indifference or defiance.

Muslim: Well....

Christian: You're not happy with what I just said, are you.

Muslim: No, frankly, I'm not. What you say is far too abstract, far too

---

1. Quoted by Ed Knippers, "The Old, Old Story," in *It Was Good*, ed. Ned Bustard, 86.

detached from the beautiful reality of the person actually filled with God's light. We call such a person "Mu'nawar," "enlightened," derived from the Arabic word *nur*, meaning light. It's a common name among Muslims. But its real importance is in honoring those in whose faces God's spirit glows.

Christian: Thank you for the correction. So maybe, despite our differences over the notion of incarnation, we have more in common than I thought. Still, wouldn't you say that Muslim artists would be reluctant to depict objects unless these objects were clearly symbols of transparency or embodied, enlightened presences (as in Peter Sanders' portraits)? Yet how interesting... Even as I say this, I'm sensing that in a way it's true for Christianity as well, though for me *every* earthly object is transparent to God's light because Christ's incarnation has made sacred *all* of matter. An eighth-century Christian monk named Saint John of Damascus put it this way: "Of old, God the incorporeal and formless was never depicted, but now that God has been seen in the flesh and has associated with human kind, I depict what I have seen of God. I do not venerate matter, I venerate the fashioner of matter, who became matter for my sake."[2]

Muslim: Your Saint John sounds a bit defensive there, as if he were arguing against a competing view.

Christian: How astute of you to notice this.

Muslim: Thank you. But I'm already quite familiar with John of Damascus. He was one of the first Christian polemicists *against* Islam.

Christian: That's true. But he was also polemicizing against fellow Christians. For at the time, in the area where John lived (what we'd now designate the Middle East), a great controversy raged over whether Christ, as God, could legitimately be represented in art.

Muslim: And this is the same era and locale where Islam was born! But Islam made clear from the start that its stance was firmly against the possibility of representing God by human art. Not even the Prophet Muhammad (peace and blessing of God be upon him) could be visually confined by a representation.

Christian: Why not? He's only human; Islam never considers him divine, does it?

Muslim: No, definitely he is not divine himself. Yet it is said that he had such transparency of soul that he did not cast a shadow. Still, there is no *picture* of him for fear of suggesting that he himself is the ultimate source of Light.

Christian: Do you really mean that? "No" pictures of the Prophet at all?

---

2. From exhibit "Idol Anxiety" at Smart Museum of Art, University of Chicago, April 8-November 2, 2008, as reported in *National Catholic Reporter*, June 13, 2008.

But there are, if I'm not mistaken, Persian miniatures that depict the Prophet astride Buraq, his winged horse, during the *mi'raj*, his ascent through the heavens to the Throne of God.

Muslim: Granted— but his face is always covered by a halo-flame or cloth.

Christian: Meaning that your reluctance to depict the Prophet is based on… how should I put this?…a *taboo* against representation? A taboo against representation not only of the Prophet, but of the human form itself in explicitly religious art?

Muslim: No, "taboo" is decidedly not the right word. It suggests a negative, fearful prohibition. Better is the Arabic word *haram*, which conveys a prohibition that is in every way positive and respectful. Haram means *sacred* — that is, too sacred to be displayed or portrayed openly.

Christian: Thank you. But I see why I'm having trouble understanding you. Secular Western culture has treated bodily display almost as a fetish. I think of the use of sexual images in advertising. Those of us influenced by that culture have a hard time understanding and valuing even the notion of modesty in dress and behavior.

Muslim: You're understanding me now, I think. And I'll add that Muslims are much more flexible about representation than the Western media claims. You're aware, aren't you, that no verse in the Qur'an nor any fully accredited *hadith* specifically bans representational images? And the work of many of today's best Muslim photographers and visual artists, people like Peter Sanders and Asma Shikoh and Huda Totonji, are deliberately using representational images to probe the contemporary dimensions of Muslim identity and indeed of human identity generally.

Christian: Yes, I'm glad you mentioned this. Because I feel free now to ask about Daisy Khan's comment that "There's a contrast between traditional Muslim artistic expression, focused on worship, and contemporary expression, which is more focused on healing on the personal and communal level, and on identity and social issues." What I'm wondering is this: Does this change of the focus of Muslim art mean that the importance of transcendence has been compromised? Is God disappearing from Muslim artists' consciousness? Is God being replaced by personal and communal needs?

Muslim: Wow! Ask me an easy question, why don't you!

Christian: I'm sorry. I didn't mean to put you on the spot. But I'd really like to know what you think.

Muslim: No problem. It's an important question, and I appreciate having it asked in a sincere and respectful way. My answer is No, I don't believe that transcendence has been compromised or that God has been replaced as the center of Muslim artists' vision. I believe instead that

Muslim artists are doing what they've always done. They're exercising their God-given freedom to seek the "signs" of God's presence in the immediacy of the world that God is creating and sustaining for them and for all of us. And they're using, again as they've always done, the artistic styles and technologies of their particular time.

Christian: So would you then say that Asma Shikoh's paintings of herself decked out in hijabs and jilbabs cut according to pop Western styles (the SuperWoman style, for example) — , would you say that these images also enable us to look beyond or through their surfaces to the light of God within them? I mean, would contemporary works like Shikoh's serve the same function as we've said the more traditional forms of Muslim art do?

Muslim: Well, I'd certainly never claim that Shikoh's work could be used for worship! Nor would she herself make that claim. Yet remember that the challenge before all Muslim artists, whether in the past or in the present, remains the same: to respond in beauty to the God who is the Beautiful One. But to respond in beauty is to make free, imaginative, and, in Shikoh's case, even humorous use of the materials of the artist's surrounding culture. Rumi did no less.

Christian: Well, I can see how Shikoh demonstrates that modern, "Western" expressive styles can be blended with more traditional Muslim styles. But what is the purpose? Forgive me, but couldn't this blending of styles end up as a form of showing-off? Or even as a dilution or adulteration of traditional Muslim styles?

Muslim: Creating art is a dangerous business, I'll grant you that. Artists like anyone else can go astray. But Shikoh isn't producing "art for art's sake." She's not simply blending styles. As she told us herself, she's searching for ways to bring her worship into harmony with her everyday life and with her own search for identity as a Muslim woman. And she does this as part of a broader project to encourage other Muslim women in their own searchings. Shikoh's art points to the transparency of intention governing this enterprise.

Christian: And the criterion for that artistic transparency, as you've been saying, involves a kind of equilibrium. Successful Muslim art, I've heard you say, should be beautiful enough to draw our attention and to delight us, but not so beautiful that it claims the attention and delight all for itself. The same is true of Christian artists, you know; in the chapter on Christian art, we heard several of them articulating this goal.

Muslim: Yes, for both our faiths, we have to distinguish between an artwork focused on God's beauty as opposed to an artwork calling attention to itself or to the genius of the artist. I think the difference, or a helpful way of measuring the difference, is in the effect on the listener or viewer. I think here of the importance of mirrors in Islam. For instance, the reflecting pool in Islamic gardens: it's a key image of the soul that is transparent to God's light. The reflecting pool can be admired for itself. But the pool's main function — and the function of all Islamic art — is to have an inward effect on the viewer. The pool's stillness must enter into the viewer's own heart if the viewer is searching. Do you agree so far?

Christian: Yes, if your term "must" doesn't mean by compulsion, but in answer to the viewer's own deep desire.

Muslim: Which the pool's own beauty may inspire or encourage.

Christian: A reciprocity between artwork and viewer…

Muslim: That's the goal of your art as much as mine, isn't it? At least it seems to me that this reciprocity describes the relation between viewer and artwork in Christian art as well. "Transparency" is a key element in that relation. I'm thinking of your photographer Krystyna Sanderson, of her photographic series, *Solitude: Light and Stillness*. That's the series focusing on women sitting in meditative stillness, while light representing eternity shines on them and as if *into* their spirits. When Sanderson describes these photographs as light streaming into her own heart and soul — as her experience of "the stillness and peace that can only come from God, and the joy of beholding God's beauty" — I think of the Sufi poets in my own tradition. They, too, sometimes use the image of light; and even when they don't, this *inner* experience of the divine is the essence of their art, of their lives.

Christian: I see what you mean about the Sufis. But I'm surprised you didn't mention Reem Al Feisal's photograph of light streaming into the interior of a mosque in her *Diwan al-Noor*. Her treatment of light as a symbol of God's presence seems close to Sanderson's, don't you agree?

Muslim: I do—thanks for reminding me.

Christian: And now that we're talking again about congruencies between our arts, what about the calligraphic work of your Dr. Ahmad Moustafa. His "landscape" painting of geometric forms plays with shade as much as with light, and with the tension between them. My impression is that he is symbolizing an intermingling of things of earth and of heaven, certainly a divine light that is also imminent.

Muslim: Right. And anyway, I never meant by "transcendent" an aloofness on God's part, a remoteness. Remember what Ibn 'Arabi said about the worshipper's dynamic movement between the God who transcends us and the God who invites us into intimacy with him? Ibn 'Arabi helps me link what you say about Ahmad Moustafa with your own painter of abstract "landscapes," Makoto Fujimura. I remember Fujimura saying that his aim in painting is to create an "ambiguous" space which seems to trap light "between the immanent reality of earth and the transcendent reality of heaven." This space —a "grace arena," he calls it — is designed to invite the worshipper into an encounter with the invisible God.

Christian: And both these painters are presented in chapters about God's "generosity," beauty's generosity, art's generosity. I wonder if we — and our artists — mean the same thing by this term.

Muslim: My instinct tells me that we do. We both start from a God who is the very essence of wondrous abundance, who pours beauty and goodness onto his entire created world and invites all his creatures to share in these freely given gifts. And our artists, while deeply humble before God's unbounded generosity, try to pass it on to others as best they can, using whatever creative talents and materials God has provided for them. They don't try to compete with God's generosity — that would be arrogant, and futile anyway — but to represent it by symbols or stories or music which strive to elicit in the spectator or reader or listener a generosity of heart in return.

Christian: And a gratitude of heart as well.

Muslim: And wonder.

Christian: And awe. And joy. And love. Which brings to mind something that one of our contemporary Christian artists — the fiction writer Mary Kenagy — said in an essay in the journal *Image*. I want to quote her words so that you can tell me if they ring true for you as well. She says, "I think the desire to make art comes partly out of a recognition that the world we know through our five senses is capable of bearing meaning, and what's more, that it is *good*." Kenagy also says, "Every artist loves the world in her own idiosyncratic way — and when art works, it's able to convey that peculiar, personal love, to illustrate it, to make it concrete and communicable, to let me in on one more vision of the world's essential goodness, even if just briefly."[3]

Muslim: I can concur in the main gist of what Kenagy is saying, especially when we're talking about today's Muslim artists, many of whom have begun to express a "peculiar, personal" vision. Throughout most of the long history of Islamic art, though, the "personal" has had no role. Art has been seen as almost anonymous, as glorifying God and keeping the particular artist out of the picture, so to speak. But this is just to remind both of us that art has developed very differently over the history of our two religious traditions. Your medieval Christian artists shared this vision of the goal of glorifying God and keeping themselves often anonymous. But then you — I mean your dominant culture, Western culture — went through the Enlightenment...

Christian: Yes, our eighteenth century Enlightenment, which glorified

3. Mary Kenagy, "The Yoke of Sympathy: The Fiction Writer and Her Characters" *Image* #53 (Spring, 2007).

human reason and human individuality. So much so that even art by devoted Christians adopted these values. Art informed by Christian faith hasn't been the same ever since. But in the hands of the greatest of our artists, this new dimension of human individuality — of what Kenagy calls the "peculiar, personal love" of each particular artist — has been a gain for Christian art, not a loss. The unique creativity of each artist has been put at the service of the single loving God who created them all.

Muslim: Well, Islamic civilization didn't experience an "Enlightenment" of this sort. Whether it is experiencing one now is a matter of great controversy. If it is, this Muslim Enlightenment will undoubtedly take a different form from your own. Yet there will also be similarities. You and I have already been discussing common features in the work of our contemporary artists.

Christian: Yes, and we can draw those likenesses even tighter, I think.

Muslim: Alright, so let's try…What about the relation between Asma Shikoh and Ginger Geyer, for example? Shikoh's humor in her art — her wonderful way of having fun while not at all disrespecting her religion — this reminds me of your Christian sculptor Ginger Geyer. She's the one who sculpted the resurrected Christ as a fire hydrant. In fact both these artists are treated in our comparable chapters on art's playfulness. I'd love to put both these women in the same art studio and see what they'd come up with creating art together.

Christian: A brilliant idea. And actually Ginger Geyer has made this very suggestion herself. "We Muslims and Christians should make art *together*," she said; "wrestling with *matter* together is bonding. I've done this with ecumenical groups — conservative and liberal Christians — and the doctrinal issues dissolve as you build these relationships through creating something meaningful out of matter together."[4]

Muslim: And here we've moved into another facet of the art of both our faiths that the previous chapters treated: the element of playfulness and surprise. We saw how Christian and Muslim artists alike use their art to awaken people to the wonders of their own faith, wonders that all people — in natural human weakness — tend to forget.

Christian: Yes, and speaking of pairing artists who delight in the play of their art form, I'd be fascinated to put together our contemporary poets Kazim Ali and Mark Jarman. Because both are comfortable with the complexity of today's post-modern Western world… with its mix of secularism and religious traditions of all stripes. As Jarman said of his poetry collection *Unholy Sonnets*, "I didn't want to rely on the traditional language of religious belief. My aim… was to surprise a reader in the midst of a religious poem."

---

4. Conversation with Peggy Rosenthal at Glen Workshop, August, 2007.

Muslim: So does the "surprise" that our artists craft into their work have the same purpose for both Christian and Muslim artists?

Christian: I'd say yes, and I'd describe that purpose in the terms in which we heard the contemporary Sengalese Sufis talked about: that God's wonders are beyond our human grasp, even the grasp of the most inventive of artists; so the job of art is to keep proliferating unexpected forms "in the quest of the One who is beyond all imaging."

Muslim: Another contemporary Muslim poet, the American Daniel Abdal-Hayy Moore, has a comment on his blog that puts art's purpose similarly. "As Dante shows us in the *Divina Commedia*, our proper attitude before Allah is one of bewilderment, where language stutters out of control to become the tongue-tied stutterings of ecstasy."[5]

Christian: "Tongue-tied stutterings": I think most great Christian artists, whatever their medium, would share this humility that Abdal-Hayy expresses. They don't pretend that their art transmits God's very words or God's infinite goodness or truth or beauty.

Muslim: Right. But at the same time, Islam does allow a *degree* of transmission. And that reminds me of a question I've been meaning to ask you.

Christian: Which is...?

Muslim: In arts informed by Christian faith, is there anything comparable to Qur'anic chanting or to Islamic calligraphy? I mean, an art form that actually transmits God's word to humankind?

Christian: Well, we do have calligraphers who make beautiful shapes of biblical passages. But they don't play the major role for Christianity that Islamic calligraphers do for Islam — simply because our scriptural words don't play the same role as the Qur'an docs. As we've had occasion to say before, Christians love the Bible as "inspired" by God, but the mainstream of Christians don't take the Bible as God's literal spoken word. Rather, for us, the Word of God is Jesus Christ: God's word made flesh, who walked among us.

Muslim: Yes, I see. I understand that this is your faith. And so you are saying that Christian art offers nothing comparable to *tajwid* chanting and to Islamic calligraphy... arts where the word of God is immediately present?

Christian: Actually, our art form that brings us most immediately in touch with God's presence is one that hasn't been mentioned yet at all: the worship liturgy. This applies only to the Christian branches that are "sacramental" in their worship practice: the Orthodox Church, the Catholic Church, and a couple Protestant churches — Lutherans and Episcopalians (in England called Anglicans). The central worship of these churches is the celebration of what they call the "eucharist" or "holy communion," when Christ truly becomes present in the bread and wine that the people consume, joining themselves as the very body

---

5. http://ecstaticxchange.wordpress.com

of Christ. The sacramental theologians of these branches of Christianity do consider their liturgy to be a sacred art form.

Muslim: Wonderful. But how about all the other arts that we've heard discussed: painting and sculpture and music and fiction and poetry and photography and film?

Christian: No, none of these would ever claim to *be* God's presence. They're like your own other art forms — dance and poetry and so on. The artists are inspired by God's beauty to create beauty which will attract their listeners and spectators and readers toward God. And often they do this by reminding us of what I've talked about above: the "sacramentality of the ordinary," that is, the holiness of each thing and each person, because Christ lives in them all.

Muslim: So we've hit upon one big difference in the art informed by our two faiths. You have no single art form — apart from the liturgy of some of your churches — which makes audibly or visually present the very word of God.

Christian: And I sense another big difference as well. I notice that nowhere in the section on Muslim art was there anything comparable to the Christian art chapter on "Broken Beauty." Of course, I wouldn't expect you to have art expressing the beauty of the Cross, because God's suffering on the Cross is not conceivable in your faith. Yet how about human suffering, pain, brokenness — which so much of Christian art through the ages has expressed. Does Islamic art ever try to deal with this unquestionable reality of human experience?

Muslim: We ran into this unbridgeable difference between us in our previous dialogue, on beauty, didn't we? Islam rejects the Christian vision of "Broken Beauty" because we do not accept your concept of "original sin." We don't accept that humankind has the capacity to damage God's good creation on the scale of a "Fall." Nor do we consider that Shaitan— whom you call Satan— has the power to league with humankind to produce such a disaster.

Christian: So you have no arts that express human brokenness?

Muslim: Well, we do have one. At least, the Shi'a branch of Islam does. It's their elaborately artistic laments for the murder of their founder, the Prophet's grandson Husayn, at Kerbala. Every year during what they call Ashura, Shi'as perform a funeral rite lamenting this murder and honoring Husayn's martyrdom. The rite includes drama, elegies, and epic poetry — all designed to indict the failure of Muslims to come to Husayn's aid and more broadly their failure to live up to the demands of Islam itself.

Christian: That last point sounds a bit like our Christian sense of "broken beauty": the lament over the failure to live up to the standards of one's faith.

Muslim: Yes, beauty is integral to the Shi'a laments, for grief and self-reproach are not all that they dramatize. They also celebrate Husayn's self-sacrifice and even see him as "redeeming" humankind by showing that humankind *is* capable of acting beautifully even in the face of the most egregious violence and ugliness.

Christian: I'd been thinking that "redemption" was a particularly Christian concept which Islam wouldn't incorporate.

Muslim: In general that's correct; but the concept *is* used of Husayn. Though of course he is a human being; he isn't "redeeming" humankind as your God-made-human did in Jesus Christ.

Christian: I want to pick up another thread, though, from your remark just above about Husayn's beautiful action in the face of violence and ugliness. I think this might lead us away from our differences back to a great congruence between our arts.

Muslim: And what is that?

Christian: I'm thinking of how the arts of both our faiths strive to represent the greatest beauty of all which we both believe in: the beauty of eternal life, the reward awaiting all those who lived well during their lifetime on earth.

Muslim: Yes, I think there is a great congruence here. And yet there *are* differences...

Christian: Oh. Well... I suppose there would have to be. And maybe in my enthusiasm to end this part of our dialogue on a positive note I've tended to downplay them. But still, wouldn't you agree that our similarities are powerful? I'm thinking of the similarity between the description we heard of the banquet in the film *Babette's Feast* and the description of the Heavenly Banquet in the Qur'anic Garden. Or if my comparing a human artwork, like a movie, to verses in the Qur'an isn't appropriate, what about imagining the Alhambra as a setting for a feast like the one Babette prepares for Martine and Phillipa's flock? Don't you find this an enticing idea? Isn't it wonderful, a cause for celebration, how many symbols of human fulfillment our religions share?

Muslim: It *is* wonderful, I don't deny that. I'd go even further and say that we share more than the symbols. I'd say we share a similar understanding of what the symbols point to: a similar understanding of human fulfillment itself. At least, when I read that description of the movie's conclusion, I felt very much that "Salaam" was the only word spoken around Martine's and Phillipa's table. I envisioned people deeply drinking of the joy of reconciliation with each other and with God... What else can the Garden mean but that? And I fully resonated with the summary statement: "Art's beauty is God's way of attracting us to the transcendent life we can experience on earth in passing moments but which awaits us for certain in heaven, in Paradise."

Christian: But there are differences, as you say…

Muslim: Yes, though I don't feel them as a "but." I don't feel them as a, well, as a diminishment. The differences sharpen my appreciation for God's creativity in rewarding us. I don't believe one of us gets "more" of human fulfillment in the Garden than the other, though I'm not sure we receive exactly the *same* fulfillment. Well, I'll go right to what I consider a key difference between us at least on the artistic level, and see what you think of it. It has to do with the role of Babette. We hear in that chapter that she takes on prominence because in the purity of her self-sacrifice she becomes "a figure of Christ, who came among us to serve, to give the entire gift of himself— his divine being— in order to draw us into the joy of the divine life." I don't have to explain to you the problems I have with that as a description of what even the greatest Muslim artist might or could accomplish.

Christian: Yes— I'm beginning to see. Or would even want to accomplish.

Muslim: Or even feel the need to accomplish. Because in one sense the feast has already happened. For the feast was laid at the dawn of time when, as the Qur'an puts it, all humankind was drawn forth from the loins of Adam to answer God's "Am I not your God?" And humankind answered in one voice, "Yes you are!"

Christian: Fascinating! And in another sense the feast is yet to come, at time's end, when God ushers the God-conscious into the Garden. The greatest Muslim artist reminds humankind of what has been prepared for it since its creation. Muslim artists are not called into union with God to produce this event. They only need to make themselves transparent to the artistic task of making vivid to their audience what their audience might have forgotten.

Muslim: Excellent!

Christian: No, it's not! Look at the way I use "only"— it comes off sounding like a disparagement of the Muslim artist. As if the Muslim artist can "only' do a lesser kind of thing…

Muslim: But to me it doesn't sound "lesser." What you say about the Muslim artist sounds natural, right, in balance. That's the problem with words of comparison. They suggest a judgment. It happens with me too. Take those words "natural, right, in balance"— Am I implying that seeing Babette "as a figure of Christ" is *not* natural, right, in balance?

Christian: No, I know you don't mean that. But what we're both seeing, I think, is that when we talk about the role of the artist in our religions, we have to speak about that role in terms of our understanding of revelation, of how God's word was and is given to us, whether in the Qur'an or in the person of Christ.

Muslim: Yes, and I suspect now that the difference we're talking about goes even deeper than the way we understand the role of the artist. The difference goes to the nature of the Heavenly Banquet itself.

Christian: 1 just remembered a verse from Revelation, the last book of the New Testament and the main source of Christian images of the life to come:

> The angel then showed me the river of life-giving water, clear as crystal, which issued from the throne of God and from the Lamb... (22:1)

Muslim: The "Lamb"?

Christian: The Risen Christ, who sacrificed himself as victim for our sakes. Christians come to the Banquet in union with him...

Muslim: So you see...

Christian: A key difference.

Muslim: Yes indeed.

Christian: And yet ... and yet our artworks, despite this difference in how we understand our fulfillment, whether it's fulfillment in Christ or fulfillment in the remembrance of our true natures— despite this, our artworks have this in common: They encourage us to become more and more transparent to our one source in God's light.

Muslim: And our transparency enables us to behave beautifully, by loving God and loving neighbor.

Christian: Is it this beautiful behavior, then, that brings out our basic commonality? Do our differences drop away as we become—or try to become—the moral beings we're meant to be?

Muslim: Great question! But we're not ready to answer it yet. Let's press on and see where it leads us!

Moving On:
And what does the life of the arts
have to do with the art of life?

We're back in our own voices again, Peggy and George, as we were in the "Moving On" reflection between Parts I and II. In that reflection, we summarized Muslim and Christian thinkers alike saying that humankind cannot live without beauty, the beauty that God calls on us to make, to enact, to live. In Part II and the Dialogue following it, we engaged this beauty as it is made by artists of both faiths. Now we're ready to move on into a key question of our book: what does it mean to *live* the beauty that this art enacts?

A passage from Annie Dillard's marvelous meditation *For the Time Being* can get us started. In this passage, Dillard is describing prehistoric knife-blades that archeologists have uncovered:

> Each of these delicate, absurd objects takes hundreds of separate blows to fashion. At each stroke and at each pressure flake, the brittle chert might — and, by the record, very often did — snap. The maker knew he was likely to lose many hours' breath-holding work at a tap. The maker worked in extreme cold. He knew no one would ever use the virtuoso blades. He protected them, and his descendants saved them intact, for their perfection. To any human on earth, the sight of one of them means: someone thought of making, and made, this difficult, impossible, beautiful thing.[6]

"Someone thought of making, and made, this difficult, impossible, beautiful thing." All art, all craft, seems impossibly difficult to make. And yet it is made — over and over again, in every culture that humankind has known. Making beautiful things doesn't require a particular religious faith. The human spirit has a deep need to create, to be creative. For some people in all cultures, this core creative impulse manifests itself in the making of art. In other people this same impulse manifests itself in ways of living: in gestures of beauty that can last an instant or shape a lifetime.

In this book we're limiting our focus to the creativity of peoples of two particular faiths because right now these two faiths seem to be locked in a dreadfully dangerous culture clash. We believe that this clash is gravely overstated by the media and by certain ideologues of both faiths who profit from demonizing the other as the locus of ugliness: the living site of vio-

---

6. Annie Dillard, *For the Time Being* (New York: Knopf, 1999), 100.

lence, of repression, of inhumanity. Our argument in this book is precisely the contrary: that at the core of each of these faiths is a vision of beauty that manifests itself in seemingly impossible yet truly beautiful works of art and of life. And our argument goes a step further: that the beauty manifested by these two faiths issues in creativity for the good not only of members of these two communities but for the whole world.

All of which is to say that we view "beauty" as a moral category, not a merely aesthetic one. Beauty as we conceive it — as Islam and Christianity conceive it — is inseparable from goodness. In Chapter One, George wrote about the Islamic quality of *ihsan*, which means "beauty" but particularly the beauty which is spiritual virtue, what Islam frequently calls "transparency of heart." The person whose heart is transparent to God's gaze acts always as if she were face-to-face with God. Christianity envisions beauty's inherent link to God and to goodness differently, of course. For Christians the living God, the Resurrected Christ, dwells through the Holy Spirit within each person. The more we let God's life live through us, the more beautiful and good are all our works. Yet Christians can comfortably concur in the statement of Islamic scholar Seyyed Hossein Nasr that "The goal of human life is to beautify the soul through goodness and virtue and to make it worthy of offering to God Who is *the* Beautiful."[7] And Muslims can comfortably concur in Christian theologian Susan A. Ross's assertion which Peggy quoted in Chapter Two, that "a central dimension of genuine beauty is the quality of generosity."[8]

"Beauty," Ross elaborates, "is not an 'add-on' to what it means to be a living being; it is, rather, partly constitutive of who we are. Thus we need to ask about its integration into our lives and its role in our moral deliberations and development." This is precisely what we'll be asking in Part III of this book.

In Part I, we presented the ways that beauty lives at the heart of both Islam and Christianity, in the Scriptures and practices that form adherents of each faith. For both faiths it is God's own beauty from which all else follows. We saw how, for both faiths, God's beauty is imaged often as "light": "Light upon light!"; "the light of all people" which "the darkness can not overcome" (John 1:4-5). For Islam, we added, God has other names as well, but collectively they are called the Beautiful Names: names like The Merciful, The Beneficent, The Fashioner, The Generous, The Great Forgiver, The Just, The Truth, The Source of Peace. All these (and more) names of God move Muslims to gratitude and joy for God's infinite care of his creatures, as well as inspiring Muslims to — as the Qur'an instructs — "act beauti-

---

7. Seyyed Hossein Nasr, *The Heart of Islam,* (New York: HarperCollins, 2002), 236.

8. Susan A. Ross, *For the Beauty of the Earth*, 14; quotation following is from p.7.

fully, as God has acted beautifully towards you" (*Sura al-Qasas* 28:77). Then we saw how Islam praises particularly the human quality of "beautiful patience," as illustrated in the Qur'anic account of Joseph and his brothers. For Christianity, we saw, Jesus himself is "the light of the world," and his followers through the ages carry on his light by striving to imitate his healing works. The beauty of his self-sacrificing actions are what move Christians the most: first the sacrifice of his Incarnation, giving up his divinity to become human for our sakes; then the sacrifice of his crucifixion, giving himself as a victim of human evil so that by going through death to resurrection he could bring all of humankind with him into eternal life.

In Part II, we presented some of the ways that artists of both faiths use their creativity to draw people towards God's beauty. For instance, God's extravagant generosity, mercy, and forgiveness of our foibles are recalled for us by art as wide-ranging as the Mosque at Córdoba and Marilynne Robinson's novel, *Gilead*. Such works of art inspire us to strive in our own lives to act generously, mercifully, forgivingly, as best we can. Sometimes it is art's playfulness and surprise that re-awakens us to the overwhelming love of God which we've grown groggy about. Some Sufi poetry is renowned for this joyfully jolting quality; we saw it also in the sculpture of Ginger Geyer and the paintings of Asma Shikoh. These arts remind us that joyful play is at the very heart of God's beauty, calling us to respond in kind with the joy that overflows from love of God to creative love of our fellow creatures. In fact, other artists whom we met take this active love among God's creatures as their primary vision. From the street-mural calligraphy of Mohammed Ali, with its invitation to solidarity among all who pass by, to W.H. Auden's poetry, with its indictment of indifference to others as our greatest sin: artists like these call on us to build neighborhoods that are modeled on God's infinite and ever-forgiving love. Finally, we saw art designed to attract us to God's transcendence: art like that of Islamic gardens or the film *Babbette's Feast*, which not only give us a foretaste of the heavenly realm awaiting us but also move our behavior in this mortal life an infinitesimal bit closer to the heavenly ideal of reconciling love.

Art's beauty, we found in Part II, acts transformatively on us. In Part III we'll see how beauty's transformative function acts further in what we might call the "art of life." Some of beauty's qualities will be familiar to us. Generosity, for instance: as we saw beauty's extraordinary generosity manifested in the arts of Ahmad Moustafa and Makoto Fujimura, so we'll now find it modeled in "artistic" lives — from the famous Saint Francis of Assisi to a nameless Pakistani woman serving refugees. And beauty's creative solidarity that we saw in Peter Sanders's photographic portraits of the world's Muslims will be manifested now in the living Sunnah, God's community modeled on the life of the Prophet Muhammad. Or the beauty of self-sacrifice at the core of Christianity: as we saw it manifested in

Rouault's paintings, now we'll find it in lives literally sacrificed in witness to God's love.

Other beautiful qualities that we'll find fully developed in Part III will be ones only slightly touched on so far: justice, for instance, and the prophetic imagination; also Shari'a (Islamic law) as the beauty of disciplined behavior directed to the flourishing of all God's children, not only of Muslims.

The life of the arts and the art of life: they are parallel and mutually reinforcing responses to God's gift of beauty. We've noted throughout Part II how the arts can inspire our behavior, how their manifestations of beauty can call and recall us to the source of all beauty in God. Professor of Theology John W. De Gruchy, in his book *Christianity, Art and Transformation*, has summarized the crucial role that art plays for the human soul: "Ultimately art has to do with the awakening of a sense of wonder, and it is in and through that awakening that aesthetic existence becomes possible and transformation begins to take place."[9] Muslim scholar Seyyed Hossein Nasr, in *The Heart of Islam*, confirms art's centrality for the life of the spirit: "By virtue of belonging to the physical level of reality, the plastic and sonoral arts are able to symbolize and reflect the highest level of reality, which is the Divine Realm. Far from being something peripheral, Islamic art is a central manifestation of the Islamic religion."[10]

Far from being something peripheral, art is central... It's a point often lost in Western culture, where art has tended to be confined to museums and concert halls — assumed to be lovely yet somehow dispensable. The contrary is a key argument of our book: that without art's manifestations of beauty, life itself is left adrift in a world where the power of ugliness so easily takes hold. Yet the reverse relation of art and life can also be true: beautiful life can inspire beautiful art. "If you're an honest person, your music will be full of beauty." So says the figure of the great composer Johann Sebastian Bach to his young son in the 2007 Spanish film *The Silence Before Bach*. Your beautiful life will produce beautiful art. The awful corollary also holds true, as painfully indicated by the Iraqi sculptor Ahmad Fadam in a *New York Times* article (April 10, 2008). The ugliness of war's violence has killed his ability to create, he writes. "I have stopped doing art since the early days of the invasion. I lost the desire to do it: the scenes of death and horror we see every day filled my mind and made me stop thinking about beautiful things any more.... Many of my fellow artists have fled the country, going to places where they might find a bit of hope... Running out of art and artists means that we are losing the civilized face of our society, and losing the appreciation of beauty... and love."

9. John W. De Gruchy, *Christianity, Art and Transformation* (Cambridge, Cambridge University Press, 2001), 8.

10. Nasr, *The Heart of Islam*, 228.

Ugliness kills the human spirit, whether it's the ugliness of war or oppressive poverty, or — on an interpersonal level — of demeaning words or acts, dehumanizing another. But wherever there is ugliness, God's transformative beauty lies in wait: such is the belief of both Islam and Christianity. God's beauty waits in each of us, waiting for us to let its creative power work through us for the good of the world. A poem by contemporary Christian poet Scott Cairns (whom we also drew on at the close of the *Moving On* section between Parts I and II) envisions how the beautiful gesture of a genuine embrace can transform dark ugliness into blessed light. The poem, which prefigures the creatively beautiful acts we'll celebrate in Part III, focuses on a famous episode in the life of Saint Francis of Assisi. In Francis's medieval world, lepers were outcasts: their decaying bodies were feared and scorned, and no one — least of all a nobleman — dared touch them. Yet Francis, a young nobleman, passed a leper on the road and impulsively embraced him. Cairns's poem "The Leper's Return" depicts the efficacy of this beautiful action — its transformation of the leper's own soul from self-hatred to joy — and it does so through the image that we've found the most recurrent one for God's grace, the image of light.

In the poem, after receiving Francis's unexpected embrace, the leper

found forgotten light
returning to his eyes, and looked to meet
the brother light approaching from the young man's

beaming face. Each man blessed the other
with this light that then became the way,
thereafter, each would travel every road."[11]

---

11. *Compass of Affection: Poems New and Selected* (Brewster, MA: Paraclete Press, 2006).

PART III: BEAUTIFUL PEOPLE, BEAUTIFUL COMMUNITIES

CHAPTER 5: CREATIVE MUSLIM LIVES

Chapter 5a. Imitating the Prophet: The Sunnah as "truly sacred art of Muslim culture"

Do the life of the arts and the art of life really have something to do with each other?

Canadian-born Ingrid Mattson, president of ISNA (the Islamic Society of North America) for several years beginning in 2006, offers a powerfully affirmative answer to that question in her article, "Finding the Prophet in the People."[1] The gist of what she has to say is that the life of the arts and the art of life have *everything* to do with each other. But then she adds that we come to this truth not speculatively, through a strictly intellectual process, but through living our lives according to a model — in this case, a model life, that of the Prophet Muhammad himself. The life of the arts and the art of life converge in imitation of a life lived beautifully.

Consistent with the answer she's offering, Mattson bases her point on personal experience, not theory. A certain kind of frustration moved her towards her answer even before she was fully able to formulate the question. Her frustration was with Western art, which made her conscious of her need for beauty but then failed to satisfy that need.

The frustration began during her college years in Paris. The Roman Catholic faith of her childhood had been rich and meaningful for her, but in adolescence she "lost my natural faith in God," as she puts it. Then while in college she worked in libraries and museums, including the Louvre, doing research there for a degree in Philosophy and the Fine Arts. What drew her to art, she says in her article, was a search for "some of the transcendence I felt as a child in the cool darkness of the Catholic church I loved." Yet, for all of her appreciation of the great artists she studied, she found such appreciation "isolating." On the positive side, she "felt some connection to the artist, [some] appreciation for another human perspective." Nevertheless, she says, "each time the aesthetic effect flared up, [it] then died down. It left no basis for action."

What does Mattson mean by "action" here? She doesn't say at this point in the essay, as if honoring the confusion of her feelings as a twenty-year-old. Clearly the aesthetic experience of beauty aroused a certain kind of desire in her. But the desire remained trapped within her even when she was able to establish "connection to the artist, appreciation for another

---

1. www.feath.com/story/findingtheprophet.htm

human perspective." Like a fitful flame or an uncertain light in the darkness, the beauty of a picture would shine brightly for her one minute, then subside the next, as if for lack of fuel for the "transcendence" she longed for. Yet transcendence didn't seem to mean escape. Transcendence seemed rather to be bound up with purposeful "action." But transcendence of what? Action of what kind? And to what kind of beauty would action lead?

Answers were revealed to her only gradually. First she discovered that beauty's light shone for her more steadily outside than inside the Louvre's walls, and not so much in paintings as in people. She glimpsed beauty's light in the behavior of poor West African immigrants living at the fringe of French society. The immigrants were Muslim:

> It was their excellent behavior that attracted me to the first Muslims I met, poor West African students living on the margins of Paris. They embodied many aspects of the Prophet's Sunnah, although I did not realize it at the time. What I recognized was that, among their other wonderful qualities, they were the most naturally generous people I had ever known.

The key term here, the one that not only binds transcendence, beauty, and action but that also brings out their interlocking meaning, is "Sunnah." What Islam means by the "Sunnah" is a community modeled on the life of the Prophet Muhammad. Sunnah outlines the steps of action necessary to transcend the usual ego-gratifying patterns of human behavior in order to walk in the beauty of God's light.

The Prophet's wife, A'isha, once referred to her husband as "the Qur'an walking." She meant that the Prophet's behavior was divinely inspired (though Muhammad himself did not thereby become divine). A'isha was articulating a belief held by every Muslim from the Prophet's own day to this. But this belief was never confined to the intellect. It manifested itself in imitation of the Prophet's behavior. To preserve accounts of his behavior, some early Muslims collected reports of his doings and sayings from those who knew him best and whose own witness was most credible. These accounts, known collectively as the Sunnah (or "custom, norm"), became detailed reference points of exemplary behavior for all Muslims, of both genders and of all times.

Yet, as we've seen, the word Sunnah had little or no meaning for Mattson at first. Admiration of the West African students was her initial inspiration. Admiration led to imitation. The students' capacity to maintain a sense of psychological and spiritual balance in the midst of their affliction encouraged her to follow them in their disciplines: to study the Qur'an and to pray the *salat* with them — disciplines modeled by the Prophet that brought her into the heart of the Sunnah before she was quite aware of the beautiful shaping she was giving herself to.

By the time she wrote her article, some twenty years later, Mattson had become fully conscious of that shaping. She was able then to articulate the effect that immersion in the Sunnah has on anyone who sincerely and thoughtfully embraces Islam:

> The Muslim who implements the Sunnah is an actor who internalizes and, without artifice, reenacts the behavior of the Prophet. The performance of the Sunnah by living Muslims is the archive of the Prophet's life and a truly sacred art of Muslim culture.

From this it's clear that the Sunnah is far more than a detailed and even exemplary system of etiquette. Imitating the Prophet is not simply a matter of copying his external behavior, however wise and noble the behavior might have been. That is why Mattson uses the word "performance" above in referring to a Muslim's implementing the Sunnah. She wants to convey the importance of imagination in such implementation. The Prophet's behavior, she says, cannot be reenacted "without artifice" until the actor "internalizes" it by making it his or her own. Performance of the Sunnah becomes a "truly sacred art," not by the actor's slavishly following the letter of the Prophet's example at the expense of its spirit, but by the actor's adapting his or her behavior in conformity to what the actor imagines would be the Prophet's own inner disposition given a certain situation.

As "a truly sacred art of Muslim culture," the Sunnah awakens believers' desire to imitate the beauty of the one they love, the beauty of the Prophet himself. This love has nothing to do with idolization. Both the Qur'an and the Sunnah warn believers about such falsely directed devotion. Muslims love the Prophet because he embodies transparency to God's beauty in the fullest way possible. By following his example faithfully, believers can embody that transparency as well and thus share in the divine beauty revealed in them all. Believers can be seen as artists of life, and their lives as artworks-in-progress, sacred "performances," as it were.

In this way the Sunnah exists on a continuum with the other arts of Islam, as we described them in Chapter 3. All these arts issue in performances that inspire and encourage other performances or ways of being. The performances magnify each other and expand what Mattson calls the "archive of the Prophet's life." The Prophet's life becomes the sum-total of believers' efforts to follow his example. The life of the arts and the art of life converge as *ihsan* — beautiful doings as a way of being.

Mattson is explicit about this converging unity among the arts of Islam and Islam's art of life. To praise an Islamic artwork is also to point to its capacity to inspire correct living. Later in her essay, for example, Mattson refers to the name of the Prophet, Muhammad, "written in curving Arabic letters on those spaces where sacrality is invoked," that is, on the front wall of almost all mosques. She immediately adds that reading his name audibly or silently "leads the believer into a reflective state about the divine message and the legacy of this extraordinary, but still human messenger of God." The reflective state is not an end in itself. It encourages what Mattson had been longing for in the Louvre, "action," now understood as the shaping of one's life after the model of the Prophet's own.

But then, to forestall idolization of Muhammad the man, Mattson directs us to another kind of artwork, one that symbolizes the source of Muhammad's reflected beauty. Though this source cannot be rendered directly, it can be hinted at in the recitation and calligraphy of the 99 Beautiful Names. Of those names Mattson lists only a few. Do they sound familiar? *The Merciful, the Compassionate, the Forbearing, the Forgiving, the Living, the Holy, the Near, the Tender, the Wise.* Mattson didn't pick these names randomly. They all fall under the category of *al-jamil*, the Beautiful One. They are the names of God's intimate engagement with the human imagination, where God most directly lends Himself to metaphors and parables. ("God speaks to humankind in symbols," says the Light Verse.) And because these names engage the imagination, they encourage artistic enhancement: "Written in beautiful script on lamps, walls, and pendants, the linguistic sign [of a Name] provokes a profoundly personal intellectual and spiritual response with each reading." The depth and extent of this "response" is her point. The arts of Islam, in the Sunnah of the Prophet, as well as in Qur'anic recitation and calligraphy, do not isolate believers from God and others in a private world of the believers' or the artists' visions. The arts of Islam lead believers and artists outside themselves, through the Sunnah towards worship of God and solidarity with the rest of God's creation.

How does this movement from the heart of the believer to public or communal solidarity actually work in the case of an individual's performance of the Sunnah? Or to state the question otherwise: What does the Sunnah look like when it is fully internalized and embodied? What does it look like when its spirit enters the heart, issuing in action that transforms both the believer and the world with which the believer interacts?

In her essay Mattson gives as an example of such a transformation an incident that occurred a few years after her stay in Paris as a college senior. Converting formally to Islam at the age of twenty-three, Mattson went to Pakistan to work with Afghani refugees. There she met the Egyptian who became her husband. Her example comes from this period:

> Soon after I met my husband, he told me about a woman he greatly admired. He spoke of her intelligence, her eloquence and her generosity. This woman, he told me, tutored her many children in traditional and modern learning. With warm approval, my husband spoke of her frequent arduous trips to refugee camps and orphanages to help relief efforts. With profound respect, my husband told me of her religious knowledge, which she imparted to other women in regular lectures.

> With deep affection, my husband told me of the meals she had sent to
> him, when she knew he was too engaged in his work with the refugees
> to see to his own needs. When I finally met this women I saw that she
> was covered, head to toe, in traditional Islamic dress. I realized with
> amazement that my husband had never *seen* her. He had never seen her
> face. Yet he knew her. He knew her by her actions, by the effects she
> left on other people.

The woman's self-sacrificing behavior, her generosity, her many acts of
solidarity with those who have been marginalized... Yes, the Prophet's
Sunnah models performances of this type. But the woman's actions are not
literal responses to command. Rather, they flow from within her in response
to the demands of times and circumstances very different from those faced
by the Prophet. And they indicate her attentiveness to people's needs in the
present moment, as exemplified in her sending meals to Mattson's soon-to-
be husband. Love of the Prophet has enabled the woman to pass through
and beyond the Sunnah's external prescriptions into inner transparency. Her
own wishes and actions are now the Prophet's, and the Prophet has been
reborn in her. The woman emerges in Mattson's account as a pure example
of the actor adding her life to the Prophet's "archive" and thus beautifully
enfleshing the "truly sacred art of Muslim culture."

My own experience of being in Mattson's presence shows another way
in which the Sunnah can be embodied creatively.

Peggy and I, along with other local people involved in interfaith dialogue, had been invited to Rochester's Islamic Center to meet Mattson
during dinner and to hear her speak afterwards to the whole community.
(This was just after Mattson's election to the presidency of ISNA.) By the
time we arrived, Mattson had already spent a full day of intense discussion
with various members. People's reactions to her varied. Mattson had held a
workshop for women during the afternoon which had been stimulating but
apparently a little controversial. The topic at one point had included whether
or not to wear the *hijab*. One Muslim woman I spoke to later during dinner,
a woman who did not wear the *hijab* and who had attended the workshop,
complained about Mattson's caution in such matters. "She's too traditional,"
the woman said, disapprovingly. Another Muslim woman I talked to, who,
like Mattson, did wear a *hijab*, thought the opposite. She thought Mattson
had struck exactly the right note by emphasizing the *hijab*'s power to raise
non-Muslims' respect and consideration for women.

What struck me about this exchange wasn't so much that Mattson had
taken a particular stand on wearing the *hijab*, as that she had wanted the
women of the Center to talk about the issue and to express their views
candidly, which they certainly had been doing! Mattson wasn't afraid of
controversy, clearly. But neither was she trying to force her views on others.
She only wanted the women to think seriously about the choices they were

making in light of the Sunnah's deepest values.

As it turned out, our group didn't get to meet Mattson at dinner. There were too many claims on her attention. Yet Mattson still found time to greet us briefly but graciously as we all were getting ready to move to the *masjid* area for prayer and then to hear her speech. A petite woman, she nevertheless suggested great physical strength, and while gentle in manner, she spoke with authority. But what most impressed me was how calm she seemed despite the fact that she was wife, mother, professor of Arabic and Islam (at Hartford Seminary), and now, through ISNA, a highly visible Muslim personage. And despite the fact that she was currently embarked on a getting-to-know-you tour of Muslim congregations throughout the U.S. and Canada. That's what had brought her that day to Rochester's Islamic Center. "She must be moving through a constant succession of hotels and guest bedrooms," I thought to myself. Somehow she had to summon her forces each day to gain the confidence of yet another of ISNA's diverse communities. And she had to do so as a convert and as a woman, to say nothing of the challenges she faced in representing those diverse communities to the non-Muslim world.

Mattson's self-possession heightened my expectation about the speech she'd soon be giving. If the topic had been announced ahead of time, I wasn't aware of it. But I sensed that whatever topic she did pick, she would challenge us. And I had a hunch that she would do so skillfully, not haranguing or agitating us, but allowing us to find our own path toward an appropriate response.

"What's your community doing about environmental issues?" — that's the question Mattson began with. Challenging, as I'd expected. But she didn't end her challenge there. Speaking without notes, she led her listeners to see the connection between environmental and social justice issues. Environmental devastation resulted from political policies that favored the rich over the poor. She didn't dwell on negatives, however. Instead, she urged the congregation to look beyond their immediate concerns to the wider world and to the effort all people of good faith should be making to bridge the gap between wealth and poverty. Charity wasn't enough, she said. We were all of us responsible for working towards change of the structures that were at the root of both environmental pollution and social inequality. This responsibility, she pointed out, followed from God's having appointed not just Muslims but all humankind as God's trustees or *khalifatun*.

Having exhorted us as communities, Mattson did not fail to remind us that solidarity is born in each individual person's response to God's beauty. To illustrate what she meant, Mattson alluded briefly to her own slowly-dawning awareness of environmentalism as a member of a family deeply concerned about the pollution of the water in the Thousand Islands area of the Great Lakes estuary where she grew up. She also talked about the understanding of social justice she'd received at school from Roman Catholic nuns. Her formation in environmental issues, a formation rooted in personal experience, in family commitment, and in two religious traditions, was obviously strong and deep. But her main focus was on us, not herself. She wouldn't let us relax with generalities. She asked each of us to think about our use of styrofoam cups at dinners such as the one we'd just had that evening. Were we aware of the environmental damage caused by such non-biodegradable products? Had we thought about the relation between environmental pollution and the incidence of poverty and crime in our own Rochester community?

I thought Mattson's presentation beautiful, and very much in the Sunnah's spirit. For one thing, Mattson's demeanor throughout her speech had exhibited *balance,* which is perhaps the salient personal quality the Sunnah ascribes to the Prophet Muhammad. Balance manifests itself not only in calm, but also in moderation, in firmness without rigidity, in sensitivity without sentimentality, and in a host of other formulations suggesting a psyche conscious of extremes of emotion and behavior as well as disciplined to find the golden mean between them. And Mattson's balance of demeanor produced a public effect just as the Prophet's had. Both possessed the power to bridge differences between individuals and groups and to unite them in pursuit of the common good.

For she had spoken healingly. Clearly all of us, Muslims and Christians alike, had a common calling to beauty manifested in social justice and in environmental stewardship. Media-induced fear had fractured that commonness, but Mattson's speech had reminded us of it, and had inched us closer to taking action on its basis.

As Mattson was leaving the *masjid,* Peggy and I and some other Christian members of the audience stole a moment of her time to thank her for her speech. I was amazed at how fresh she still managed to look. She calmly accepted our praise, and then said, "Thank you all for your support of this community. They need it right now. Because they're young. So connecting with groups more established in social justice will help everybody."

And so it will. One lesson I learned from Mattson's presentation is that Muslim beauty, while rooted in the particularities of the Prophet's life and behavior, is nevertheless inseparable from every other kind. We cannot have our "own" beauty anymore than we can have a planet that is pure in some places, polluted in others, socially just in some places, unjust in others. Trusteeship is given to us all.

Given, yes — but the giving is just the starting point. The Sunnah becomes sacred art to the extent we honor the gift. We all want the Prophet for ourselves. How we share him with others is the test.

Professor and poet Shabana Mir, in her poem "To Everyone I Disagree

With,"[2] shows what it means to pass such a test with a smile. Her speaker begins in clipped indictments:

> I can see that you're clearly wrong.
> Your opinions are your personal views.
> They certainly don't come from Islam.
> They clash with the Qur'anic text,
> Out of synch with the Prophet's way...

At the height of her indignation she pauses, and that's enough space for second thoughts to raise their timid heads:

> But then
> In the relative sort of way
> That I exist, so do you too.
> Though I think there's no room for you
> In the world, yet here you are, because
> God made sure you'd be around.

While the speaker never budges one inch in her estimate of the "other," she comes to see at the end how both of them are noisy children in God's eyes:

> So even as I know I'm right
> I dust the chair beside me so
> That you can sit and take your place
> In the rowdy classroom of the world.

Now, finally, sitting together edgily but peaceably, maybe they can open their common primer, the Prophet's Sunnah, and discover the beauty that eluded them as long as they stuck to their private claims. Making that transition is the first step towards the generous behavior Mattson says attracted her to Islam in the first place.

---

2. Published online by The American Muslim at http://www.theamericanmuslim.org/tam.php/features/articles/to_everyone_i_disagree_with/

Chapter 5b. The Beauty of the Shari'ah: Source and Goal of the "Greater Jihad"

Shari'ah...

For non-Muslims who have never heard this word, a neutral definition would be like this one from Wikipedia: "Shari'ah is the body of Islamic religious law..., the legal framework within which the public and private aspects of life are regulated..., including politics, economics, banking, business, contracts, family, sexuality, hygiene, and social issues."

But no one in the West, once they hear the word used in the media, ever thinks of Shari'ah neutrally. The media almost universally associate Shari'ah with images of ugliness: of heads and hands lopped off by public executioners, of women shut up inside *burqas* and *chadors*, of novels consumed in bonfires while death-sentences are pronounced on their authors. And behind such hideous actions loom frowning, merciless Mullas and Ayatollahs, and behind them that Draconian code of law, the Shari'ah, which not only justifies but also sanctifies violent condemnation of the least departure from its oppressive strictures. And behind the Shari'ah that God of Wrath himself, Allah, the Shari'ah's inventor and ultimate enforcer on the Day of Judgment...

Caricatures? Yes, of course. Caricatures that both reflect and inflame the West's long-standing ignorance and fear of Islam.

I can speak with authority about those caricatures because I was for many years a typical victim of them, although I would never have admitted such a thing. For in order to admit to it, I would have had to confess my almost total ignorance of all things Islamic— a degree of ignorance that had allowed the caricatures to worm their way into my imagination.

How, by the grace of God, I was able to cast out those wormy caricatures and allow Islam's beauty to fill and enliven my imagination instead is a story I've told in an earlier book, *Meeting Islam: A Guide for Christians*.[3]

I will repeat one key moment in that story, however. The caricatures took flight forever on the evening I first entered Rochester's Islamic Center in the fall of 1993 to take lessons in Arabic. I was met, not by the suspicion and hostility the caricatures had taught me to expect, but by a warm welcome both from the teacher, Dr Shafiq (the Center's imam, whom I've spoken of frequently in these pages), and by my fellow students — all Muslims. (I had had no idea till then that only one fifth of Muslims are Arabic-speakers. Many Muslims are as ignorant of Arabic as I was at that time.)

Unknowingly, in just those initial gestures of welcome, I had begun to experience the effect of Shar'iah.

---

3. George Dardess, *Meeting Islam: A Guide for Christians* (Brewster, MA: Paraclete Press, 2005).

In the weeks and months and years that followed until the present, I've experienced this effect many times, not just in the gracious hospitality that Muslims everywhere have shown to me, but in the gracious hospitality I've seen them show to other non-Muslims. Hospitality is a way of manifesting God's love of beauty, and the love of beauty is at the heart of Shar'iah.

I didn't fully grasp this truth until many years after my first visit to the Islamic Center in 1993. It was a truth confirmed through study. But the meaning of Shar'iah was instilled in my heart and imagination long before I became aware of it cognitively. I am glad its meaning has unfolded in me in this slow, gradual way. Its root is all the deeper for having worked its way into the light from a multitude of unselfconscious kindnesses extended to me by Muslim friends over the years.

Nothing in what I've just said denies the fact that there have been and continue to be applications of Shari'ah law in Muslim-dominant countries that appear to confirm the truth of the caricatures that once sent me into a panic and that still torment our national psyche. Shari'ah as practiced by the Taliban of Afghanistan and by the Wahhabi jurists of Saudi-Arabia seems to consist of little more than restriction and punishment. No "love of beauty" there!

Whether such impressions tell the whole story about Shari'ah even in Afghanistan and Saudi Arabia is doubtful. Western news media have been notoriously unreliable in giving us an accurate understanding of the complexities of life in Muslim countries. Nor have they helped us see how extremes of behavior in such countries are often partly the product of the West's own interventions in those same lands, first through colonialism, later through support of authoritarian local governments.

Yet any good thing can be made ugly; and Shari'ah, in human hands, is not invulnerable to abuse. But whatever the juridical form Shari'ah takes at any particular time or place, its essential nature is to provide the path for creation's continuing well-being — the well-being of all creation, not just of the Muslim part of it. Personal gestures of hospitality from Muslims to non-Muslims are small-scale embodiments of the welcoming guidance Shari'ah provides to everything under the sun.

This understanding of Shari'ah comes from the belief, shared normatively by all Muslims, that God is not a punishing, angry deity, but *ar-rahmani ar-rahim*: The Most Beneficent, the Most Merciful. Having in his Beneficence created the universe and every single thing that fills it, God in his Mercy sustains it from one second to the next. Time is the vital factor here. Creation is not static. Indeed, change is a condition of creation. Yet change in itself could entail disintegration. So God gifts creation with Shari'ah, that is, with guidelines it must follow in order to flourish in and through time. But just as God brings forth a diversity of created beings, God also shapes the Shari'ah of each being according to that being's created nature or *fitrah*. Birds have their form of Shari'ah. Clouds have theirs. Rocks have theirs.

And we human beings have ours. Our Shari'ah, revealed through the Prophets, is, like the fitrahs or natural regulations given all other created things, specifically suited to our nature. In our case, Shari'ah is designed to accommodate God's unique gift to us of free will. Shari'ah is not imposed on us, as it is on other creatures, but is submitted to our assent (or denial). Further, God molds this universally human Shari'ah in even finer forms, ones best suited to the particular communities to which God sends His Prophets. Speaking to Jews, Christians, and Muslims in *Sura al-Ma'idah* 5:48, God says, "To each of you we have given a particular law (*shir'at*, a form of Shari'ah) and a particular way of life...."

To Muslims, God gave a particular Shari'ah that shapes their every moment. There is no domain of life, no thought or action to which the Muslim Shari'ah does not apply. To believe otherwise would be to suppose that there was some corner of creation that God did not create. It would be to posit a second or at least a different creator. But who or what could such a creator be? Would God be God if God had such a rival?

Non-Muslims might find something to praise in Islam's strict monotheistic logic. But they might, even with the most generous intentions, feel uneasy with the Muslim Shari'ah's dominance of the most ordinary acts of life. How can our human free will be honored when we must follow law, even Divine Law, so strictly? Does a Muslim have to live his or her entire life with a rule-book in hand, fearful of forgetting or transgressing what must be an infinite number of prescriptions? And doesn't individuality suffer and shrink as people attempt to conform to laws seemingly designed for the community's rather than the individual's well-being?

Yet the Islamic Shari'ah is not and could never be a detailed rule-book dropped down from on high. The Islamic Shari'ah's general principles are revealed in the Qur'an, yes, but specific applications of that law (according to the majority Sunni view) may be determined by *ijtihad*, independent reasoning. To have it otherwise would be as if God took away with one hand the gift He has given with the other: human free will. But then, to prevent chaos in the proliferation of individual interpretations, *ijma* or consensus must be sought as well — though consensus must never smother creativity and new insight.

Another way Shar'iah resists legalism is by assuming a human face in the Prophet's Sunnah. This connection between the communal and personal may seem paradoxical until we realize that the Prophet Muhammad's realization as a person could only have been achieved through his service (*abadah*) to God and community. That modeling of double realization is enjoined on all. The Prophet Muhammad exemplifies what it means to live the Shari'ah fully. Living according to the Shari'ah as the Qur'an reveals it and as the Prophet Muhammad embodies it is therefore not just a matter of following revelation and laws but also of walking in a revered brother's footsteps. A whole community walking in those footsteps searches together through *ijtihad* and *ijma* for the best application of the Qur'an's general principles. When Muslims follow the Sunnah faithfully in their personal lives, they naturally find themselves bringing the Shari'ah to life in a communal effort to achieve flourishing for all.

And "effort" is the operative word, just as "action" was in Ingrid Mattson's account of the Sunnah. The Islamic Shari'ah is not about standing still. It is not about being frozen in time. It is about forward movement. We see this clearly when we note that the word Shari'ah contains within it the Arabic root-word for "path" — *shar'*. "Path" brings to mind people walking together towards a common and desired destination. This image was a key part of the word *shar'* from the first. The nomadic people of the Prophet Muhammad's time visualized this *shar'* as a "path to the water-hole" — as the way to life, and an absolutely indispensable one for desert-dwellers. Deliberately ignoring the *shar'* or wandering from it into the trackless desert was a death-warrant.

Of course, in Muslim usage of the word Shari'ah, we're not asked to visualize a water-hole as our final destination. We're asked to visualize the Garden of Paradise, *al-jannah*, the place of human fruition after death and judgment as described in Chapter 3f. But the urgency of people's finding and keeping to the path remains the same as it was in nomadic times. So too does people's need to adapt to the shifting contours of the landscape as they travel together towards the Garden through time. That is why God or *al-Shari'*, the Path-Giver, does not reveal the Shari'ah in rigid detail. To do so would be unthinkable in a God who endowed us with free will for life in a world of time and change. Beauty is the light in which the signs of change along the way are read and reinterpreted. Then the people, refreshed in understanding and reoriented, resume together their journey to the Banquet.

This at least is a picture of how the Islamic Shari'ah *should* work. That it does so more effectively in some places and times than others should not surprise us. God's submission of Shari'ah to human free will means that we human beings are always capable of resisting our particular Shari'ah, either through defiance or forgetfulness, or of manipulating our Shari'ah to serve our own ends. But when Shari'ah is treated in any of these ways, then Shari'ah as God designed it and as we interpret it becomes two different things. Or more accurately put: Shari'ah, when perverted for selfish ends, is not Shari'ah at all but its corruption.

Muslim thinkers are well aware of the many instances where their own Shari'ah has suffered corruption. Many of them are working hard to restore its luster. Many do so by citing broad affinities between the basic principles of the Islamic Shari'ah and of Western rights traditions and by urging collaboration among the most creative scholars, jurists, legislators, and religious leaders from both worlds. The temperament of such thinkers is extroverted, their approach ecumenical, their rhetoric public and persuasive. (We'll look in the next chapter at the creative work being done by representative members of this group.)

Yet these broadly-based efforts to restore Shari'ah's beauty don't originate on public platforms. They may eventually play out in dialogue-groups, conferences, in law-courts, even in legislative sessions, but they don't draw their strength from there. The efforts begin within the heart. They begin in jihad, or struggle.

Specifically, they begin in what Muslims call the "greater jihad."

A famous *hadith* tells the story of the Prophet Muhammad's rebuking a troop of his warriors when they boasted of their successful armed jihad against their Meccan enemies. He told them they had been engaging only in the "lesser jihad" of physical struggle. The "greater jihad," the Prophet said, is the struggle against one's baser instincts. The logic is as follows: We must struggle against ugliness within our hearts before we can struggle against ugliness within our community and world. *Ihsan*, beautiful doings and ways of being, is both motivating source and goal of the jihad that must be begun and won inside us before it can be carried on outside us.

I myself was unaware of the connection between Shar'iah and the "greater jihad" until I heard Dr Shafiq give a lecture on the topic a few years ago. He did so as part of a public forum put on by one of our interfaith groups, Rochester's Commission for Christian-Muslim Relations. As a member of the group, I had just introduced Dr Shafiq to the audience and then sat down, quietly (smugly?) confident that I knew what Dr. Shafiq would say. He and I had already touched on the topic of Shar'iah during one of our conversations. He would stress, I believed, the careful way Shar'iah negotiates the tricky ground between privacy and public behavior. The rules against adultery, for example, as first outlined in the Qur'an and then as elaborated by Muslim jurists over the ages, are very difficult to impose. Four witnesses have to catch the couple in *flagrante delictu*. But the punishment for perjured testimony in such cases is extremely severe, almost as severe as for the offense. The point of the rules is to preserve public order, not to encourage or reward witch-hunts.

Dr. Shafiq did in fact make that point later in his talk, but he did not begin there. He began where I began just above, with the "greater jihad." He stressed the struggle each Muslim has to undertake and persist in, to get control over each of the organs of the body, over the eyes, the ears, the tongue, the hands, the feet, the reproductive organs, and to put each of them in service first to personal then to communal flourishing. Shaitan (Satan) hovers ready in opposition, ceaselessly whispering in our inner ear in order either to distract us from our jihad or to induce us to deform or misdirect it. The Shar'iah emerging under such baleful influence is bound to be deformed or misdirected as well.

To say that I was struck by Dr Shafiq's presentation puts it mildly. Yet the more I thought about his speech's starting point, in the "greater jihad," the more sense it made. I also realized that everything I'd heard about Shar'iah up to that point had come through criticisms of particular applications of it. In addition, the criticisms were almost always made by non-Muslim commentators, usually by people who knew no more about Shar'iah than I did. Now I was eager to plumb Shar'iah to its root. What did it mean to say that Shar'iah was the result of struggle for what is beautiful in the person and the community? Dr Shafiq had outlined the nature of the struggle in general terms. But what did it feel like in a specific case?

Sometime later I happened upon the book that answered my questions, *The Search for Beauty in Islam: A Conference of the Books* by UCLA Law Professor and Muslim jurist Khaled Abou El-Fadl.[4]

El Fadl wrote his book not simply to explain but to dramatize the intimate relation between Shari'ah and the human heart. Unlike his other books in defense of Shari'ah, which are discursive and philosophical in approach, *The Search for Beauty in Islam* is personal, vulnerable, agitated, lyrical, metaphoric. El Fadl speaks in it as Shari'ah's lover and ardent advocate, like the Hebrew Psalmist who sang, "Your word is a lamp to my feet and a light to my path" and "Oh, how I love your law! It is my meditation all day long" (Psalm 119:105, 97).

And like the Psalmist as well, El Fadl believes that the Law consists not in fixed certainties but in a continual search to adapt one's ways to God's will. It is a search that a believer cannot carry out alone, however. Already for centuries this search has been carried out in the books of the great Muslim jurists, each book responding to the other. So it is within this imagined juristic "conference" that El Fadl places himself. He then invites us to enter with him into the flow of words coursing among the saints and spiritual masters who abound in all Islamic countries and cultures and who dedicate themselves to inner purification, the beautiful results of which are manifested in their day to day affairs and livelihoods. The talk is passionate, as vibrant now as it was centuries ago. Arrogance, corruption, and ignorance might marginalize this murmur to dusty corners and prison cells, but anyone searching for beauty in Islam can rediscover it. "If you listen carefully enough, in the dead of night" El-Fadl says, "you will hear the whispers, the arguments, the debates. You will hear the constant search for the Divine and the aching sublimation."[5] You will hear, in other words, the struggle

4. Khaled Abou El-Fadl, *The Search for Beauty in Islam: A Conference of the Books* (Lanham, MD: Rowman & Littlefield, 2005).

5. El-Fadl, *Search*, 1.

of your own conscience, in concert with similar struggles engaged over the centuries. El-Fadl

In this conference there is no grabbing after power or after false certainty but instead the unending quest to know how God wants us to respond, as individuals and communities, to the changing landscape of our *shar'*, our path. The quest's unendingness is not a negative, however. Its unendingness teaches humility, and the quest itself brings out the limited but real beauty of each book's engaged moral imagination. Every new reader entering the conversation plays a role in connecting one book's beauty with another's. In this way reader and books move together through moments of self-doubt and joyful discovery, through lamentings, chastisings, repentings, self-reproachings, delightings. These emotional states themselves aren't the goal, however. They are evidence of the commitment to the effort, to the jihad. Their goal is the most humane possible articulation of *ihsan*, "the intuitive sense of the ethical, the just, and the beautiful," given the exigencies of time and place.[6] The ultimate audience of the conference and the judge of its success is God, not the reader or the jurists themselves.

El Fadl never talks about *The Search for Beauty in Islam* as itself a work of art. But I have no problem talking about the book in that way. While reading its pages, I've found myself recalling more than once that Rumi was a jurist before he was a poet, and that, from all accounts, Rumi's prestige as a jurist did not suffer because of his verses. Far from it! The search for beauty requires the whole person, not one part only. Islamic civilization during its most creative periods always acted on this truth. El Fadl, writing his book in order to "to create a cultural ethos of beauty in contemporary Islam",[7] hopes to usher in another such period. His goal could never be merely aesthetic. *Ihsan*, beauty, always carries a moral dimension. And Shari'ah, the way to the waterhole, is never less than a guide to human flourishing. Yet human flourishing, prepared for by God, delights and attracts us all, whether we're Muslim or not. Probably most of us are attracted also by books like *The Search for Beauty in Islam*, which open a window on what the struggle for that flourishing feels like. The struggle is infectious. The books of the "conference" become beautiful by making beauty desirable once again.

I enter Rochester's Islamic Center for a meeting of one or another interfaith gathering or committee… and I, along with all the other non-Muslims, are immediately offered a cup of tea. Are we comfortable? How's your family? We settle in our chairs to plan a program or talk about a current world event. We disagree at times. But we don't try to score points. We enjoy our differences and try to learn from them. Over time, and as friendships grow, teases and jokes take root. We pray for each other during illness and dif-

---

6. El-Fadl, *Search*, 71.
7. El-Fadl, *Search*, xix.

ficulty.

These small interactions promote the well-being of whatever segment of God's creation one has some influence over. They constitute the pulse of the human family on its way to the thirst-quenching water-hole. I have experienced this pulse; indeed, I have added my own beat to it for so long that I feel as if our many different hearts were all connected to one artery. And I feel in a new way the truth of the Qur'anic verse: "We are closer to you than your jugular vein" (*Sura al-Dhariyat* 51:16).

Of course, these moments at the Islamic Center have been and continue to be happy, fulfilling ones, where those on the path explicitly and intentionally search for beauty together. But even enemies can find themselves united willy-nilly on that path.

Mahmoud Darwish, the late great Palestinian poet, imagines such a moment in his poem "In Jerusalem."[8] At the beginning of the poem the speaker abandons himself to Jerusalem's powerful prophetic voices. "The prophets over there," he tells us, "are sharing the history of the holy…" The holy becomes a light transfiguring the speaker as he continues to wander along. "All this is light for me…./ I walk as if I were another. And my wound/ a white Biblical rose. And my hands like two doves/ On the cross hovering and carrying the earth." The speaker's absorption then appears to be shattered by ugly reality when an Israeli guard confronts him:

> A woman soldier shouted:
> Is that you again? Didn't I kill you?
> I said: You killed me… and I forgot, like you, to die.

The guard's murderous action is transformed in the light of her and the speaker's forgetfulness. Death caused by the one and suffered by the other places both protagonists beyond the ugliness of the moment of an earlier meeting we hear about only now. But now they are freed to search for the source of the beauty that has always surrounded them.

---

8. http://www.poets.org/viewmedia.php/prmMID/19183

Chapter 5c. Rebuilding Córdoba: "A time of transformation"

Shari'ah, the way to the waterhole, begins in the heart, where God plants beauty's seed as *ihsan*, our "intuitive sense of the ethical, the just, and the beautiful." Then the new growth, properly cultivated, begins to spread outside the individual, like the offshoots from a plant. It meets similar spreadings from other individuals. Like a ground-covering vine, these spreadings weave together to form a solid pathway on which all can safely walk towards beauty's fulfillment, in *al-jannah*, the Garden. "Safely" does not mean "easily," however. The community of beauty-seekers will meet ugliness along the way. They will have to reweave the path constantly to cover the changing terrain. But if the members of the community remember beauty, beauty will remember them, and they will reach beauty's abode at journey's end.

The tragic events of September 11, 2001, threatened to put the lie to such hopeful language. Here was ugliness on a scale to wither beauty's sturdiest shoot. Here was ugliness enough to cover the Qur'an, the Prophet, and sixteen centuries of Muslim artistic and social achievement under layer upon layer of grey debri. No path here, but a smoking pit in the ground.

There was and is no way to deny or tidy up that ugliness.

On the other hand, there was and is no way to deny or smear the beauty rising from the ashes.

Towards evening on September 11 a large group of ministers and rabbis from Rochester, New York's extensive interfaith community assembled at the front steps of the Islamic Center to act as a nonviolent shield against individuals or groups that might have been inflamed by anti-Muslim rhetoric already beginning to erupt in the media. The religious leaders' witness at that place and at that time was a statement of their confidence in the beauty of the interfaith enterprise and of their determination that the search for that beauty not be abandoned, no matter how great the temptation to succumb to rage.

Some members of the group assembling that evening had brought flowers for everyone to hold. A merely sentimental gesture? The commonness of flowers as symbols of beauty can diminish their meaning and effect. But on stressful occasions flowers can reveal symbolic power. Flowers, carefully chosen and presented, can restore faith in human flourishing despite the fear and resulting violence that may seem to engulf that faith. And so it was that the flowers held by religious leaders on the Islamic Center's steps that infamous day became a solemn symbol of beauty persisting right in the midst of the ugliness poisoning the air, literally so in lower Manhattan.

The flowers of September 11 were symbols of beauty ready to hand. More complex symbols required greater inspiration and labor to assemble.

One of the first major displays of Muslims' own efforts to produce complex symbols appeared a little over three years after September 11. On January 19, 2004, not far from the site of the World Trade Center, at the Cathedral of Saint John the Divine, six hundred people gathered for an afternoon of multi-media artistic exhibitions and performances entitled "Reflections at a Time of Transformation: American Muslim Artists Reach Out To New Yorkers." The event had been inspired and organized by Daisy Khan, the Executive Director of the New York-based American Society for Muslim Advancement (ASMA). Daisy herself had interrupted her own career as an artist in interior design and architecture to assume ASMA's executive position in the wake of September 11.

An article entitled "The Milder, Gentler Side of Islam"[9] by Hisham Aidi, research fellow at Columbia University's Middle East Institute, gives a picture of what was seen and heard that evening: displays of Mohamed Zakariya's calligraphy, of Salma Arastu's painting of the falling towers, of Mumtaz Hussain's sculpture of Ground Zero; performances by Muslim jazz trumpeter Barry Danielian of pieces he'd composed in response to 9/11; readings by poets Daniel Abdal-Hayy Moore and Michael Wolfe of their post 9/11 expressions of grief and hope. And these were just a few of the Muslim artists represented.

None of the artists ignored or whitewashed the recent ugliness. All of them sought ways of bringing the ugliness into the light of a greater vision where it could begin to be transformed.

The challenge the artists faced on this occasion was all the greater for their being Muslim artists. The fact that fellow Muslims — however debased their religious understanding and un-Islamic their act — had conceived and perpetrated the events of September 11 dealt a blow to all Muslims everywhere.

But Islam came to the artists' aid by reassuring them of God's mercy for them as well as for all his creation. September 11 was big, but it was not bigger than God. The artists, fully grounded in their faith, could trust that the ugliness would yield to beauty and to all that beauty offers for human flourishing. But the process of transforming the ugliness would be difficult and unpredictable. The process must pass through ugliness, not avoid or deny it. The artists would have to share Abou El Fadl's faith, in *The Search for Beauty in Islam,* that "it is through the process of engaging those unseemly realities that the search for beauty takes place."[10] And they would have to hold on to that faith even while knowing that their search must seem hopelessly overmatched by the scale of the evil they were trying to absorb and re-imagine.

Feisal Abdul Rauf, Daisy's husband, is ASMA's founder as well the Imam of the Al-Farah Mosque, located twelve blocks from Ground Zero.

9. http://www.asmasociety.org/calendar/pastevents.html
10. El-Fadl, *Search*, vii.

Imam Feisal acknowledged the apparent overmatch in his welcoming speech.[11] "Life happens," Imam Feisal said. "And 9/11 happened, creating a tidal wave of human shock and emotion, with a desire to do something about it." What artists can do, he went on, is to "touch the life of their fellow-citizens" — because the arts have enormous power:

> The greatest moments in Islamic history, those epochs when Islamic civilization peaked, were periods when the arts were highly prized. From Córdoba to Cairo, from Istanbul to Agra, Muslim artists and artisans expressed themselves in the best modalities of their time. It is fair to state that if a civilization fades when it ignores its arts, the opposite is also true, that a civilization's star brightens as it supports the arts.... Although there should be no need to prove the importance of the artistic quest, it should be remarked that for the modern Muslim, a crisis in the area of art has contributed to perhaps the profoundest crisis Muslims face, a crisis of the soul.

The "crisis of the soul" Muslims face did not originate on September 11. September 11 merely revealed it for all to see. And while this crisis has many causes, one of them would be, following El Fadl's analysis in *The Search for Beauty in Islam*, a fascination with ugliness. A minority of Muslims—just how many is debatable— have been tempted by the effects of Western colonialism to withdraw into a tensely defensive, reduced form of their religion and to barricade themselves behind walls of self-righteousness. The moral ugliness of their response has encouraged certain sociopathic individuals among them to kill and terrorize civilians, thereby breaking all Islamic laws. By committing crimes in the name of Islam, these individuals have condemned Muslim people everywhere to suffer the consequences: prejudice, alienation, fear, and hatred.

The "crisis in the area of art" rises from the ugliness like a noxious plant. The crisis becomes evident when traditional artistic forms are repeated and recycled, without any struggle to enliven them with fresh experience. Art then reduces itself to little more than a tool of propaganda or to a badge of tribal belonging.

"Crisis" does not mean "final catastrophe," however. The word "crisis" means "decision." "Crisis" means that a fundamental option exists, not that there are no options left. Muslims are not without power, moral power, to reject ugliness and to choose beauty. In fact, Imam Feisal suggests in those opening remarks that this power is no more clearly defined and available than right at that moment, even as he speaks, just three years after the Twin Towers came crashing down.

He's also suggesting that the fundamental option emerging under circumstances of crisis goes far beyond simply taking one side or another in

11. Unpublished ms., previously on American Society for Muslim Advancement website www.asmasociety.org

a contest. That's why the title of the Hisham Aidi article mentioned above — "The Milder, Gentler Side of Islam," — is misleading, regardless of the good intentions that surely motivated it. Talking about "the milder, gentler side of Islam" implies that this side is matched by a correspondingly harsh and violent one. It implies that the pitifully misguided souls who drove the planes into the Towers are simply the flip sides of their "softer" cousins displaying their paintings or reciting their poetry at the Cathedral of St John the Divine. It implies that both bombers and artists define opposite and incompatible extremes of the same phenomenon, called "Islam."

But that is not the Islam either Imam Feisal or the many Muslim artists represented on January 19 were trying to put their audience in touch with. The word "transformation" in the program's title, "Reflections At a Time of Transformation: American Muslim Artists Reach Out To New Yorkers," shows what they had in mind instead. Islam itself *is* transformation, and art contributes to Islam by reinvigorating awareness of transformation's beauty. In Imam Feisal's words:

> There is no real art if there is no personal and positive transformation; anything else is ostentatious display. Muslim artists, who as Muslims are after all dedicated to perfecting their faith, must constantly make their art a bridge on which the average person is prompted to embark upon the goal of human perfection as embodied by the Prophet Muhammad's example.

We cannot speak, then, of a "good" Islam and a "bad" one, two equal and irreconcilable extremes of an incoherent reality forever frozen in time. We cannot speak of it as in spasmodic motion, either, as if Islam were forever lurching between extremes, even if one of the extremes appears to be a peaceful, "safe" one. We have to speak instead of Islam as dynamic in an orderly way, as powerfully and fruitfully transformative. Muslim artists, for their part, have to feel and act upon this transformative power by encouraging others to feel and act upon it as well.

When Muslim artists are able to do this, they catch the kind of truth laid out poetically in an especially compelling Qur'anic verse:

> For consider, in the creation of heaven and earth
> In the succession of night and day
> In the ships that cross the seas bearing things useful for humankind
> In the rains God sends down from the heavens
> Giving life to the earth after a period of lifelessness
> In the creatures of all sorts God scatters over it
> In the changing of the winds and of the clouds
>
> Racing on their appointed ways between heaven and earth —
> In all these are signs for a people using its understanding.
>
> (*Sura al-Baqarah* 2:164)

The "signs" the Qur'an invites us to understand are those revealing the meaning of a world created for fruitful change. This change depends upon the balanced play of differences: differences between heaven and earth, night and day, rain and dry; and upon the way the natural world dances to the interweaving of those differences. Humankind flourishes when it trusts in the play and joins the dance in its turn, sending cargo-laden boats across the ocean swell to skim the interface between the firmament above and the firmament below. Humankind flourishes even more beautifully when it trusts in the play of its own differences. "We have created you all [i.e. Christians, Jews, Muslims] as different communities and nations so that you may learn from each other," the Qur'an says (*Sura al-Hujurat* 49:13). Entering into the play of our differences in religion and culture is the basis of human transformation.

So when on January 19 the Muslim artists brought the horrific events of September 11 into the frame of artistic transformation, they were doing only what God had shown them how to do in *Sura al-Baqarah* and elsewhere. They were "using their understanding." They were reading the "signs." And they were helping their audience read them too. Even from the ashes and debris of 9/11 the artists were finding the materials to "build a bridge on which the average person is prompted to embark upon the goal of human perfection," as Imam Feisal put it.

For the other Muslims in the audience, that goal would be "embodied by the Prophet Muhammad's example." But there weren't only Muslims in the audience that day. The January 19 event was explicitly directed "to New Yorkers," of whom Muslims actually form a very small part. And Imam Feisal spoke of the audience in even wider terms, as "fellow-citizens." Yet even "fellow-citizens" is restrictive. Though the January 19 event arose out of the heart of a specifically Muslim artistic inspiration, the event's message was intended to engage the imaginations of people everywhere. It was intended to remind people everywhere of the power of beauty to transform their lives as well and to reorient them on their own paths to what God intends to be a common human fulfillment, not just a Muslim one. For, as God says in the Qur'an:

> We have designed you as a community in pursuit of the middle way,
> resisting extremes,
> so that you can be a witness to humankind
> just as the Prophet Muhammad is a witness to you.
>
> (*Sura al-Baqarah* 2:143)

Not only in their art but also in the way they live their lives, Muslims are to embody a mediating, dialogic principle. They are to embrace a "middle way" personally and publicly. They are to keep opposed feelings and ideas always in play, never dressing up passing thoughts as absolutes, never allowing temporary emotions to become idols or obsessions. They are to resist the idolatry of selfishness in all its forms, from blatant greed to the subtlest whispering of ego. They are to resist as well the tribalism of their own religious practice by recalling that the one God they worship has created one humanity. To the extent that Muslims do this, they become a "witness" to a species otherwise the victim of its own extreme impulses. That is the quality of the moral beauty Islam offers the world. As Imam Fesial had put it in his January 19 address, Muslims today are called to "build a bridge" on which all humankind can walk together through a world of change towards *shalom*, *salaam*, peace and fullness of life.

Imam Feisal's own efforts, and his wife Daisy's as well, show that this bridge is already under construction.

Like El Fadl, Imam Feisal has assumed the life mission of revealing Shari'ah's true nature as the search for beauty. But his approach is much more broadly public than El Fadl's. Imam Feisal emphasizes Shari'ah's societal principles, as opposed to its strictly religious ones. What the Islamic Shari'ah shares with the Shari'ahs given other communities is the obligation to be good stewards of God's creation, with particular attention to the upholding of the human rights of all God's people, regardless of their religion (or non-religion).

The title of one of Imam Feisal's most influential books proclaims this common element with admirable directness: *What's Right with Islam is What's Right with America*. The book's key argument is summed up in an early section entitled, "America: a Shari'ah Compliant State." Imam Feisal's point here is that "the American Constitution and system of governance uphold the principles of Islamic law." The Constitution's enshrined values of "life, liberty, and the pursuit of happiness" are, as Imam Feisal shows, enshrined as well in the Shari'ah. And he goes on to say that

> Any system of rule that upholds, protects, and furthers these rights is therefore legally "Islamic," or Shari'ah compliant, in its substance. Because these rights are God-given, they are inalienable and cannot be deprived of any man or woman without depriving them of their essential humanity.[12]

The corollary of the argument is that Muslims have a special obligation to uphold and defend the Constitution's values: Shari'ah, seen here as the guarantor of universally human societal values rather than of strictly religious Muslim ones, compels them to do so.

Imam Feisal has clearly felt compelled to do more about the connections between Constitutional and Islamic values than simply to describe

---

12. Imam Feisal Abdul Rauf, *What's Right with Islam is What's Right with America: A New Vision for Muslims and the West* (New York: HarperCollins Publishers, Inc.; HarperSanFrancisco, 2004), 86.

them. His purpose in founding ASMA, in 1997, was to foster an American-Muslim identity and to build bridges between American Muslims and the American public. The sponsoring of conferences, cultural events, and interfaith programs principally in New York City, where Imam Feisal's mosque is located, marked ASMA's initial range. The January 19 gathering at St John the Divine was in that sense a typical effort on ASMA's part. But Imam Feisal broadened ASMA's mission and geographical scope in 2002 by co-founding the Córdoba Initiative with former Aspen, Colorado mayor John S. Bennett. The Initiative takes its name from the city of Córdoba, in Spain, the site during the early Middle Ages of perhaps the greatest flowering of mutually creative understanding among Jews, Christians, and Muslims. In the spirit of that city, the Córdoba Initiative sees itself as a "multi-faith organization whose objective is to heal the relationship between the Islamic World and America through civil dialogue, policy initiatives, education, and cultural programs."

The Córdoba Initiative has already hosted a number of impressive cultural programs both in the U.S. and abroad. The programs cover topics such as religious extremism, the connection between contemplation and community, and the commonalties among the religions of Abraham. But perhaps its most interesting policy initiative is the Shari'ah Project. The Project's goal, announced at its first meeting in Kuala Lumpur in 2006, is "to enumerate the societal — as opposed to religious — obligations that Shari'ah requires of a nation governed according to Islamic principles. The project will strengthen the capacity of moderate Muslims, who form the vast majority, to employ the vocabulary and principles of Islam to reduce conflict and promote democratic values in Islamic societies." The Shari'ah Project's scope indicates that Imam Feisal's mission to illuminate the United States Constitution's implicit "Shari'ah compliance," ambitious as that mission seems, does not end there. He seeks to shine a similar light on the governing principles of Islamic societies throughout the world. By doing so, he hopes to spur fellow Muslims to work towards "Shari'ah compliance" in autocratic regimes that are only nominally Muslim. (The irony of finding greater "Shari'ah compliance" in the U.S. than in countries like Egypt or Saudi Arabia is not lost on him. "Many American Muslims regard America as a better 'Muslim' country than their native homelands," Imam Feisal admits.[13])

Could Imam Feisal have achieved so much without the help of his wife Daisy? I doubt it. The couple work as a team, as Peggy and I discovered when we sat down to talk with them one sunny morning not long ago at The Chautauqua Institute in upstate New York. (Daisy and Imam Feisal are members of the Advisory Council of Chautauqua's Department of Religion, and both are frequent speakers there.) Each contributes his or her

13. Abdul Rauf, *What's Right*, 86.

special strengths to the furthering of their common goals, the celebration of *ihsan* in art and in life and the revitalization of Shari'ah. In fact, those goals are one. The effectiveness of their teamwork testifies to that unity. Daisy's artistic talents and organizational skills brought "Reflections at a Time of Transformation" into being. And because of that, Imam Feisal had backing for his claim that "a civilization's star brightens as it supports the arts." Likewise Imam Feisal's stature as a Muslim pastoral leader and as founder of ASMA gave Daisy the platform to assume a new and unexpected role after September 11, 2001: that of empowering Muslim women around the world.

Daisy spoke about her new role, not during our conversation, but in a public talk later that afternoon. Prior to September 11, she said, she had been losing track of her Muslim faith in her pursuit of a career in interior design. Yet in the tragedy's aftermath her husband's prominence put her in the spotlight. She was frequently asked to speak about her identity as a Muslim woman — a question that had seldom been posed to her before, and never with such urgency. But in the light of events, and recalling her Kashmiri upbringing in a family intensely dedicated to social justice, Daisy felt compelled to try to raise the consciousness of Muslim women everywhere and especially to try to empower Muslim women in traditional societies to be respected by their communities. In launching this initiative, Daisy took American feminists like Helen LaKelly Hunt and Gloria Steinem as her role models.

Yet when she formed the Women's Islamic Initiative in Spirituality and Equity (WISE) in 2006, she and her new group reached back for guidance to Shari'ah traditions. WISE's goal, as expressed in its vision statement, would be "to generate a space in which Muslim women actively dialogue, debate, and collaborate on pressing issues of social justice, in order to articulate an ethical and egalitarian Islam."[14] The mechanism for implementing this vision would be through the traditional juristic form of the *shura* council. *Shura*, meaning "consultation" in Arabic, was the Prophet Muhammad's own preferred model for Muslim governance. After his death, the shura council became the site where specific applications of Shari'ah could be debated and rules established through consensus, *ijma*.

What Daisy and her group were proposing was, she admitted, "radical." Shura councils had almost always been totally male. In contemporary Muslim countries governed by puritanical interpretations of Shari'ah, they tend to be the exclusive province of men, and their *fatwas* or ordinances have diminished women rather than empowering them. WISE, however, intends to put Shari'ah in the hands of those who are prepared to bring out its beauty, by ensuring that consultation governs its process and that equality and equity, both for men and for women, governs its result.

14. http://www.wisemuslimwomen.org/about/shuracouncil/#vision

Daisy's and Imam Feisal's re-imaginings of Shari'ah and their efforts to broaden participation in its workings are not isolated initiatives. Muslims in all parts of the world are resisting ugliness and searching for beauty, *ihsan*, first in their own hearts, then in the life of the broader community, a community embracing all God's creation, not just privileged parts of it.

One of the American Muslims embarked on that mission is Eboo Patel, the dynamic young executive director of the Interfaith Youth Core (IFYC), a Chicago-based organization that, according to its mission statement, "promotes mutual respect and pluralism among people from different religious traditions by empowering them to work together to serve others." During our visit to Chautauqua to meet Imam Feisal and Daisy, I heard Patel speak to an enthusiastic overflow audience. "An interfaith youth movement has to focus on the areas on which we agree on Earth," he said. "On shared values of mercy, of compassion, of hospitality, of service. And ask how we can apply those values together." So successful has Patel been in bringing young people of all faiths into the Youth Core that he has achieved national recognition. Patel has been selected to serve on President Obama's new Faith Advisory Council. He has also been named a Fellow of the Ashoka Foundation, a network of social entrepreneurs dedicated to restoring a balance between citizen and corporate interests worldwide. In 2009 he became the first Muslim to receive the prestigious Grawemeyer Award from the Louisville Presbyterian Theological Seminary and the University of Louisville. In addition, *U.S. News & World Report* magazine named him one of "America's Best Leaders 2009," and Harvard's *Kennedy School Review* cited him as one of "five future policy leaders to watch."

Patel didn't mention Shari'ah explicitly, but the search for beauty underlies efforts like his, as it does the efforts of another American Muslim leader, Hamza Yusuf. Along with Dr. Hesham Alalusi, Hamza Yusuf founded California's Zaytuna Institute in 1996 as a site for interfaith education and understanding. On its website (www.zaytuna.org/about.asp), the organization asserts its belief that "Islam offers a cohesive understanding of the world and a praxis for it that is able to cut through the illusion of contemporary nihilism and materialism." And further:

> We believe the problems facing this generation are those very problems mentioned in our Prophet's final sermon, upon him be prayers and peace: economic injustice, racism, the oppression of women, and the manipulation of natural order. We believe these human illnesses can only be treated through healing the hearts of humanity with spiritual truths of the impermanence of the world and the need to understand our purpose while we are here and act accordingly. This can only be done with sound and true knowledge. It is our goal to acquire and disseminate that knowledge.

A similar spirit pervades the work of Sufi shaikh and scholar Kabir Helminski, founder of The Threshhold Society, an educational foundation based like The Zaytuna Institute in California but explicitly rooted in the traditions of Sufism and inspired by the life and work of Rumi. The Threshhold Society welcomes to its gatherings people of all faiths and backgrounds, seeing its purpose as "facilitating the experience of Divine Unity, Love, and Truth in the world at a time when humanity is reaching a point of cultural convergence, ecological crisis, and rapid social change."[15] The energy, creativity, and wisdom of both Kabir and his wife Camille are central to the success of this effort to encourage the search for beauty.

Imam Feisal's Córdoba Institute , Eboo Patel's Youth Corps, Yusuf Hamza Zaytuna Institute, and Camille and Kabir Helminski's The Threshhold Society are by no means alone in their mission to rebuild Córdoba. Many more such groups could be mentioned. (We'll touch on a few of them in our Conclusion.) Different as their specific focus may be, the groups all project the vision of a world enriched by human differences. The vision entails more than building castles in the air, however. The Twin Towers came down within the space of a morning. Rebuilding Córdoba takes patience and a clear-eyed assessment of the forces within us all that would prefer to dwell in the smoking ruins.

What Imam Feisal told me during our conversation at Chautauqua about his own spiritual journey is the case, I believe, for all people, and not just Muslims, who are engaged in the search for beauty. "My journey," he said:

> has led me to look at the world through God's eyes. Which means looking at myself through the eyes of the other. What God sees isn't the religions. What God sees are two groups of people, those who are on the good and beautiful side, and those on the evil and ugly side. Or in other words people of the right hand and of the left, as the Qur'an calls them— those who behave ethically or not, those who are beautiful or ugly in their ethics, regardless of their religion. What is required of the people of the right hand is that they take on the people of the left in battle. But we ourselves aren't to fight left-handedly! Our opposition has to be ethical. As it says in Qur'an 41:34, "The beautiful and the ugly are not equals or opposites. Therefore repel ugliness with beauty."

Syrian-American poet and professor Mohja Kahf slyly makes a similar point in her poem "Most Wanted."[16] The "most wanted" in this instance is God. But how are we to understand what "most wanted" connotes? Is God "most wanted" because most desirable? Or is God "most wanted" because he is most feared and hated, like an escaped criminal? Kahf plays on the

---

15. http://www.sufism.org

16. http://progressiveislam.org/literature_mohja_kahfs_most_wanted First published at MuslimWakeUp.com. Quotations from unpublished revised version courtesy of the author.

possibility that it's the second of those meanings we often have in mind:

> Warning: God has slipped the noose.
> We must confirm the worst
> of our righteous fears—
> God has escaped the mosque,
> the synagogue, the church
> where we've locked him up for years...

God's offense, it turns out, is that he has been dispensing his love and mercy on others besides Muslims, Jews, and Christians. The poem ends with an all-points warning:

> Henceforth beware:
> You may find him in heathen beauty.
> You may stumble upon him unaware.
> Take appropriate measures:
> You may have to behave
> as though each human being
> could reflect his Face.

What a disaster! With beauty to illuminate the path and Shari'ah to guide us along it, we may all have to find our way to the water hole...together!

CHAPTER 6: CREATIVE CHRISTIAN LIVES

Chapter 6a. Standing with Jesus: "The art of daily life"

Rowan Williams, the Archbishop of Canterbury (head of the world-wide Anglican Christian Church, based in England), has written about what "the art of daily life" means for Christians. As Williams explains it in his book *Christ on Trial*, "the art of daily life" is grounded in our "standing with Jesus." And where does Jesus stand? Unequivocally in the profound certainty of being "at home" in God.[1]

For Jesus what this means is that he lives securely in God's "kingdom" — which is nowhere on earth yet everywhere on earth — rather than under the authority of any of the world's powers, idols, or ideologies. Jesus refuses to play by the world's rules of violence and manipulative force. The cost for him of this refusal is death. Yet precisely because Jesus refuses to respond with violence to the violence inflicted on him, in his Passion the world's violence is "overcome and silenced," as Williams puts it. Secure in the knowledge that his true home is the whole of God's marvelous creation, Jesus is freed from fear of whatever harm any worldly powers could do to him. His sense of freedom is expressed most fully in a long discourse to his disciples on the eve of his Passion, related in John's Gospel, where Jesus — in his confident and expansive absorption of God's love — invites all to join him in the peace of God's kingdom. Jesus at that moment, and indeed throughout all the Gospels, becomes the incarnation of God's "hospitality."

Williams goes on to elaborate what this means for followers of Jesus throughout the ages, what it means for us today in our daily lives. To "stand with Jesus" does not at all mean, Williams cautions, that Christians are to seek persecution and suffering. Quite the contrary. If we seek high drama in which we are the grand victimized hero, we are actually perpetuating two kinds of violence. One is the violence of aggrandizing the self over and against all else; the other is cutting oneself off from the "other" who is seen as enemy and hence as unworthy of God's hospitality.

Rather, Williams insists, the challenge is to live Christ's freedom in "the undramatic context of daily life." This requires "imagination," for "I have to make an art of ordinary living."

How does one create such an art? Williams reminds us how often in the

---

1. Rowan Williams, *Christ on Trial* (Grand Rapids, Michigan: Eerdmans, 2000). Our quotations are from pp. 89-111.

Gospels we hear Jesus say "Do not be afraid." In a range of contexts, this is his greeting to his fearful friends. Fear is what limits our imaginations, cramps our freedom to breathe our lives into the peace of God's hospitality.

> To the extent that our daily life is conditioned by fear (of failure, of others, of too much of the same, of too much change, of death, of our own desires and our own weaknesses), it is indeed in this 'theatre' that we have to display the sovereignty of the power that gives life to us. Making an art of our daily life is really about living without fear; doing what we do not out of anxiety... but out of the inner pressure to 'incarnate' what has been given to us, to give it flesh, voice and locality."

Reflecting on the essence of what we normally think of as the arts — music, literature, painting, and so on — Williams notes that "Art always has about it the dimension of freedom. It is not there to do a job or prop things up; it exists, most artists would say, because some form, some vision presses itself upon us, in ways we cannot fully perceive in advance. So if we talk about 'the art of daily life,' we are evoking this strange freedom — not a freedom to make things up from nothing, to do and say whatever we please, but a freedom from the need to meet obligations all the time, a freedom (in the case of the believer's life) to give to human actions a shape and meaning rooted in what has been given to us."

And what *has* been given to us? The gift of God's hospitality. Surrendering to this gift — letting ourselves be at home in God's creation — displaces "the busy and frantic ego, trying to impose an individual will on the world. That displacement is freedom."

Rowan Williams's concept of living in God's "hospitality" recalls for me theologian Susan A. Ross's notion of beauty's extravagant "generosity," which we saw at play in Chapter 4a. I quoted there from Ross's book *For the Beauty of the Earth*, where she argues that "a central dimension of genuine beauty is the quality of generosity" and indeed that generosity is "intrinsic" to beauty. "Beauty is always ready to give more. When we encounter a beautiful work of art, we find ourselves unable to exhaust fully the beauty that it offers." Ross grounds her theology of beauty in the Gospels. "Such generosity," she writes, "is one of the main ways in which Jesus describes God... the God whose love is so immense that this God is with us in our very flesh." And alive in our flesh, the beauty which is God's infinite love "enlarges the heart" so that "to be generous with one's own beauty means to welcome others to one's self... A theology of beauty that is incarnate and grows from our sense of beauty in the natural world is also a theology of generosity: to oneself and to others."[2]

Expanding on what beauty's generosity entails, Ross says that "Real

---

2. Ross, *For the Beauty of the Earth*, pp. 28-30.

beauty does not exclude; rather, it invites. Real beauty does not 'count up,' but rather flings its gifts to anyone who asks." In Chapter 4a, I found this quality of beauty exemplified in the paintings of Makoto Fujimura; now I want to talk about how it is exemplified in the life of Saint Francis of Assisi.

We've met Saint Francis in this book before: in his influence on bringing Western art back to a celebration of the body (in Chapter 4d); and further (in Chapter 4e) in his modeling of an intimacy with Christ that unfolded in classic Christian art images like the Pietà. These were influences that Francis — and the spirituality that he inspired — had on movements of Western-Christian art. But Francis himself was an artist in his own right, and in a unique way. Though he did write some poems, most famously his "Canticle of Brother Sun," the art of life itself was where his fullest poetic mastery lay.

Indeed, Francis's life is often spoken of as his greatest work of art. His biographers tend almost unconsciously, it seems, to liken his life to a poem. One, for instance, writes of Francis's qualities of "not only fearless sincerity, but also a persuasive personality, a poetry of action that attracted all who met him."[3] This "poetry of action" which was Francis's shining quality is a major motif in the book *Poetry As Prayer: Saint Francis of Assisi*, by contemporary Franciscan priest and poet Murray Bodo. Sketching Francis's life, Father Bodo repeatedly calls on language with which we'd describe a work of art.[4]

Bodo begins with the essential background facts: that Francis was born (in 1181 CE) into a wealthy home; that his father, Pietro Bernardone, was a successful cloth merchant very attached to his riches. As a young man, Francis assumed he'd live the life of a noble soldier. But unexpected failure in this endeavor brought him to a deep inward reflection on what his life was truly meant for. He went literally into a cave in the mountain above Assisi. There, Bodo writes, "In his soul he heard the Gospel, he meditated on the images that rose from the Gospel stories, and he wondered how and when he would begin to live the Gospel that had become the poetic landscape of his meditative soul."

Soon, unexpectedly, he was given the opportunity, while riding his horse outside of town.

> Suddenly, a leper stood there before him on the road. Instinctively, Francis reined in his horse and attempted to turn and ride in the opposite

3. T.S.R. Boase, *Saint Francis of Assisi* (London: Thames & Hudson, 1968), quoted in Gerard Thomas Straub, *The Sun and Moon Over Assisi* (Cincinnati: St Anthony Messenger Press), 2.

4. Murray Bodo, *Poetry As Prayer: Saint Francis of Assisi* (Boston: Pauline Book and Media, 2003. Our quotations are from pp.19-54.

direction in fear and disgust at the sight of the disfigured person. But something in his Gospel-touched inner landscape stopped his retreat. He dismounted his horse, walked up to the leper, and placed coins in his hands. Then, in a gesture he did not fully understand, Francis embraced the leper.

The incident is one of the most famous of Francis's life. Bodo explains its significance. After embracing the leper, when Francis mounted his horse and turned back to wave to the leper, he "saw no one on the road. He knew then that he had seen and embraced the Savior himself, and he realized that if he would know Jesus Christ, he would have to seek out the lepers who lived in the swamp-like conditions of the plain below the city."

Thus began the transformation of the wealthy youth into an embracer of poverty. He began to pray in the poor, dilapidated churches of the area, sure that here was the home of his poor Savior Jesus. In one of these churches began his second transformative experience. While praying in the run-down chapel of San Damiano, he heard a voice telling him to "go and repair my house which, as you see, is falling into ruins." Knowing the voice to be God's, Francis rushed to take cloth from his father's business, sold the cloth, and returned to San Damiano's priest, offering this money to repair the church. The priest, suspicious of the zealous young nobleman, rejected the money, so Francis went up the mountain to collect stones himself to repair the church. "Poetry is revealed," writes Bodo, "both in the act of embracing the leper and in rebuilding San Damiano. Francis's gestures become symbols of a deeper reality, much as a verbal metaphor holds more meaning than it first appears. When Francis embraced the leper, he simultaneously embraced Christ, and in embracing Christ, he embraced the entire Mystical Body of Christ. For, as Saint Paul wrote so beautifully, 'If one member suffers, all suffer together with it; if one member is honored, all rejoice together with it. Now you are the body of Christ and individually members of it' (1 Corinthians 12:26-27)."

Later, Francis would realize that God's command to "repair my house" referred metaphorically to God's house as the entire Christian faith, which had lost its authentic Gospel spirit and become compromised by wealth and privilege. But "like a true poet," says Father Bodo, "Francis always began with concrete things such as stone, and his work with them made of them symbols of an inner reality."

Soon came the famous incident in which the twenty-four year old Francis, with finality and theatrical flair, rejected his father's materialistic values to give himself over totally to the Incarnate God of the Gospels. The scene came when his father, fed up with his son's scandalous association with lepers and other outcasts, had a summons issued for Francis to appear before the local bishop. There, in front of not only the bishop but a crowd of townspeople as well, Francis made the dramatic gesture of handing over all his money to his father and then stripping himself naked of his clothes, laying them at his father's feet. With these actions, Francis declared:

> Up to now I have called Pietro Bernardone my father! But now that I am determined to serve God, I give him back not only this money that he wants so much, but all the clothes I have from him! From now on, I can advance naked before the Lord, saying in truth no longer 'my father, Pietro Bernardone,' but 'our Father who art in heaven!'

Father Bodo comments, "Francis the poet once again enacted a metaphor; the son of a cloth merchant used his unclothing as a symbol of renouncing his father's values."

So Francis was free, freed from possessions that could possess him (as they possess most of us and had certainly possessed his father), free to become a poor wanderer in the footsteps of his Savior Christ. Instead of embracing possessions, he "embraced all of creation as his brother and sister," Bodo writes. "His own daily experience became Gospel metaphors for Francis, because he saw the actions of Christ's life everywhere. He walked into water, and it was holy because Christ said that he is living water... The earth... was holy because Christ walked upon the earth. Air was holy because Christ breathed it; fire was holy because Christ said he was a living flame who came to cast fire upon the earth."

Francis began attracting many followers to his way of radical poverty: men (whom he called simply "brothers") as well as women, starting with Clare, a noblewoman of Assisi who in his spirit established the Order of Poor Ladies. So Francis journeyed to Rome to ask the Pope for official approval of his Gospel-inspired "way of life"; and the Pope approved it. Followers multiplied, reaching over 5,000 during the course of Francis's lifetime.

"Gradually, Francis himself became more and more a contemporary icon of the poor Jesus," writes Bodo. But Francis put a unique spin on his embodiment of his Lord. Playing on his era's courtly love tradition, where the knight wooed his noble lady, adoring her from afar, Francis declared his devotion to "Lady Poverty." In typically flamboyant and joy-filled fashion, he announced "I am going to espouse a more noble and beautiful lady than you have ever seen; she will surpass all others in beauty and wisdom." As the "rule" of his Order (for every holy order of men or women approved by the Pope must write out the "rule" it will follow in living the Christian life), Francis chose the words of Jesus from three Gospel passages:

> If you wish to be perfect, go, sell your possessions, and give the money to the poor. (Matthew 19:21)

> Take nothing for your journey. (Luke 9:3)

> If any want to become my followers, let them deny themselves and take

up their cross and follow me. (Matthew 16:24)

These imperatives, followed literally as Francis did, sound severe to us today. But for Francis they were joy itself. Extravagant joy was the core of his being. He sang all the time, singing praises to God, composing his own poems of praise. But clearly, as Bodo concludes, his life was his greatest poem. "Saint Francis's whole life was a metaphor of the poor, crucified Christ. His contemporaries called him the mirror of Christ, so closely did the gestures of his own life conform to the public life of Jesus, even as he followed Christ as a man of his own times, using the imagery and language of the troubadours, the posture of the true knight. Saint Francis was a medieval Christian whose living out of the Gospel became a poem that people could read. And they read there the Gospel of Jesus Christ come to life in their world."

But what of us today? Can we possibly live the "art of daily life" as Francis did? Many women and men around the world, joining Franciscan orders, do commit themselves to following his rule. But for the rest of us? Francis's art of life sounds too hard, too scary in its demands of radical poverty. He truly — to return to Susan Ross's words about beauty — "flung his gifts to anyone who asked."

Ross is confident that we all *can* do this, that living in beauty is the call and competence of us all. In fact, she insists that "Beauty is not an 'add-on' to what it means to be a living being; it is, rather, partly constitutive of who we are." Beauty can and must play an instrumental role "in our moral deliberations and development."[5]

Coleman Barks, best known for his translations of the Sufi poet Rumi, gives us a clue for how to live in Francis's spirit. "Saint Francis," Barks has said, "was so empty of nervous haste and fear and aggression that the birds would light on him."[6] This insight recalls for me Rowan Williams's comment that "Making an art of our daily life is really about living without fear; doing what we do not out of anxiety... but out of the inner pressure to 'incarnate' what has been given to us, to give it flesh, voice and locality." And what has been given to us is God's wildly extravagant gift of open-ended hospitality.

When I think of the art of life as the beauty of living God's hospitality, I think immediately of neighbors who lived across the street from us for many years. They were a large family — seven teenagers and their parents when we first moved to the neighborhood — and during the warm months turned their front porch into a living room. Sitting there happily chatting together, they cast a warm "hello" to everyone who passed by: the neigh-

5. Ross, *For the Beauty of the Earth*, 7.
6. Quoted without citation in Bodo, *Poetry as Prayer*, 12.

borhood kids on bikes, people walking their dogs, older couples out for a stroll. And not just a hello. It was always followed by "come have a seat... have some lemonade..." — and often we and others would accept the invitation to sit and chat and laugh for a while. The parents, who of course were setting the tone for the family, never seemed to be in a rush. Even when they were going out to their car for an errand, if I happened to be outside they'd pause to ask how things were going, or about some particular issue in my life.

When we first moved in and met them, George and I weren't yet Christians, and it took a while for me to figure out the source of their marvelously comfortable, welcoming ways. But gradually I learned that they were devout Catholics; the mother even went each morning to Mass ("the only time I can be alone all day," she'd say, laughing). Their "extravagant generosity" (as Ross would call it) was God's hospitality incarnated in them. They were, to recall Rowan Williams's terms, so "at home in God's creation" that with natural grace they invited everyone into their home.

I don't mean to suggest that people without religious faith can't embody a warm and loving hospitality. I know many who do. But for Christians who are *conscious* of being at home in God, their hospitality is grounded in a special dimension. An infinite dimension. The eighteenth century American preacher Jonathan Edwards articulated how the beauty we're called to live as Christians is a reflection of divine beauty. Edwards is most famous for his rather strict Puritan sermonizing, but beauty — the beauty of "true virtue" — was also a passion of his. Beauty, he wrote, is the "union of heart" which manifests itself in "general good will," that is, in benevolence toward others.[7]

Beauty as behavior. Marilynne Robinson, in her novel *Gilead*, which we touched on in Chapter 4c, has her narrator (who is also a Protestant preacher) muse on this theme:

> Calvin says somewhere that each of us is an actor on a stage and God is the audience. That metaphor has always interested me, because it makes us artists of our own behavior, and the reaction of God to us might be thought of as aesthetic rather than morally judgmental in the ordinary sense. (p.124)

We are "artists of our own behavior," actors on God's stage. Jesus in the Gospels does call on us to act; in Matthew 7:24 he commends those who "hear these words of mine and act on them." To act in God's grace, to throw oneself open to the beauty of God's hospitality, to fling this beauty to anyone who asks, inviting all our sisters and brothers to share in it: this is to become the actor whom God applauds.

---

7. Jonathan Edwards, quoted by Gesa Elsbeth Thiessen, *Theological Aesthetics: A Reader*, (Grand Rapids, Michigan: Eerdmans, 2004), 157.

As artists of our own behavior, we live in the challenging freedom —
the "strange freedom," Rowan Williams calls it — to give our actions "a
shape and a meaning" informed by the God who is Beauty. Poet Jeanne
Murray Walker offers an image for this shape and meaning in her poem
"Sister Storm."[8] Her title derives from Saint Francis's "Canticle of Brother
Sun," in which he intimately invokes various elements of the cosmos as
brother or sister, through whom God's praise is sung. So God is praised
through "Sister Moon and Stars," "Brother Wind," "Sister Water," and so
on. In Walker's poem, however, Sister Storm is a nasty kin, her lightning
as threatening as "your ugly cousin, war." The poem's speaker "defies" the
storm's destructiveness and in its stead invokes her own image of creativity
rather than destruction. The image of creativity is the homey one of knitting, with needles and crochet hook.

> My house is knit to other houses,
> living rooms hooked to front yards,
> neighborhood to neighborhood,
> hooked to that bright creative engine,
> to whose rule, before the sun, moon
> and stars, we hold out our hands.

This is the poem's end. Its image of neighborhood created by the knitting
together of homes hooks itself allusively to the famous ending of the *Divine
Comedy*, where Dante stands finally speechless before the grandeur of "the
Love that moves the sun and the other stars." Walker's divine Love is "that
bright creative engine." With Dante's sun and stars, with Francis's Brother
Sun and Sister Moon and Stars, Walker's house opens from "my" to "our":
all the neighborhood of people and cosmos "hold out our hands" in both
praise and petition to God.

Knitting neighbors and cosmos together in God's creative love. What
an apt image for the art of daily life.

---

8. Jeanne Murray Walker, "Sister Storm," *Image* #53 (Spring, 2007).

Chapter 6b. Beauty as Justice, Justice as Beauty: "Imagining how to live an alternative life"

Beauty as justice; justice as beauty. The equation emerges from what is called by theologians the "prophetic imagination."

I was just starting to ponder how to begin this chapter on the prophetic imagination when my priest gave a Sunday sermon about "imagination" as an essential faculty for living the Christian life. He began by citing a scene in George Bernard Shaw's play *Saint Joan*, the scene where Joan of Arc is being interrogated by Captain Robert de Baudricourt about why she wants to fight as a soldier in France's cause against the English:

> ROBERT. What did you mean when you said that St Catherine and St
>   Margaret talked to you every day?
> JOAN. They do.
> ROBERT. What are they like?
> JOAN [*suddenly obstinate*]. I will tell you nothing about that: they have
>   not given me leave.
> ROBERT. But you actually see them; and they talk to you just as I am
>   talking to you?
> JOAN. No: it is quite different. I cannot tell you: you must not talk to me
>   about my voices.
> ROBERT. How do you mean? voices?
> JOAN. I hear voices telling me what to do. They come from God.
> ROBERT. They come from your imagination.
> JOAN. Of course. That is how the messages of God come to us.

"Your imagination," my priest repeated; "Of course. That is how the messages of God come to us." He elaborated: "Imagination is indeed central to our Christian faith; it *is* to our imaginations that God speaks. We see this in today's Gospel reading: Jesus speaks to us in parables, which are stories that call our imagination to life."

The parables in the day's Gospel were from Matthew 13:24-43, part of a wonderful series of what are generally called "parables of the kingdom." These are separate, vivid images for what the fulfillment of God's reign will be like.

> The kingdom of heaven is like a mustard seed that a person took and sowed in a field. It is the smallest of all the seeds, yet when full-grown it is the largest of plants. It becomes a large bush, and the birds of the sky come and dwell in its branches.

> The kingdom of heaven is like yeast that a woman took and mixed with three measures of wheat flour until the whole batch was leavened.

In trying to evoke for his listeners a sense of the fulfillment that God promises, Jesus turns throughout the Gospels to images like these, images that

are familiar and homey yet portray wondrous life-giving growth. *Images…
imagination*. The two words are close kin; our imagination is our faculty of
both absorbing and creating images.

And what are images? Simply pictures taken or adapted from reality.
Images aren't always beautiful; they can be pictures of ugliness as well:
acres of blacktop weighed down with gigantic concrete boxes collectively
called shopping malls; starving children in front of tattered refugee tents in
a devastated landscape; bloodied bodies on the street of an urban battlefield.
Similarly, our imaginations can produce ugly, evil images: schemings for
how to "get back at" a colleague who has slighted me; strategies to demean
people in one's power; sinister ways to torture prisoners. The imagination
itself can be an agent for either evil or good.

When Jesus calls on our imagination, he is of course calling on it for
the sake of the good: for the building of God's kingdom here on earth.
That mustard seed, for instance. It is "the smallest of all the seeds"; yet if
I sow it, it will grow into a bush so large that birds will come dwell in its
branches, a bush full of colorful life and song. How do I sow this marvelous
seed in my own life, my own community? This is the question that Jesus'
parable invites me to ask. Similarly with the woman's yeast: a tiny thing
that, when mixed and kneaded correctly, will yield a large batch of bread.
In what small way am I making bread for the world — making it for others
who are hungry rather than consuming it all myself?

Because he often speaks in parables — in images that only the imagination can "hear" and respond to — Jesus is sometimes called a poet. And,
indeed, in these parables he is inviting, even urging, our imaginations to
take the world creatively into our hands (to sow the seed, to knead the
bread) exactly as contemporary American poet Scott Cairns invites us in his
poem "The Theology of Delight," which begins:

> Imagine a world, this ridiculous,
> tentative bud blooming
> in your hand. There in your hand, a world
> opening up, stretching, after the image
> of your hand. Imagine…[9]

Or as twentieth century British-American poet Denise Levertov wrote in
an essay: "Because I'm a poet, and I do have faith in what Keats called
the *truth of the imagination*; and because, when I'm following the road of
imagination (*following a leading*, as the Quakers say), both in the decisions of a day and in the word-by-word, line-by-line decisions of a poem in
the making, I've come to see certain analogies, and also some interaction,

---

9. Cairns, "The Theology of Delight," *Compass of Affection: Poems New and
Selected*, (Brewster, MA: Paraclete Press, 2006).

between the journey of art and the journey of faith."[10]

Analogies between the journey of art, the journey of faith, and — I'd add — the journey of everyday life. There are communities today who are intentionally seeking to create their daily lives out of the imaginative power that Jesus speaks of in his parables. Communities of mustard seeds, of yeast.

There are many such communities in the U.S. alone. To choose one isn't to slight the others. I could focus on Jubilee Partners, a Christian Service Community in rural Georgia, whose mission statement says: "We seek to understand and live by the radical implications of following Jesus Christ. We are deeply concerned about how to be effective peacemakers and how to promote justice and understanding among our neighbors and around the world."[11] Or I could focus on Rutba House, in Durham, North Carolina, one of the many intentional Christian communities forming themselves under the umbrella term "The New Monasticism." For Rutba House, living this "new monasticism" calls for lifestyle commitments such as: relocation to places abandoned by mainstream society and government; sharing economic resources with the needy of the neighborhood; hospitality to the stranger; intentional formation in the way of Christ; peacemaking in the midst of violence, and conflict resolution within communities along the lines of Matthew chapter 18; and care for God's earth along with support of local economies.[12] Or I could focus on any of the hundreds of Catholic Worker Houses around the country, inspired by the foundational vision of Dorothy Day and Peter Maurin in the 1930s.

But to give a fuller sense of how these communities are living out the imaginative power of Jesus' parables of the kingdom, I'll take as example The Simple Way community, settled in the destitute neighborhood of Kensington in North Philadelphia. I choose The Simple Way because one of its founding members, Shane Claiborne, has made it internationally famous through his book *The Irresistible Revolution: Living as an Ordinary Radical* and his speaking tours that have followed from the book's success.[13]

The Simple Way's mission statement on their website could hardly sound simpler: "*To Love God. To Love people. To Follow Jesus.*" But nothing could be more difficult, more challenging, than to live this simple love in the midst of a consumerist society that thrives on wars abroad while

---

10. Denise Levertov, "Work that Enfaiths" (1990), in *New & Selected Essays*, (New York: New Directions, 1992), 248-9.

11. www.jubileepartners.org/

12. www.newmonasticism.org/12marks.php/index/html

13. Shane Claiborne, *The Irresistible Revolution: Living as an Ordinary Radical* (Grand Rapids, Michigan: Zondervan, 2006). Quotations are from pp.117-134.

marginalizing (indeed, trying to make invisible) its own poor. Founded in 1996 by a group of college friends, The Simple Way has developed into an extensive network of outreach programs and sister communities. At their heart is the Potter Street Community, a home where members live out their commitment to Christian community along the lines of the New Monasticism principles listed above.

Shane's own upbringing was in an evangelical Christian church in Tennessee. The current "evangelical" branch of Christianity stresses a personal relationship with Jesus, and so Shane's writing and conversation speak of "Jesus" constantly as of a close friend and mentor. The evangelical church that formed Shane focuses on the blessed life promised Jesus' followers in heaven, but Shane writes:

> I am convinced that Jesus came not just to prepare us to die but to teach us how to live. Otherwise, much of Jesus' wisdom would prove quite unnecessary for the afterlife. After all, [referring to Jesus' command to "love your enemies"] how hard could it be to love our enemies in heaven? And the kingdom that Jesus speaks so much about is not just something we hope for after we die but is something we are to incarnate now. Jesus says the kingdom is "within us," "among us," "at hand,"...
>
> No wonder the early Christian church was known as the Way. It was a way of life that stood in glaring contrast to the world. What gave the early Christians integrity was the fact that they could denounce the empire and in the same breath say, "And we have another way of living. If you are tired of what the empire has to offer, we invite you into the Way."

Hence "The Simple Way" as the name of the new community that Shane and his friends founded in an "abandoned place of the empire," as they and others in the New Monasticism movement put it. With contemporary biblical scholar Walter Brueggemann, they see current American society as an "empire" — in its worshipping of the idol of wealth and its manipulation of people's fears and anxieties in order to maintain the power of the rich, while keeping poor people poor and impotent. Brueggemann, in his voluminous writings and lectures, calls on Christians to free themselves from empire's grip by "*imagining* how to live an *alternative* life," and acting on their imagination's vision through grand leaps of "generosity."[14] Christians are called, says Brueggemann, to live out a "prophetic imagination" — prophetic in the sense of the Hebrew Scripture's prophets, who condemned the oppressive power structures of their own day and envisioned human relationships in which justice would reign.

Shane, too, speaks frequently and enthusiastically about the imagination's

---

14. Walter Brueggemann, lecture at Saint Paul's Church, Rochester, NY, Nov.4, 2007.

power for good. Interviewed by Krista Tippett on National Public Radio's *Speaking of Faith* (May 17, 2007), he comments that "We have to learn to live with some imagination and give ourselves for something bigger than our own small circle." When they first began, Shane explains in his engaging and gently joyous Tennessee drawl, their Simple Way community was just responding to whatever needs their homeless neighbors brought to their door. But then they saw how a greater imaginative visioning was necessary. "At a point you say with Dr. Martin Luther King 'you keep lifting people out of ditches but eventually you come to the point where you say maybe the whole road to Jericho needs to be transformed.' So we started to look at an economy which in our neighborhood has left about 200,000 people without jobs and abandoned housing everywhere and we see one in every three African-American men going to prison, and just horrific things that are clearly not in line with God's dream for the world. So we start to re-imagine that."

The Simple Way's website (www.thesimpleway.org) lists some of the ways that they and others in the Christian social justice movement are "re-imagining that." They urge college students, for instance, to "Find out who makes the clothes for the athletic department and if those companies reflect the values of Christ"; "Ask to see the budget of your school. What do the workers get paid compared to the administrators? Make sure folks know — if you are proud of this, affirm the folks who make those decisions. If not, begin a conversation with both workers and administrators of how this could be better"; "Ask where the campus gets its energy. Is it renewable? If not begin a plan for moving toward renewable energy…"

These are all instances of the prophetic imagination to which Brueggemann calls Christians — instances of creative actions for the justice which is God's kingdom. "Prophecy," wrote the major twentieth century Catholic writer of fiction Flannery O'Connor, "is a matter of seeing near things with their extensions of meaning and thus of seeing far things close up. The prophet is a realist of distances."[15] O'Connor was speaking of the novelist's task, but her words apply just as well to the prophets of everyday life in today's imperial society. So The Simple Way links also to many neighboring groups who "see far things close up": who see a future of justice that's not yet present in their current lives. These groups include the Kensington Welfare Rights Union, a movement of poor and homeless families committed to ending poverty (and sometimes driven to civil disobedience — always creatively nonviolent — in order to win their rights). Also included as a "sister community" of The Simple Way is "New Jerusalem," a community of people in recovery from chemical addictions, who have a banner on their wall saying "we cannot recover until we help the society that made us sick recover."

They are all small groups; but out of "small things done with great love" comes God's kingdom, says The Simple Way's newsletter (Fall 2007). Small

---

15. *Mystery & Manners* (New York: Farrar, Straus & Giroux, 1961), 44.

things like the mustard seed of Jesus' parable: that tiniest of seeds which grows into a plant so hugely embracive that "the birds of the sky come and dwell in its branches." In fact, another of The Simple Way's links is to the "Mustard Seed Associates — a network of people committed to being faithful to the mustard seed revolution in an ever-changing McWorld." Mustard seeds are evidently being sown everywhere in the network of New Monasticism, and the parable is a favorite of Shane Claiborne's as well. He writes in *The Irresistible Revolution* that "Jesus has called us to littleness and compares our revolution to the little mustard seed, to yeast making its way through dough, slowly infecting this dark world with love."

"Of course, everyone was forewarned," he writes elsewhere in the book (paraphrasing well-known Gospel passages), "that in this kingdom everything is backward and upside-down — the last are first and the first are last, the poor are blessed and the mighty are cast from their thrones. And yet people were attracted to it. They were ready for something different from what the empire had to offer." They were ready, he adds, for "justice." But "that's when things get messy," he admits:

> When people begin moving beyond charity and toward justice and solidarity with the poor and oppressed, as Jesus did, they get in trouble. Once we are actually friends with folks in struggle, we start to ask why people are poor, which is never as popular as giving to charity. One of my friends has a shirt marked with the words of late Catholic bishop Dom Helder Camara: "When I fed the hungry, they called me a saint. When I asked why people are hungry, they called me a communist." Charity wins awards and applause, but joining the poor gets you killed. People do not get crucified for charity. People are crucified for living out a love that disrupts the social order, that calls forth a new world.

Major contemporary Christian theologians affirm what Shane is saying and what his community and others like it are acting on: that the prophetic imagination generates actions of justice, actions which re-conceive the current social order. Such creative acts of justice, these theologians and scholars insist, are exactly what Christian "beauty" means. "Justice," writes Professor of Theology Jeremy Begbie, "concerns right relationships and the same goes for beauty — the beauty God desires for the human community is the proper dynamic ordering of lives in relation to each other. Justice is beautiful."[16] Scholar Richard Viladesau, in his book *The Beauty of the Cross*, concurs. "Christ's beauty is not apparent except to those who know how to discern spiritual beauty. That beauty consists above all in goodness or justice, which we are called to imitate, and thus become similarly beautiful."[17]

So it's not surprising that one of Shane's recurrent words, in his writ-

16. Jeremy Begbie, "Beauty, Sentimentality and the Arts," in *The Beauty of God*, ed. Daniel J. Treier et al, (Downers Grove, IL: InterVarsity Press, 2007), 65.

17. Richard Viladesau, *The Beauty of the Cross*, 323.

ing and his talks, is "beautiful." Describing the leper colony that he was assigned to when he and a college friend went to India to be mentored by Mother Teresa, he passionately tells Krista Tippett that these hundred or so families of lepers "had created a *beautiful* culture together. They made their own clothes, made their own bandages, ran their own clinic.... It was there that I caught that vision of 'let's build something new together' — or as one of my heroes, Dorothy Day, said, 'Let's build a society where it's easier for people to be *good* to each other.'" Beauty and goodness: for Shane they are a single breath, a single joy. Later to Krista he mentions that The Simple Way receives about twenty letters and phone calls a day from people, especially young people, inspired by the community's way of life. "These are people who want to know where their clothes are made, where their food comes from. And that's a *beautiful thing*!"

"A beautiful thing." It's the refrain ringing throughout *The Irresistible Revolution*:

> It is a beautiful thing when folks in poverty are no longer just a missions project but become genuine friends and family with whom we laugh, cry, dream, and struggle. One of the verses I have grown to love is the one where Jesus is preparing to leave the disciples and says, "I no longer call you servants.... Instead, I have called you friends" (John 15:15).
>
> Dorothy Day of the Catholic worker movement understood this well. She said, "Love is a harsh and dreadful thing to ask of us, but it is the only answer." This love is not sentimental but heartwrenching, the most difficult and the most beautiful thing in the world.
>
> I almost feel selfish sometimes, for the gift of community. The beautiful thing is that there is enough to go around.

With the "beautiful" blossoming from his mouth, and community so close to his heart, Shane naturally, unselfconsciously, becomes a kind of artist: an artist whose creation — with his colleagues — is a community of love. To Krista Tippett he describes himself almost offhandedly in the artistic image of a singer: "I try not to be a soloist but to *harmonize* with all the other voices who express a Christianity that reflects who Jesus is." The great Christian theologian of beauty, Hans von Balthasar, implicitly affirms the artistic vocation of Shane and all who live the prophetic life when he writes that "God needs prophets in order to make himself known, and all prophets are necessarily artistic."[18] How appropriate, then, that in listing on its website its foundational principles, The Simple Way describes one of them in exactly the language that Christian artists use of their vocation: "we are created Imago Dei [in God's image] to be creators." For The Simple Way and all in the New Monasticism movement, that creativity manifests itself in a "communal art"

---

18. Hans von Balthasar, *The Glory of the Lord*, 43.

which recognizes each individual's "unique and special creative abilities."[19]

"Also" this website statement continues, "we value the role that art has in breaking the cycle of poverty and liberating emotional and spiritual deprivation." With this vision and value of art's liberating possibilities, The Simple Way has quite naturally developed as one of its outreach projects an arts program for residents of the neighborhood. "Collaborate Art and Imagination is Taking over the City!" shouts The Simple Way in boldface caps on its website, as if warning that artistic imagination is a danger — which it *is* to the status quo. As the Russian Christian philosopher Nicolas Berdaev wrote, "A creative act always rises above reality; it means imagining something other and better than the reality around us."[20]

Christian prophetic communities living and loving in the places abandoned by their society's power structures: they are artists of life. So it's delightful to learn from Shane's National Public Radio interview that one of his role models is Saint Francis of Assisi, that consummate artist of life. Speaking of Francis re-building the Church of San Damiano, Shane muses, "God has this special way of breaking into the ruins and brokenness of society — which is exactly what happened with Jesus showing up."

Creativity as moral power: that's what the prophetic imagination is all about. For Christians it is Christ's beauty in action, in the action of justice. The late nineteenth century British Jesuit poet Gerard Manley Hopkins envisioned this in his untitled poem "As kingfishers catch fire..." After proliferating images for how each "mortal being" enfleshes Christ by living out its unique calling, the poem ends with the calling of "justice:

...the just man justices;
Keeps grace: that keeps all his goings graces;
Acts in God's eye what in God's eye he is —
Christ — for Christ plays in ten thousand places,
Lovely in limbs, and lovely in eyes not his
To the Father through the features of men's faces.

---

19. www.thesimpleway.org/PSC/community/function.html
20. Nicolas Berdaev, *Dream And Reality* (London: Geoffrey Bles, 1950), 218.

Chapter 6c. The Beauty of Christian Witness and Sacrifice: Giving our Life out of "love for enemies"

Not many Americans had heard of Christian Peacemaker Teams until one of their members, Tom Fox, was murdered by his Iraqi kidnappers in March, 2006. He and the three others of this particular CPT group — two from Canada, one from Britain, and Tom from Virginia — had gone to Iraq for the reason that Christian Peacemaker Teams go everywhere: to witness to the power of God's healing love in a place ripped apart by violent hatred.

In the midst of Iraq's complex and factionalized carnage, on the evening of November 25, 2005 — the very evening, it turned out, before the group was kidnapped — Tom wrote out a reflection that he titled "Why Are We Here?" His answer was that we are here, in this life, in this war zone, "to take part in the creation of the Peaceable Realm of God." As his fellow CPT hostage James Loney paraphrased Tom's reflection later for *The Christian Century* magazine (July 24, 2007), "we help create" this Realm of God when (in the Bible's words) "we love God, our neighbors, even our enemies 'with all our heart, our mind and our strength.'" So creativity is at the core of the CPT mission, and the creative force is love — even love of enemies. Explaining what this creative love entails, Loney moves between paraphrasing and quoting Tom's words:

> In the context of Iraq, where "dehumanization seems to be the operative means of relating to each other," and where U.S. forces kill innocent Iraqis in "their quest to hunt down and kill" those they've dehumanized as 'terrorists,'... the first step down the road to violence is taken when I dehumanize a person.... Why are we here?" he asked again. It was not a rhetorical question. "We are here to root out all aspects of dehumanization that exist within us. We are here to stand with those being dehumanized by oppressors... We are here to stop people, including ourselves, from dehumanizing any of God's children, no matter how much they dehumanize their own souls."

For trying to live out these convictions, Tom Fox gave his life. The rest of his group were rescued two weeks after his death. But they, too, had given of their lives: risked their lives for the sake of witnessing to another way than war: the Way — as CPT sees it — of following Jesus.

Christian Peacemaker Teams were born in response to a rousing speech by activist theologian Ron Sider addressed to the 1984 Mennonite World Conference in Strasbourg, France. Mennonites (also called Anabaptists) are Christians who formed in sixteenth century Europe under the belief that Jesus came to bring peace and that his disciples must therefore refuse participation in all wars. Along with the other "historic peace churches" (as they are called) — the Church of the Brethren and the Society of Friends (or Quakers) — Mennonites have traditionally identified themselves as Christian pacifists. Sider's speech, called "God's People Reconciling," challenged his fellow believers to go further than a pacifism that had become a comfortable isolation from the world's troubles.[21] Speaking at the height of the nuclear arms race of the Cold War, Sider voiced an urgency that the planet's very survival depended on a profoundly more active and creative way of following Jesus the Peacemaker. This was the way of the Cross.

Jesus' approach to the evils of his time "was not one of passive nonresistance," Sider insisted. Jesus blisteringly condemned the hypocrisy of the religious authorities of his day, and he "would never have ended up on the cross if he had exemplified the isolationist pacifism of withdrawal." Rather, Sider went on:

> Jesus said that God's way of dealing with enemies was to persist in loving them. 'Love your enemies and pray for those who persecute you.' Why? 'So that you may be sons and daughters of your Creator in heaven.' In fact, Jesus went even further. Jesus said that God's way of dealing with enemies was to take their evil upon himself. The crucified criminal [Jesus] hanging limp on the middle cross is the eternal Word who in the beginning was with God and indeed was God, but for our sake became flesh and dwelt among us. Only when we grasp that that is who the crucified one was, do we begin to fathom the depth of Jesus' teaching that God's way of dealing with enemies is the way of suffering love. By powerful parable and dramatic demonstration, Jesus had taught that God forgives sinners again and again. Then he died on the cross to accomplish that reconciliation. The cross is the most powerful statement about God's way of dealing with enemies.

And because of this, Sider continued, "we know two interrelated things. First, that a just God mercifully accepts us sinful enemies just as we are. And second, that God wants us to go and treat our enemies exactly the same way. What a fantastic fulfillment of the messianic promise of *shalom* [the Hebrew biblical term for 'peace,' meaning 'right relationships']."

Then came Sider's direct challenge to his fellow Christians in the peacemaking churches: "We must take up our cross and follow Jesus to Golgotha. We must be prepared to die by the thousands. Those who have believed in peace through the sword have not hesitated to die... Why do we pacifists think that our way — Jesus' way — to peace will be less costly?"

> Unless comfortable North American and European Mennonites and Brethren in Christ are prepared to risk injury and death in nonviolent opposition to the injustice our societies foster and assist in Central America, the Philippines, and South Africa, we dare never whisper another word about pacifism to our sisters and brothers in those desperate lands. Unless we are ready to die developing new nonviolent attempts to reduce international conflict, we should confess that we never really

---

21. www.cpt.org/resources/writings/sider

meant the cross was an alternative to the sword. Unless the majority of our people in nuclear nations are ready as congregations to risk social disapproval and government harassment in a clear ringing call to live without nuclear weapons, we should sadly acknowledge that we have betrayed our peacemaking heritage. Making peace is as costly as waging war.

Then, in conclusion, Sider got scarily specific:

> What would happen if we in the Christian church developed a new nonviolent peacekeeping force of 100,000 persons ready to move into violent conflicts and stand peacefully between warring parties in Central America, Northern Ireland, Poland, Southern Africa, the Middle East, and Afghanistan? Frequently we would get killed by the thousands. But everyone assumes that for the sake of peace it is moral and just for soldiers to get killed by the hundreds of thousands, even millions. Do we not have as much courage and faith as soldiers?
>
> Again and again, I believe, praying, Spirit-filled, nonviolent peacekeeping forces would by God's special grace, be able to end the violence and nurture justice. Again and again, we would discover that love for enemies is not utopian madness or destructive masochism but rather God's alternative to the centuries of escalating violence that now threatens the entire planet. But the cross — death by the thousands by those who believe Jesus — is the only way to convince our violent world of the truth of Christ's alternative.

Sider was speaking many decades after Gandhi had proven the power of "nonviolent action," so Sider's audience would have been familiar with what nonviolence entailed. They'd have known that it called for a lifelong inner discipline of purging hatred and violence from one's own heart, along with carefully organized mass actions to enlist the power of love against those perpetrating the violence of injustice or war.

Sider's listeners heeded his impassioned plea "to take the lead in the search for new nonviolent approaches to conflict resolution." Just two years later, at a December, 1986 conference in Illinois, Christian Peacemaker Teams were officially founded. Their mission statement confirmed their commitment to offer "an organized, nonviolent alternative to war and other forms of lethal inter-group conflict," grounded in "the Gospel of Peace" which "calls us to new forms of public witness which may include nonviolent direct action."

The creativity and courage of CPT since its founding have been impressive. Since 2001, for instance, CPT has maintained a continuing presence in the dangerous Magdalena Medio region of Colombia, standing alongside local communities which have bravely risked declaring themselves Humanitarian Spaces: refusing, that is, to take sides in the ongoing violent conflict between the Colombian Armed Forces, left-wing guerrilla organizations, and right-wing paramilitaries. CPT members live with the villagers, witnessing their harrassment and inevitably being subject to it themselves. What creativity it must take to respond nonviolently to events like those in CPT's 2007 Colombia Human Rights Report:

> June, *La Guasima, Micoahumado, Morales:* Soldiers from the Nueva Grenada Battalion arrived at the home of a young mother, beat her and threatened to burn her 8-month-old baby.

> June 22, *La Plaza, Micoahumado, Morales:* Under the command of Sergeant Monsate, soldiers fully uniformed and heavily armed occupied homes and camped in the community's cemetery, less than 100 meters from civilian homes. Despite petitions from CPT and community leaders, the soldiers did not leave the community. Additionally, soldiers demanded gasoline from one resident of the community, who refused to supply it, and they obliged a man to drive to pick up their supplies. On June 24, they moved camp to the opposite end of the community, surrounding a civilian home.

> November 4, *Barrancabermeja:* Two armed and hooded men forced their way into the apartment of Yolanda Becerra, president of the Popular Women's Organization, ransacked the apartment, pushed Becerra, held a gun to her head and threatened to kill Becerra and her family if they did not leave the city within 48 hours.[22]

If a CPT member happens to be present in the home of Yolanda Becerra on November 4, that member must instantly improvise a response that will deflate rather than intensify the violence. And how to respond during those tense June days in the village of La Plaza, negotiating with hostile soldiers in an attempt to prevent their exploding into violence? This too requires improvisatory creativity. Taking on the role of nonviolent witness in areas of conflict is an art learned through disciplined training and continual practice. Like jazz, it's the art of improvisation — but with the risk of death if you slip off-beat or miss a note.

There's a playful seriousness as well in the punning phrase that CPT chose as its motto: "Getting in the Way." CPTers "get in the Way" exactly like the earliest followers of Jesus, who named their new life "the Way" because Jesus called himself "the Way" — the Way to enter God's peaceful kingdom. But for CPT there's an added twist to "Getting in the Way." As in those incidents in Colombia, CPTers don't get *out* of the way when violence threatens; rather, they deliberately get *in* the way of violence — with the aim of deflating and transforming it by direct nonviolent intervention and creative public witness. CPT groups of recent years have been "getting in the way" in conflict-ridden areas of the world including not only

---

22. www.cpt.org/work/colombia/human_rights/2007

Colombia but also Israel/Palestine, the Congo, and even North America, where indigenous peoples are harassed when they assert their treaty rights to waters and land. Tom Fox and his CPT colleagues in Iraq had been sent to put themselves in the way of authorities who were abusing detainees and denying them basic legal and human rights.

Though initiated by the historic peace churches — Mennonites, Brethren and Quakers — CPT welcomes members of all Christian denominations and even other faiths to join them. Tom Fox, for instance was a Quaker, and among his three CPT colleagues were a Baptist (Protestant), a Catholic, and a Sikh.

The most poignant part of Fox's experience as a hostage, according to James Loney's account in *The Christian Century*, was Tom's daily inner struggle to keep violence from overtaking his own heart. With extraordinary discipline, "he turned his captivity into a sustained, unbroken meditation," recalls Loney.

> The chain that bound his wrist became a kind of rosary, or *sebha* (the beads Muslims use to count the names of God). He would picture someone: a member of his family, a member of the Iraq team or the CPT office, one of the captors — whoever he felt needed a prayer. Holding a link of the chain, he would breathe in and out, slowly, so that you could hear the air gushing in and out of his lungs, praying for the person he was holding in his mind.

The physical effort of prayer under the shadow of death: it recalls for Christians Jesus' own agonized prayer in the garden of Gethsemane the night before his crucifixion; in Luke's account Jesus prayed so earnestly that "his sweat became like great drops of blood falling down on the ground" (22:44).

If suffering for the sake of the world's good takes creative power — as it did for Jesus and does for today's Christian Peacemaker Teams — it is a creativity so demanding that only God's love can inspire and sustain it. Like Tom Fox transforming his chain into prayer beads, every CPT member must work to cultivate the inner strength of a loving, peaceful heart. Each must develop the discipline of an art: the art of self-sacrifice.

The twentieth century's most famous Christian theologian of self-sacrifice for the good of the world — Dietrich Bonhoeffer — actually wrote of the Christian calling in terms of art.

Bonhoeffer had just finished his doctorate in theology and begun his academic career when, in 1933, the German Reichstag passed the "Aryan Clause," a law excluding all Jewish people from government service. When the official German church supported this law, Bonhoeffer was outraged and spoke publicly against this unchristian affront to humanity. In the face of inhumane laws, he insisted, the church is obliged to oppose and disobey them. It is the church's task, he declared, not only to "bandage the victims under the wheel, but to jam the spoke in the wheel itself."[23] During the tense years that followed, as Hitler consolidated his power, Bonhoeffer did all he could to jam the Nazi's wheel. In 1943, the Gestapo finally arrested him for his resistance activities. He remained in prison until he was executed in April, 1945, a week before his prison camp was liberated by the Allied armed forces.

Prison was not easy for Bonhoeffer; he deeply missed his family, his friends, his fiancée. In letters to them, later published as *Letters and Papers from Prison*, he articulated a theology of living as a true Christian in a secularized age, a theology of engaging the world's evil as well as its good. This theology — developed out of his earlier writings, including his book with the foreshadowing title *The Cost of Discipleship* — continues to be immensely challenging to Christians, not least because Bonhoeffer literally gave his life for his religious principles.

Music had always been dear to Bonhoeffer, and he drew on it comfortably in developing his prison theology. His most extended musical metaphor came in a phrase he himself coined: the "polyphony of life." Polyphony was an invention of medieval music, a way of interweaving melodic lines in counterpoint. Bonhoeffer developed it as a theological term in letters to his close friend Eberhard Bethge, at a time when both men suffered deeply from enforced separation from their loved ones: Bethge as a soldier on the Italian front, Bonhoeffer in prison. In May, 1944, on the day after Bethge, home on leave, had visited his imprisoned friend, Bonhoeffer wrote to him about this new idea, "what I might call the polyphony of life."

> What I mean is that God wants us to love him eternally with our whole hearts — not in such a way as to weaken or injure our earthly love, but to provide a kind of *cantus firmus* [a preexistent melody underlying a polyphonic musical composition] to which the other melodies of life provide the counterpoint. One of these contrapuntal themes… is earthly affection. Even in the Bible we have the Song of Songs; and really one can imagine no more ardent, passionate, sensual love than is portrayed there…. Where the *cantus firmus* is clear and plain, the counterpoint can be developed to its limits. The two are 'undivided and yet distinct,' in the words of the Chalcedonian Definition [a fifth century formulation of Christ's dual nature], like Christ in his divine and human natures. May not the attraction and importance of polyphony in music consist in its being a musical reflection of this Christological fact and therefore of our *vita christiana* [our Christian life]? This thought didn't occur to me till after your visit yesterday. Do you see what I'm driving at? I wanted to tell you to have a good, clear *cantus firmus*… Only a polyphony of this kind can give life a wholeness and at the same time assure us

---

23. "The Church and the Jewish Question," April 1933; quoted in *The Modern Theologians*, ed. David F. Ford (Malden, MA: Blackwell Publishers, 1997), 38.

that nothing calamitous can happen as long as the *cantus firmus* is kept going.[24]

There's a lot packed into this passage. Even Bethge asked for elaboration. In response, Bonhoeffer wrote about the idea of "aesthetic existence," a term he took from Kierkegaard but dramatically reconceived. As South African professor of theology John W. De Gruchy explains it in his book *Christianity, Art and Transformation: Theological Aesthetics in the Struggle for Justice*, Kierkegaard had seen "aesthetics" as a personal, existential way of living, whereas "for Bonhoeffer social relations are primary, and that is why he seeks to recover 'aesthetic existence' within the believing community." Bonhoeffer saw 'aesthetic existence' as a realm of "freedom for creativity," De Gruchy explains, but not a freedom without limits. Rather, "The necessary and inevitable improvisation that life demands, to use a metaphor from jazz, only makes sense when it reworks the familiar. Artistic freedom demands discipline, coherence, and form. Hence Bonhoeffer's insistence on a *cantus firmus*…"[25]

And hence the apt image of improvisatory jazz for the art of a life of dedicated self-sacrifice: as apt for Bonhoeffer as we found it was today for Christian Peacemakers Teams.

Here is the art of living the "Beauty of Christian Witness and Sacrifice," as this chapter has called it. But we mustn't think that living this particular beauty always leads to sacrificing one's very life. We mustn't think that the beauty of witness to Christ's active love in the midst of violence requires our death — as it did for Dietrich Bonhoeffer and Tom Fox. So I want to end this chapter by turning to a community where the beauty of witness to God's love has blossomed into fullness of life for all involved. And, appropriate for this book, it is a community dedicated specifically to enhancing Muslim-Christian relations.

I speak of the monastery of Deir Mar Musa in mountains of the Syrian desert. Founded in the sixth century by a Christian monk, Deir Mar Musa flourished for several centuries and then gradually withered away until it was abandoned in the early nineteenth century. But in the 1980s it was revived by a young Italian Catholic of the Jesuit order, Paulo Dall'Oglio. A student of Arabic, he visited the abandoned site and was inspired to stay, to

---

24. Dietrich Bonhoeffer, *Letters and Papers from Prison* (London: SCM Press, 1971), 303.

25. John W. De Gruchy, *Christianity, Art and Transformation: Theological Aesthetics in the Struggle for Justice* (Cambridge: Cambridge University Press, 2001), 163-4.

renew it as a Christian monastic community devoted to love of Islam.[26]

He became Father Paulo, ordained to the priesthood in the local Syrian Catholic Church. With the local Christians' help, he was able in 1991 to open Deir Mar Musa as a monastic community of men and women including Syrian Orthodox and Catholic Christians. Along with the usual Christian monastic vows of poverty and chastity and the usual monastic practices of contemplation and hospitality, they added the commitment to love Islam. To aid in this commitment, they conduct all their worship in Arabic and hence address all their prayers and praise to "Allah" (simply the Arabic word for "God"). This is one way that, as Deir Mar Musa's website puts it, "we seek to give up a culture of separation in order to build gradually a culture of communion."

In an interview after receiving the 2006 Euro-Mediterranean Award for Dialogue on "Mutual Respect among People of Different Religions or any other Belief," Fr. Paulo describes other ways that Deir Mar Musa seeks today to build a culture of communion between Islam and Christianity.[27] The interviewer kept asking him how Deir Mar Musa furthers "respect," but Fr. Paulo insisted on going way beyond what mere respect entails. "Respect," he insisted, can be negative, "as we teach children to have respect for electricity." Instead, the foundational principle of Deir Mar Musa is "love" — as "a basic feeling, an attitude that can help to avoid war and the tensions that lead to war." And for Deir Mar Musa, love enfolds "hospitality: to be able to welcome others 'under our tent.'... In hospitality, especially Semitic/Arabic hospitality, your guest is not somebody you will take advantage of, nor that you need for your own purposes. By the very fact of being 'other' (nation, tribe, religion) he becomes an icon, an embodiment of 'otherhood', which, for religious people, is God Himself. In the name of God, the host receives the guest, recognizing in his face the image of God the Guest." Gracious hospitality, seeing the guest as God, is a core practice for both Christianity and Islam.

Deir Mar Musa's mission is to throw open its hospitality so widely and warmly that the monastery can be (in fact has become) "a place of meeting" the other, as the website phrases it. Fr. Paulo offers in his interview a beautiful image of Deir Mar Musa's hospitality in action:

> One, it offers a large room in our hearts and minds to Islamic/human/cultural reality, a warm room of consideration, curiosity, appreciation, with a desire for friendship, communion and interaction, mystical, spiritual, embodied in a monastery, where there is the priority of prayer in human life. Thus we know deeply that we have brothers and sisters in the Islamic/Sufi tradition. In this monastery, we have been trying to re-

---

26. Dana Greene, "Witness in the Desert," *National Catholic Reporter*, Dec. 29, 2006.

27. www.deirmarmusa.org/page/AnnalindhInterview2006-10eng.HTM

discover and re-express... the ancient structure of inter-relationship between this kind of Christian institution and the still young Islamic community. Prophet Mohammed (peace and blessings be upon him from the Lord), had been in contact with monks and the monastic tradition from his childhood, when he came in caravans....The Caliphs, the first generation after the Prophet, brought deep respect but also real protection to the monasteries, discovering places of interaction and deep meeting with Christian communities.

When asked by the interviewer whether "lack of mutual respect is one of the most burning problems in our Euro-Mediterranean region," Fr. Paulo again rejects the term "respect" but this time launches into a contextual history of why Islam and the West are so at odds today. Westerners can't understand "why Islam is so aggressive towards the occidental way of life and pyramid of values, principles and life style."

> The West finds it difficult to understand how deep the contention is. Why so much negativity? It depends probably on two things: first, we have to accept that the Islamic world around the Mediterranean has been victim of colonial projects.... After colonialism, the creation of national entities was seen under the direct influence of the West, through a national ideology which is external to the Islamic world.

Then came the founding of Israel "in the heart of the Arab world (Islam and Oriental Christian). Furthermore, two empires, (capitalism and communism) both of them from the West, came to impose their logic and their own internal fight upon the Arab/Islamic world." And now today "the feeling of being economically colonized is so deep, the regimes being so dependent on Western economic interest":

> The impression that the Israeli/Arabic war is also a way of expanding spaces for Western markets, arms, and then after the end of the Cold War, this enormous feeling of being victim of a process of globalization, in which Western lifestyle is imposed as being the only reasonable, really human, feasible one, without the people in the West having the capacity to question the model.
>
> Having in Islam an enormous desire for emancipation, having a project for a future built on its own values, hope in its own literature, imagination, desires, aesthetics: Muslims in many different ways feel a need for fighting to resist Western/worldly power, and for fighting back in order to create a space for Islamic hope. It is clear to me that there are many different 'Islams' as there are many different 'Wests'.

"The Islamic criticism of the Western economic, capitalistic model, secularized society and desecrated personal and family life, stays as a voice to be heard and paid attention to," Fr. Paulo adds. Reading his interview, one can tell that Fr. Paulo has gained the wisdom of a life dedicated to *listening* to the other. It's fine, he says, to talk of "mutual respect about differences

— but what about liberation processes from unjust regimes, from aristo-cratic privileged systems, old-fashioned kingdoms or remnants of tyranni-cal, hyper-nationalistic power systems? What about liberation of territories from illegal occupation, what about this prison of border-control, unobtain-able visas?"

Then comes his positive vision, again the fruit of *listening* with an open heart to the other, to the aspirations of Islamic peoples. "I think that we need today more and more a movement of global democracy... orga-nized like syndicates, surely larger than nations and more universal than religions, although not violently opposing religions. I dream of a system of dynamic, internet-based federations in which the elaboration of common current aims defines an opinion front, able to put pressure on both civil and religious authorities."

"Internet-based federations" might sound surprising coming from the head of a remote Syrian monastery, but Deir Mar Musa is very much in tune with what the internet can offer to inter-religious dialogue. "A virtual monastery is being built in cyberspace," their website proudly announces. Through internet connections with people of good will around the world, along with those (and there are droves by now — Muslims, and Christians, and those of other faiths or even no traditional religious faith) who come in person to Deir Mar Musa for workshops and dialogue, the monastery is boldly creative in "scrutinizing the mystery of 'otherness.'" Recognizing that "the presence of the Other as other in front of me has been perceived through centuries as an insoluble fact and a source of anguish, tensions and wars," Deir Mar Musa has a different vision and a different experience. As Fr. Paulo puts it, "Our experience in Deir Mar Musa is deeply the one of a common worship and a common relationship with the One God, the Merci-ful Creator, the One who sides with the poor, oppressed, abandoned, those little ones who are thirsty and hungry for justice."

This is the witness of a Mid-East desert monastery in our day. Its spirit is captured (appropriately, since the Deir Mar Musa community feels deep affinity with the Sufi mystic tradition) in a short poem by the medieval Sufi poet Rumi, who lived not far from where Deir Mar Musa stands. Though certainly not a Christian, Rumi could write these joyously challenging words to his fellow Muslims:

> I called through your door,
> "The mystics are gathering
> in the street. Come out!"
>
> "Leave me alone.
> I'm sick."

"I don't care if you're dead!
Jesus is here, and he wants
to resurrect somebody!"[28]

---

28. from *The Essential Rumi*, translated by Coleman Barks with John Moyne (New York: HarperCollins, 1995).

Closing Dialogue: A Muslim and a Christian, walking together in God's light, reach toward the Good of the world

Muslim: I'm speechless before the beauties of behavior that pour forth from people who give themselves over to God's beauty, God's hospitality.

Christian: Speechless before the moral power of creativity issuing from love of the God who is love.

Muslim: But speechlessness won't get us far into our final dialogue, will it?!

Christian: No. But where shall we begin then?

Muslim: We began our previous dialogues with the light. The "Light upon Light" of the Qur'an's Light Verse; the God who in Jesus Christ, for you, is the Light of the world. So can we begin again with this Light?

Christian: I don't see why not. We've certainly seen God's light shining through the lives of the Muslims and Christians we've just been hearing about. The marginalized West African immigrants who showed God's light to Ingrid Mattson in their following of the Prophet's Sunnah.

Muslim: The light kindled in the hearts of those dear young people creating prophetic Christian communities devoted to bringing justice to life in the poorest of city neighborhoods.

Christian: The light of Shari'ah when it leads El Fadl, Imam Feisal, Daisy Khan and many other Muslims to proclaim imaginatively the beautiful guidelines given by God for the good of the world.... But tell me something. I don't mean to be collapsing the very real differences between us that we've discussed in our previous dialogues in this book. But isn't it fair to say that Christians and Muslims who walk in God's light — like the people we've just been talking about — tend to look a lot alike? I know that our vocabularies are different: you speak of following "the Prophet's Sunnah" and "the Shari'ah"; I speak of "the prophetic imagination" and "Christian witness." But beyond, or underneath, the different terminology, the different concepts, here's my question: Do Christians who are dedicating their lives to service of God's people and God's creation behave differently from Muslims who do the same? Or does their common commitment to justice bring them closer and closer, in solidarity not only with those they're serving, but also with each other?

Muslim: I'd say it brings them closer and closer. And why wouldn't it?

The light we're talking about isn't a Christian light or a Muslim light. It's not two lights. It's one light, God's light, given to Muslims and Christians in different ways, to be sure, through Christ and through the Qur'an, but unified at the invisible source.

Christian: I thought as much. But I wonder if there is a concrete example of this growing closeness…

Muslim: How about the Muslim Peacemaker Team? Here's a terrific instance showing how Christians and Muslims are allowing themselves to be influenced by the moral example of each other's creativity.

Christian: You're talking about the group of Muslims in Iraq encouraged by the Christian Peacemaker Teams — and in turn encouraging their Christian counterparts?

Muslim: Yes. But the driving force behind the MPT is a Muslim, Sami Rasouli. Sami fled Iraq in 1975 when he was twenty-three years old to escape Saddam Hussein's regime. He then moved to Minneapolis where he became a successful restaurateur and community leader. Horrified by the destruction visited on Iraq by his adopted country's invasion, he gave up his business and returned to Iraq in 2003 to see if he could be an agent of peace amid the violence. Sami says that in Kerbala he was "fortunate to meet some beautiful Christian peacemakers" from the U.S., the United Kingdom, Canada, and other places. "They were there to promote the same things I wanted, and their stories were inspirational."[1]

Christian: Well? What happened next? How did Sami get started?

Muslim: Sami found his first opportunity to put nonviolence in practice in Najaf, his hometown. A Sunni himself, Sami was able to persuade fifteen Shia Muslims there to form the first Muslim Peacemaker Team. The Team's mission was to bring peace to the warring Sunni and Shia factions of Iraq by encouraging them to work together to rebuild Iraq's ruined cities. They decided to begin in perhaps the most devastated Iraqi city of all, Falluja. Right away they met resistance from a local Sheikh who distrusted any collaboration with Christians. "We have been destroyed twice by the U.S. Christian army," the Sheikh asserted to Sami. But gradually, after much patient negotiation, the Team was able to persuade representatives of all parties involved, of the Allied central Command as well as of the remaining residents of Fallujah, to begin the work of reconstruction, one house at a time.

Christian: So the personal examples of the Christian Peacemaker Team members were important for Sami, especially their commitment to follow the nonviolent Jesus?

Muslim: Of course — but note that he embraced the commitment to nonviolence as a Muslim. "*Salaam* (that is, peace and fullness of life) is not

1. *International Falls Daily Journal*, May 1, 2008.

just a greeting. It is the goal." Sami observes the Sunnah as faithfully as the members of the CPT root their behavior in the Gospels. No religion "owns" nonviolence. But we all share in the vision of our goal, and we all identify similar aspects of the kind of life we have to lead if we and all the rest of God's children hope to get there. That's why Sami also expresses his religious grounding in universal terms. It isn't just Muslims and Christians who walk in God's light, you know! He puts it this way: "I believe our creator created all of us out of love, and loves us all without discrimination. He could be called Allah, God, Yahweh. Our religious journeys never stop. They are an acclimation and a learning process that keep going as long as the universe continues."[2]

Christian: And yet…

Muslim: What's the matter?

Christian: Well, just being reminded of so much devastation made me think about the fact that despite all this light and all this beauty, there's so much darkness and ugliness…

Muslim: "Despite" the light and the beauty? You mean, the darkness and ugliness are greater than the light and the beauty?

Christian: No, I don't believe that any more than you do… It's just that, well, we live in a time when darkness and ugliness are nearly all we hear about…

Muslim: They're always in the headlines…

Christian: Yes, exactly. But not only that, the darkness and ugliness we hear about are often associated with, and sometimes even blamed on…

Muslim: …blamed on me, you mean, blamed on Islam.

Christian: Yes, blamed on Islam. Which is unjust, of course. But the result of the stereotyping and blaming of Islam is that the kinds of claims made in Chapter 5 — about the grounding of the Prophet's Sunnah and the Shari'ah in the search for beauty — that these claims can sound completely unrealistic, pie-in-the-sky, wishful thinking of a Pollyanna-ish sort, or even worse: like a devious whitewashing of the brutal facts.

Muslim: And by "brutal facts" you mean the kinds of things that were mentioned in Chapter 5: inhuman applications of Shari'ah, the tragic events of September 11…?

Christian: Yes —

Muslim: But you're forgetting that those uglinesses *were* talked about in that chapter. They weren't ducked, they weren't hidden away. And in Chapters 1 and 2 we saw how ugliness and darkness play key roles in our respective revelations. The fact is that darkness and ugliness give urgency to our dialogue, give it point and purpose. Don't you remember El Fadl saying that, "it is through the process of engaging those unseemly realities (that is, darkness and ugliness) that the search for

---

2. *International Falls Daily Journal*, May 1, 2008.

beauty takes place"? Without the light, darkness would be unrecogniz-
able. The light enables us to see what we're struggling against. And
gradually, as we get stronger, we're able to see that there's actually no
"battle" at all between light and beauty on the one hand and darkness
and ugliness on the other since the two aren't equal. Your Gospel of
John puts it well when it says: "The light shines in the darkness, and the
darkness did not overcome it."

Christian: Yes, I do remember all these things. But I'm afraid I haven't said
what I've really been feeling. What's really on my heart is that you and
I are praising beauty even as we both stand right in the middle of the
darkness and ugliness. I mean right in the middle of the ongoing political and cultural strife between the Muslim world and what I'll call the
"West" — though I know the term "West" is misleading, since millions
and millions of Muslims now live and make their homes in the West.

Muslim: Well, I agree. There are times when I feel that the ugliness is engulf-
ing me, like a mudslide. But while a lot of that mud comes from outside
— Fr. Paolo spoke eloquently about the reasons why many Muslims feel
hostile to the West (thinking of the West strictly in its political and cultural dimensions) —, a lot of it comes from within as well. From within
the culture surrounding Islam, I mean, from within what you call the
"Muslim world." If we're talking about the ugly way certain people who
profess our faiths are behaving towards each other, then we'd have to say,
I think, that there's plenty of blame to go around.

Christian: Yes, I must sadly agree that Christians — or more broadly the
Western culture that has derived from Christianity — have instigated
many of the horrors for which they blame Muslims.

Muslim: Yet even granting the ugliness of the place where we stand, whether
neck deep in mud or blundering in thick darkness or imprisoned in
some other way, what better place from which to seek beauty? Remember our Yusuf — your Joseph in the Bible? It was while he was sitting
in the depths of the well in which his brothers threw him that the light
of God's revelation first came to him.

Christian: Thank you— that's so helpful, what you said. Helpful in jogging
my memory of what was said about the "Reflections at a Time of Transformation," the artistic event ASMA sponsored on January 19, 2004. I
recall how the ugliness and darkness of September 11 presented a crisis
or opportunity for beauty. It's so true that beauty is no mere opposite of
ugliness, any more than light is of darkness. Beauty and light transcend
all ugliness and darkness — because they come from God and draw us
to God.

Muslim: Which we have seen so dramatically in the lives sketched in Part
III: the beautiful lives, beautiful communities, all opening themselves
to the moral power of creativity…

Christian: ... when that creativity is inspired by — or you would say "transparent to" — the Creator of us all, the Creator of beauty itself.

Muslim: As Professor Ed Fadl has put it, in a rhetorical question: "Isn't justness of character at the epitome of beauty?"

Christian: I want to tell you about a community that has acted on that conviction in an unusually creative way.

Muslim: Yes?

Christian: In the city of Erie, Pennsylvania, there is a community of nuns, Sisters — women in the Benedictine monastic tradition — who have focused many of their ministries in the poverty-stricken section of downtown Erie. One of these ministries, going strong now since 1995, is called Neighborhood Art House. It's located in an abandoned Goodyear Tire building which the Sisters bought in 1994. They renovated the building and turned it into a center where neighborhood kids come for free lessons in all the arts: drawing, painting, ceramics, writing poems and stories, playing musical instruments, dancing, theater acting, and more. Thirty different classes offered every day!

Muslim: Because the arts create beauty, and the human soul cannot thrive without beauty.

Christian: Exactly. That's the premise. Here's how their mission statement puts it: "The mission of the Benedictine Sisters of Erie Inner-City Neighborhood Art House is to enable children to experience beauty, grow in positive self-expression and self-discipline, and develop into full and productive human beings... We believe the human soul is shaped by beauty and the arts."[3]

Muslim: So these Sisters are genuinely acting on the conviction that beauty shapes the human character. That without beauty, the full human being — one's love of justice and truth, one's self-knowledge, one's caring for the good of the world — cannot develop. Just as our Muslim scholar Seyyed Hossein Nasr has said: "beauty, far from being a luxury, is as necessary for the soul as the air we breathe is for the body."[4]

Christian: Indeed. The motto of Art House is "Bringing Beauty to Life."

Muslim: I like the pun in the "life" of that motto. Beauty is brought to life in the sense that it is *animated* through the arts. And at the same time beauty is brought *into* the lives of these children. Children, I'd guess, whose lives are otherwise saturated with ugliness.

Christian: Yes, alas, "saturated" describes it well. The kids who come to classes at Art House — and there are about 600 of them each year — live in neighborhoods approaching 95% poverty. With poverty like this, as with all inner-city poverty across the U.S., come hideously mul-

---

3. *Inner-City Neighborhood Art House* (Erie, PA: Benedictine Sisters of Erie, 2007).

4. Seyyed Hossein Nasr, *The Heart of Islam*, 226.

tiple forms of ugliness: the visual ugliness of run-down and boarded-up houses, of litter in the streets; the moral ugliness of drug-trading on the corners, of violent language heard inside the home and out, of violent behavior seen and threatened all around them.

Muslim: My heart aches for these children. Because, as the Qur'an says, God "made everything that He created beautiful" (*Sura al-Sajdah* 32:7). So these children who are born into ugliness are being denied the very essence of God's creation, the beauty that God made of *everything*. Except when they enter Neighborhood Art House...

Christian: Ah, yes! when they enter Art House they enter a haven of beauty. A haven of beauty's joy and colorfulness, beauty's creativity and delight. From an ordinary downtown street corner, the children walk (or probably run or skip, being children) up attractive salmon-colored cement steps through a peacefully landscaped front garden with flowering trees, into the welcoming glass doors of the building. Inside, suddenly all is bright and light. Cheerfully painted walls; the children's colorful, inventive art work hanging everywhere; shelves upon shelves stacked with kids' books; room after room of art supplies, musical instruments, costumes for dramatic productions. And children filling every room with their creativity, mentored by nearly 30 adult staff and around 2000 volunteers per year.

Muslim: What effort it takes to bring beauty to life where ugliness has such a strong hold! And yet Neighborhood Art House — the vision and commitment that make it happen, that make it a reality — gives me hope. I'm reminded of what the famed Muslim poet Muhammad Iqbal said in 1928 (he lived in the part of India that became Pakistan): that "the spiritual health of a people largely depends on the kind of inspiration which their poets and artists receive."[5]

Christian: How similar Iqbal's vision is to that of Erie Benedictine Sister Joan Chittister, a famed writer herself. Speaking of the motivation behind Neighborhood Art House, she said: "If we put food and shelter into the inner-city we will reap survival. If we put art and beauty and values there we will reap soul."

Muslim: Yes, and actually the Muslim Peacemaker Team could have used Sister Joan's quotation, along with Muhammad Iqbal's, in their website's description of the Iraqi Art Project. The Iraqi Art Project reminds me very much of Art House. The artists in this case are adults. But the vision is similar: to reinforce the idea that *salaam* is impossible without an honoring of beauty. Here's how the IAP describes itself: "The Iraq Art Project brings you art and culture from the Cradle of Civilization with images, created by Iraqi artists, of the people and the land. Build-

---

5. Quoted on website of Farrah Hafeez at www.arthafez.com/Biography/Biography.htm

ing on the transformative power of art, this project helps to personalize relationships with Iraqis. It bridges American communities with Iraqi artists. Some of the art carries messages that invite the Children of Abraham — Christians, Jews and Muslims — to recognize their common roots." Sami Rasouli brings examples of this art with him on his trips back to the U.S. They've become a key part of his effort to help Iraqis and Americans get to know each other as human beings, rather than scary stereotypes.

Christian: His "effort"; yes. What the Erie Sisters and the Muslim Peacemaker Team and other groups like them are doing is hard work, isn't it?

Muslim: Indeed. So the imagination's pursuit of beauty requires dedicated, disciplined effort towards a still-distant goal.

Christian: It requires the "greater jihad."

Muslim: Thank you. Yes, yes. And art itself plays an important role in the greater jihad. Art refreshes our vision of the *salaam* or fullness we are striving for. It also enables us to experience a taste of that fullness, even in the midst of our present brokenness. And art's discipline strengthens us to endure the struggles that still await us before that *salaam* becomes perfected in God's time. But art also requires openness. That's because beauty itself never works by coercion but rather by attraction and invitation. We've seen this again and again in this book: that beautiful lives must be lived in freedom — the very freedom of imagination that issues in all the arts — or they are not truly beautiful.

Christian: Yet there's a divine imperative as well, is there not? I love how your Qur'an expresses it in a line quoted already in this book: "Act beautifully, as God has acted beautifully towards you" (*Sura al-Qasas* 28:77).

Muslim: I can certainly say *Ameen* to that. So shall we say it together? — however slightly differently we pronounce this word which means simply "this is true."

Christian: Of course. It's the way we both end our prayers. And our prayer is the same: that both our faiths reclaim the beauty that is God's gift to us for the good of the world.

Christian and *Muslim: Amen, Ameen; Ameen, Amen.*

Conclusion: The Beauty
of Interfaith Action

We began this book on a personal note. We recounted how our own experience led us to bring these two great faiths, Islam and Christianity, together into dialogue about beauty. We end now by celebrating the experiences of those many others who are already out in the world manifesting the beauty of interfaith action. The beauty of what these Muslims and Christians are doing derives from their faiths, but it doesn't end there. It moves out to embrace all God's world and all the creatures in it. Beauty doesn't belong to a privileged few. It infuses the entire creation.

We've already mentioned, in Chapters 5c and 6c, some of the more successful interfaith initiatives and established programs. Chapter 5c, entitled *Rebuilding Córdoba: "A time of transformation,"* highlights Imam Feisal's Córdoba Initiative, Hamza Yusuf's Zaytuna Institute, Kabir and Camille Helminski's The Threshhold Society, and Eboo Patel's Interfaith Youth Core. Our Chapter 6c, entitled *The Beauty of Christian Witness and Sacrifice: Giving our life out of "love for enemies,"* calls attention to Fr. Paolo's efforts at Syria's Deir Mar Musa monastery to promote Muslim and Christian dialogue in a region of the world where such dialogue is both most dangerous and also most needed.

We said back in Chapter 5c that "many more such efforts could be mentioned." What an understatement! The frustration in celebrating contemporary Muslim and Christian interfaith efforts is that we can't possibly name them all. In the U.S. at the present time we would be hard put to find any major urban area that does not a offer a group or groups engaged in interfaith action. Sometimes these initiatives are faith-based, in mosques or churches or monasteries. Sometimes they find a home in academic settings or in community groups. But all are dedicated to promoting the beautiful behavior that Islam and Christianity call us to.

Just as a taste of these riches of current interfaith work, consider the Rumi Forum for Interfaith Dialogue, dedicated to promoting peace in the world and contributing to a peaceful coexistence of the adherents of different faiths, cultures, ethnicities and races; the Common Word project, an interfaith dialogue initiated by an October 13, 2007 letter from a wide array of Muslim scholars to Pope Benedict XVI and other Christian leaders, highlighting the foundational principles of both faiths as love of the one God and love of neighbor, and arguing that these shared fundamental convictions compel us to work together for justice and peace in the world; the Monastic Interreligious Dialogue, sponsored by North American Benedictine and Cistercian monasteries of men and women committed to fostering interreligious and inter-monastic dialogue at the level of spiritual practice; the Islamic Society of North America, providing a common platform for presenting Islam to non-Muslims and fostering good relations and creative initiatives with other religious communities as well as civic and service organizations; the Center for Interfaith Studies and Dialogue at Nazareth College (Rochester, New York), which offers programs to students and the general public, all designed to promote unity and understanding of both the self and of the global community; and the MacDonald Center at Hartford (Connecticut) Seminary, committed to the premise that through intensive study and academically guided dialogue, mutual respect and cooperation between Muslims and Christians can develop.

Local communities across North America have formed as well their own grassroots interfaith dialogue groups. Such groups spring up from the good will of individuals in local mosques, synagogues, and churches — often with no budget but with a surplus of energy for creating opportunities to help people of different faiths to form close friendships and to work together on common projects. Typical are the Interfaith Mission Service of Huntsville (Alabama), which sponsored a 2009 Interfaith Summit on common global values; or the Faith Alliance of Metro Atlanta (Georgia), whose World Pilgrims program creates interfaith travel experiences to parts of the world with religious significance for each faith.

Though each of these groups — and the countless others like them — has a different setting, all see Muslim-Christian dialogue in the larger context of dialogue with the other great faiths as well. Beauty informs these other faiths as profoundly as it does Christianity and Islam. There is no mystery in this. The One God may for His own purposes reveal His designs differently to different communities of faith. But the beauty towards which and through which He calls humanity is One. For Christians and Muslims to believe otherwise would be to deny the core teaching of their faiths, the teaching that beauty encourages us to embrace: We human beings are all made to worship God and God alone...

...And also to love one's neighbor.

Here is the surest sign of the success of interfaith dialogue: the degree to which it issues in beautiful actions of solidarity with the neighbor, and especially the neighbor in need.

Solidarity with the poor: we Christians and Muslims certainly recognize the centrality of this teaching. But why does our interfaith dialogue so often stop short of engaging it?

A key reason for what can go wrong with dialogue is its failure to focus on beauty, perhaps because beauty seems only a minor concern of religion or merely an aesthetic concern. We hope our book has shown how misguided such assumptions are. We hope we have demonstrated the importance of imagination in fulfilling the obligation God has imposed on us.

In our Introduction, we gave examples of different kinds of beauty: the beauty of a sunset, the beauty of a Schubert string quartet, the beauty of a neighbor's tender care for her elderly father. We close now with another example of beauty, a much less comforting one than any of these. In fact, this example thrusts itself at us out of the deepest ugliness, challenging not only Christians and Muslims but people of faith everywhere to recognize both their complicity in the ugliness as well as their responsibility to transform it by bringing, with God's help, light out of darkness.

The example comes from Benedictine Sister Joan Chittester. Sister Joan, a passionate advocate of interfaith dialogue as of so many prophetic causes, wrote not long ago about a time when "beauty shocked me into a new sense of what it means to be human in an inhuman environment." The event happened in "the slum of all slums" in Cité Soleil in Haiti:

> Here people live in one room hovels made of corrugated steel over mud floors. They bear and raise one child after another here. They eat the leftovers of society. They scrounge for wood to cook. They sleep in filth and live in rags and barely smile and cannot read. But in the middle of such human degradation they paint bright colors and brilliant scenes of a laughing, loving, wholesome community. They carve faces. They paint strident colors on bowls made out of coconuts. They play singing drums across the bare mountains that raise the cry of the human heart. They manufacture beauty in defiance of what it means to live an ugly forgotten life on the fringe of the wealthiest nation the world has ever known. They are a sign of possibility and aspiration and humanity no amount of huts or guns or poverty or starvation can ever squelch.[1]

This "sign of possibility and aspiration and humanity" emerges from those whom the rest of the world, led by France and the United States throughout Haiti's tragic history, has done its best to dehumanize and erase. And what Sister Joan writes here is not the half of it. The Cité Soleil she describes here could at least be characterized as a slum. This was before the January, 2010, earthquake reduced the slum to an even deeper level of ugliness: to utter ruin. Called by many a natural disaster, the devastation of the Haiti earthquake is more accurately seen as the result of systematic impoverishment of the island and its people.

Christians and Muslims reacting to the Haiti earthquake or to any of the other uglinesses resulting from racism, greed, and obsession with power — the devastation of Iraq, the oppression of Palestinians, the persecution of immigrants, the policies contributing to climate change, the widening gap worldwide between rich and poor — have to keep in mind what God has

---

1. Newsletter *The Monastic Way*, November, 2009.

revealed to them: in Muslim terms, that "He is beautiful and loves beauty"; in Christian terms that He has created all of us "in his own image." To reflect on this revelation is to acknowledge, as poet and essayist Lucy Shaw puts it, that we were "created to create." Or in Seyyed Hossein Nasr's terms: "to beautify things is to see God's beauty reflected in things and therefore to turn to God."

Here then is the challenge for interfaith dialogue: If Haitians can create images of beauty even in the midst of their recent near-annihilation, how much more does God call us, as beneficiaries of the current economic and political system, to create the beautiful image of a just society, one where all persecuted and impoverished people are treated with dignity, the dignity that is theirs not because the privileged happen to assign it to them but because it is their gift from their loving creator.

As the Rumi Forum quotes on its website from Rumi's poetry:

Come, come, whoever you are...
Come and come yet again...
Come even if you have broken your vows a thousand times
Wanderer, idolater, worshipper of fire...
Ours is not a caravan of despair,
This is the date of hope,
Come, come yet again, come.[2]

---

2. www.rumiforum.org.

Glossary of Christian Terms

Apostle: Literally, "one sent forth." The term is used of the twelve men who accompanied Jesus throughout the three years of his ministry of teaching and healing as recounted in the Gospels. After his resurrection, Jesus instructed them to "go and make disciples of all nations" (Gospel of Matthew 28:19).

Baptism: The rite by which people become Christians. It is celebrated within the worshipping community by a water bath (sometimes total immersion, sometimes simple sprinkling of the head) accompanied by the words derived from the Gospel of Matthew 28:19, "I baptize you in the name of the Father and of the Son and of the Holy Spirit." At baptism, Christians believe, they die with Christ so as to be raised to new life in Him. They no longer live a separate, sinful existence, but Christ now and forever lives in each of them. As members of Christ's image and embodiment, Christians are empowered to go forth and continue Jesus' healing, forgiving, life-renewing mission.

Benedictine: A monastic tradition that traces its roots to Saint Benedict, who lived in the sixth century CE. Today, Benedictine monastic communities of men or women around the world follow a life of prayer and service to neighbors. Cistercians (also called Trappists) are a worldwide branch of the Benedictine tradition who live within monastic enclosures, devoted to the vocation of prayer and the contemplative life.

Bible: Name used for the Christian Holy Scriptures. The Bible includes both the Old Testament or Hebrew Scriptures (see definition) and the New Testament (see definition).

Christian humanism: A Renaissance philosophical movement stressing the compatibility between Christianity and the Greco-Roman valuing of the human person. The great Renaissance art that relishes the body's beauty is an outgrowth of this movement.

Christian non-violence: Not passivity before violence and evil, but a creative effort to engage evil so as to transform it into good. Christian non-violence is inspired by Christ's own refusal to deal with his enemies on their own terms but rather to allow himself to become the means by which his enemies might experience change of heart.

Christian denominations: The various distinct Christian worshiping communities as they have developed since the emergence of the church at Pentecost, fifty days after Christ's resurrection. (This event is described in the New Testament's Acts of the Apostles 2:1-4). Denominations tend to be divided by language and ethnicity, but more fundamentally by differences in doctrine and church authority. The history of the development of the Christian denominations is extremely complex and difficult to separate from historical, cultural, and political factors. The earliest major denominations, the Roman Catholic and Orthodox, grew out of the separation of the Roman Empire into a western half, centered in Rome, and an eastern half, centered in Constantinople. The Reformation (initiated by Martin Luther) led to the separation from the Catholic Church of dissenting communities which became known collectively as Protestant (see definition). Today, Catholicism is the largest denomination, comprising about half of the world's Christian population.

Christ: The Greek translation of the Hebrew honorific title "Messiah" (meaning "anointed one") first used of Jesus by his disciple Peter. Paul in his Letters (see definition) uses the word Christ not as a title but as part of the name of the risen Jesus. Christians have never separated the human Jesus from the divine risen Christ. According to the Council of Chalcedon (451 CE), Jesus Christ combines both human and divine natures within one Person and, together with the Father and the Holy Spirit, forms the Holy Trinity (see definition).

Christmas: The feast day celebrating the birth of Jesus Christ as the incarnate Word of God.

Cross: The wooden instrument of torture on which Jesus was crucified. Sometimes used as synonym for Jesus' Crucifixion. For Christians, the cross is transformed by Jesus' self-sacrificing love into an object of veneration. Christians often have crosses in their homes or carry them on their persons. The Cross as symbol gives them reassurance that God not only accompanies them in their sufferings but also gives them a share in his transformation into glorious eternal life.

Crucifixion: The physical event of Jesus' horrific death on a cross, but glorified by Christians as the definitive sign of God's love for humankind, hateful as our behavior can be. As Paul says in the Letter to the Romans 5:8, "God proves His love for us that while we were still sinners Christ died for us."

Disciples: Refers both to followers of Jesus while he lived, and also to all Christians ever since. "Discipleship" is a synonym today for the desire to live as Jesus lived and taught.

Easter: The celebration of Christ's resurrection from the dead. By "resurrection" Christians are referring neither to the resuscitation of Jesus' dead body nor to his re-creation in physical form but to his re-ascent to heaven, returning transformed in body, mind, and spirit to "sit at the right hand of the Majesty on high" (Letter to the Hebrews 1:3). Christians use phrases like "Risen Christ" and "Risen Love" to refer to the ongoing power of this transformation to bring them into Christ's glorified life.

Enlightenment: A philosophical movement growing out of Renaissance humanism. The Enlightenment celebrates the "light" of human reason (unaided by divine revelation) as the source of all truth.

Fall: The disastrous effect on all future generations of Adam's and Eve's disobedience to God. As the story is told in Genesis (the opening book of the Bible), Adam and Eve disobey God's prohibition against eating from the tree of the knowledge of good and evil. As punishment for their disobedience, God not only expels them from the Garden forever but also consigns them to a life of toil and pain: the woman to pain in childbirth, the man to arduous work tilling the rough ground for his food. Furthermore, their days will end in "dust"; they will die. Christian theology calls this event "the Fall" because Adam and Eve fell away from God's grace. The disobedience that caused their Fall came to be called "original sin" (see definition).

Fallen world: Christians believe that Adam and Eve's Fall (see definition) damaged not only humankind but the rest of creation as well, subjecting each thing, whether animate or inanimate, to tragic disfigurement. As a result, creation has become an environment hostile to God's love. Yet this hostility is temporary, Christians believe, since Christ's redemption (see definition) includes the entire cosmos. As Paul says in the Letter to the Romans 8:19-22: "The creation waits with eager longing for the revealing of the children of God…. We know that the whole creation has been groaning in labor pains till now…."

Good Friday: The celebration of the day of Jesus' crucifixion and death. The original English phrase "God Friday" later became "Good Friday" to honor Jesus' total act of self-sacrifice on this day. Easter (see definition) is celebrated on the following Sunday.

Gospels: The New Testament accounts of Jesus' life, death, and resurrection by four different authors (Matthew, Mark, Luke, and John). The word "gospel" is derived from Old English gōd spell or "good news." Quotations from the Gospels are cited by using the attributed author's first name: for instance, John 1:4-5 refers to chapter 1 of John's Gospel, lines 4 and 5. Often in citations, the name is abbreviated: Mt, Mk, Lk, Jn.

Grace: God's free and unconditional gift of love to humankind. By opening itself to this undeserved gift, humankind is rescued from Original Sin (see definition) and restored to its rightful status as made in the image and likeness of God (see Genesis 1:26).

Hebrew Bible: The Jewish Scriptures which Christianity adopted under the name of the "Old Testament." Books of the Hebrew Bible often quoted and reinterpreted in the New Testament include Genesis, Exodus, Proverbs, Psalms, Isaiah.

Holy Spirit: For Christians, neither a power nor an attribute of God, but God's own self, in the third Person of the Trinity (see definition).

Incarnate/ Incarnation: God's choice, out of love for humankind, to take on flesh for a time in the person of Jesus of Nazareth.

Jesus: Born a Jew in Bethlehem of a human mother, Mary, through the power of the Holy Spirit. Grew up in Nazareth. Taught and did works of healing during three years of active ministry. Was crucified under the Roman governor Pontius Pilate but rose again to become the Savior of humankind. Jesus is also referred to in the New Testament as Messiah, Christ (see definition), Word of God, Son of God.

Last Supper: Jesus' final gathering with his apostles on the evening before he was arrested by the Roman authorities. The meal Jesus shares with them on that occasion, described in all four Gospels, is the model of Christian communion in all churches.

Lent: A forty-day period of fasting, self-denial, penitence, Bible study, and prayer celebrated by most Christian denominations in preparation for Easter (see definition).

Letters of Paul: Thirteen letters within the New Testament, nine of which Paul wrote to communities he had either helped found or was eager to visit, and four to individuals. (Disagreement continues among Christian scholars about the actual authorship of certain of the letters.) The letters to communities are central to the development of Christian faith. The letters are named after the community or individual written to and are often cited by using the addressee's name: for instance, Romans 1:5 refers to Paul's Letter to the Romans, chapter 1 verse 5.

Liturgical churches: A phrase specifically referring to denominations (Catholic, Orthodox, Anglican, Lutheran) united by a belief, expressed in different ways, in the Real Presence of Christ in communion. Worship is structured around the occurrence of this event, so much so that the service includes a prayer in which Christ is invited to enter the bread and wine. By consuming the bread and wine (now become sacraments—see definition), the people enter more fully into Christ's life. Liturgical churches treat Jesus' offering of bread and wine to his disciples at the Last Supper (see definition) as an ever-present gift. Non-liturgical churches tend to treat the events of the Last Supper as an historical moment in Jesus' life which they honor and memorialize. Their celebrations typically focus on other elements of worship, like singing, preaching, and individual or group petition.

Liturgy: Literally, "work of the people." The order of public worship performed by a specific religious group, according to its particular traditions. Some of those traditions are elaborate, as in Orthodox and Roman Catholic churches; others simple, as in many Protestant churches. All Christian liturgies seek to enable the worshiping community to enter more deeply into the life of the risen Christ through repentance, praise, petition, and thanksgiving.

Minister: Derived from the Latin *minor*, lesser, reflecting Jesus' warning that "Whoever wants to be first must be last of all and servant of all" (the Gospel of Mark 9:35). The term refers to anyone called by a worshiping community to perform religious functions.

New Testament: Christian sacred scripture, the part of the Bible (see definition) consisting of the Four Gospels, the Acts of the Apostles, the Letters of Paul, James, John, Peter, and Jude, the anonymous Letter to the Hebrews, and the Book of the Apocalypse (or Revelation). These writings are the works of human beings, though definitively inspired by the Holy Spirit.

Original Sin: The tragic disfigurement of human nature in all its aspects through Adam's and Eve's disobedience. This disfigurement of humankind's initial goodness was so severe that all creation, not just humankind itself, lost connection to God. Christians believe that only through God's grace (see definition) is the lost connection restored.

Our Father (often referred to as "the Lord's Prayer"): The prayer Jesus offers to his disciples in response to their request that he teach them how to pray. It is found in slightly different versions in the Gospel of Matthew 6:9-13 and the Gospel of Luke 11:2-4. The Our Father closely resembles Islam's Fatijah (see definition in the Glossary of Muslim terms) in length, structure, and in function as a model for prayer.

Passion: Refers not only to Jesus' suffering on the cross, but also to his suffering during the events in Jerusalem leading up to his crucifixion: his betrayal by his disciple Judas at the Last Supper, his abandonment by his closest friends after his seizure by the Roman authorities, the torture and mockery then inflicted on him. Christians celebrate Jesus' Passion on Good Friday (see definition).

Protestantism/Protestant: Originally defined by its opposition to the Roman Catholic Church at the time of the Reformation in the sixteenth century, Protestantism has become a collective term for perhaps as many as 30,000 distinct Christian communities world-wide. While practice and belief can differ greatly among Protestant communities, they have traditionally emphasized three elements of faith: the Bible as sole authority (rather than Pope or clergy), justification by faith (as opposed to works), and the priesthood of all believers (rather than of clergy only).

Priest: The person in the Catholic, Orthodox, and Anglican churches who blesses the bread and wine during liturgy and petitions the Holy Spirit to transform them into the body and blood of Christ (whereby they become sacraments). A priest of the Catholic and Orthodox churches, currently always male, is addressed as "Father," irrespective of his age. (Father is usually abbreviated Fr.)

Redemption: God's saving activity through Christ's self-sacrifice on the Cross, releasing not only humanity but all creation from the bondage of Original Sin (see definition).

Sacrament: A religious sign or symbol that conveys the presence and blessing of the risen Christ to the Christian who freely and wholeheartedly opens him or herself to them. All Christian denominations recognize the sacrament of Baptism (see definition).

Salvation/ salvific: The effect of redemption (see definition). The restoration of humanity and all of creation to wholeness and to friendship with God.

Sin: Any intentional act that separates a human being from God's love. Because of Original Sin (see definition), Christians through their own efforts are not capable of counteracting the effects of their sin and restoring themselves to God's favor. But they *are* responsible for accepting and faithfully abiding by the grace (see definition) that Christ unfailingly offers them, with its power to heal sin's most calamitous effects.

Transfiguration: Jesus' glorious transformation on the mountaintop where he led his disciples Peter, James, and John. There, "he was transfigured before them, and his face shone like the sun, and his clothes became dazzling white" (Gospel of Matthew 17:2). The transfiguration is a sign of Jesus' intimacy with God the Father.

Trinity: The Christian doctrine of the Trinity was developed in church councils of the fourth and fifth centuries CE. The doctrine of the Trinity affirms that God exists in three Persons: Father, Son, and Holy Spirit. "Person" in the doctrine's usage does not refer to a separate existence (as it does when we refer to a human person), but to God's will to exist as relationship or divine intercommunion.

Way: The word used by the earliest followers of Jesus to name their new life (see the Acts of the Apostles 19:3). Probably the name derived from Jesus' own characterization of himself in the Gospel of John 14:6, "I am the way, and the truth, and the life."

Glossary of Muslim Terms

Adhan: The Call to Prayer, announcing the times of Salat.

Allah: Literally, "the deity." God's name in Arabic.

Arabesque: Flowering design reminiscent of Arabic calligraphy.

Ayatollah: Literally, "sign of God." The highest rank among Shi'a clergy.

Beautiful Names: The ninety-nine names of God, most of which are found in the Qur'an. In *Sura al-A'raf* 7:180, Muslims are enjoined to recite the Names in order to bring themselves closer to God.

Bismillah: Abbreviated form of the Arabic phrase "bismillahi arrahmani arrahim," meaning "in the name of God the Most Beneficent, the Most Merciful." The phrase appears at the beginning of all the suras except one and is voiced by Muslims as a blessing before undertaking an activity, much as "In the name of the Father, Son, and Holy Spirit" is voiced by many Christians.

Chahar-bagh: Literally, "four-gardens," referring to a fountain or pool at the center of a space divided into four quarters and planted with a variety of shade-producing shrubs or trees, along with flowers and sometimes even vegetables. Usually channels of water mark off the quarters. An emblem and foretaste of Paradise.

Fatihah: The first sura (see definition) of the Qur'an. Literally meaning "the opening," the Fatihah closely resembles Christianity's "Lord's Prayer" in length and structure, and serves like the Lord's Prayer as a model for prayer.

Fatwa: General term for a judge's ruling, based on Shar'iah law. A Fatwa is *not* equivalent to a "death sentence" except in those instances where judges have made that determination.

Five Pillars of Islam (*Shahadah, Salat, Sawm, Zakat, Hajj*): The five guiding principles of Muslim belief and practice. All Muslims without exception subscribe to the Five Pillars. (See separate definitions of each of these.)

Hadith (plural ahadith): Literally, "report." Accounts of the Prophet Muhammad's own words as authenticated by scholars tracing the reports to reliable sources among the Prophet's own followers and companions. A hadith qudsi (literally, "holy report") is the account of God's own words as the Prophet recalled them (i.e., not as they were directly revealed in the Qur'an itself).

Hajj (pilgrimage): One of the Five Pillars of Islam. The pilgrimage to Mecca during a stated time in the Muslim lunar calendar. Enjoined once in one's lifetime on all Muslims financially and physically able to comply.

Hijra: Literally, "emigration." The exodus in 622 CE of Muhammad and his followers from Mecca to the town of Yathrib (later called Medina) to escape persecution. The Muslim calendar begins on this year.

Ihsan: Literally, "doing what is good and beautiful." More particularly the beauty which is spiritual virtue, what Islam frequently calls "transparency of heart."

Imam: Literally, "pattern," "example." In Sunni Islam, an imam is the person qualified by knowledge and moral character to lead prayers at Salat (see definition). In Shi'a Islam, an imam must be a direct descendant of the Prophet Muhammad's daughter Fatima and of his son-in-law, Ali; believed to inherit the Prophet's extraordinary spiritual gifts, the imam becomes the leader of the Shi'a community.

Jahannama: Hell, answering to desert-dwellers' worst nightmare: becoming perpetually lost in the sand-dunes at a perpetual noon of blazing fire and heat. The Arabic word is derived from the Hebrew "Gehenna."

Jannah: Literally, "garden." Paradise, the final oasis and reward for those who have been faithful to God.

Jihad: Literally, "striving for what is good." According to a hadith (see definition), the Prophet identified a Greater Jihad (striving for self-control, i.e. striving against injustice within oneself) and a Lesser Jihad (striving in defense of the community against the injustice of neighbors).

Khalifa (plural Khalifatun): Literally, "successor," with secondary meaning of "trustee" or "vice-regent." In *Sura al Baqarah* 2:30, God tells the angels that "I will create a successor on earth," i.e. humankind. Corresponds to Genesis 1: 26, where God appoints humankind "to have dominion...".

Light Verse: One of the most beloved verses in the Qur'an (*Sura an-Nur* 24:34). Often the subject of the calligraphy adorning mosques.

Masjid: Literally, "place of prostration." Muslim worship space. The word from which English "mosque" is derived.

Mecca: In the Prophet Muhammad's time, a town along a caravan route running north-south not far from the Red Sea in what is now Saudi Arabia. Also the site of a pilgrimage shrine known as the Ka'bah, once containing the 360 idols of the surrounding tribes. Birthplace of the prophet Muhammad in 560 CE and eventual center of Muslim worship.

Medina: The town to the north of Mecca to which Muhammad and his followers emigrated to escape persecution by Mecca's authorities, who feared Islam's challenge to their selfish behavior and to their profits from pilgrimage traffic.

Mi'raj: Literally, "ascent," referring to the Prophet Muhammad's Ascent through the heavens to the Throne of God. The story of the *mi'raj* is not told in the Qur'an, though the event is alluded to in *Sura al Isra* 17:1.

Mihrab: The niche located in the middle of the mosque wall that faces Mecca. The imam or prayer-leader leads salat from the mihrab.

Mu'adhdhan: Literally, "the one calling to prayer," often transliterated *muezzin*. The call itself is the adhan.

Muhammad (pbuh): The Prophet Muhammad. Muslims never pronounce his name without adding the Arabic phrase meaning "Peace and blessing upon him."

Mulla: Muslim religious leader by virtue of his expertise as a jurist.

Muslim Dress (for females): *hijab* (or head scarf), *qameez* (the loose-fitting tunic), *shalwar* (the flowing ankle-length skirt), *jilbab* (the full-length gown worn over both *qameez* and *shalwar*), *burqa* (full face and body covering, consisting of *jilbab*, *hijab*, as well as *niqab* or face-veil).

Naskh, thuluth: Two of the many styles of Islamic calligraphy.

Qari: Literally, "reciter," from the same root as Qur'an. An expert in the chanting of the Qur'an.

Qur'an: Literally, a "reciting," that is, an "audition" in the sense of the human voice being directly subjected to the divine Word and stretched to utter it. This understanding of the "reciting" goes back to the very first revelation that came down to Muhammad in the cave on Mt. Hira' where he had gone to meditate. "Recite!" is the first word Muhammad was given on that occasion (in 610 CE). The revelations that he received intermittently over the next twenty-two years until his death in 632 CE constitute the totality of the "qur'an's" which we know as *the* Qur'an.

Ramadan: The ninth month of the Muslim lunar calendar, believed to be the month when the Qur'an was revealed to the Prophet Muhammad. Ramadan is celebrated by sawm (fasting) and by nightly recitations of the Qur'an. It culminates in zakat (the giving of alms) and the great community celebration known as the Eid al-fitr, literally "feast of the fast-breaking." Corresponds to certain elements of Lent (fasting and penitence) and Christmas (celebration of revelation).

Ruh: Literally, "spirit." A power of God, but emphatically *not* a divine Person, *not* a member of the Trinity. In *Sura al-Hijr* 15:29, God breathes the spirit into Adam, thus providing Adam with free will. The spirit strengthens Jesus in *Sura al-Baqarah* 2:87 as well as all believers in *Sura al Mujadilah* 58:22. Through the spirit, the Qur'an is first revealed to the Prophet Muhammad in *Sura al Qadr* 97:4.

Salat (ritual prayer): One of the Five Pillars of Islam. Enjoined on all Muslims five times each day (from dawn till just before sunrise, after mid-day till afternoon, from late afternoon till just before sunset, after sunset till daylight ends, after daylight ends until dawn).

Sawm (fasting): One of the Five Pillars of Islam. Fasting from eating and the satisfaction of other appetites from dawn to sundown. Enjoined on all Muslims during the month of Ramadan.

Shahadah (confession): One of the Five Pillars of Islam. By publicly stating in Arabic that "I confess that there is no god but God and that Muhammad is his Prophet," a person is initiated into the religion of Islam.

Shari'ah: Literally, "path to the water-hole." Concretely, the body of Islamic religious law, the legal framework within which the public and private aspects of life are regulated including politics, economics, banking, business, contracts, family, sexuality, hygiene, and social issues. More broadly, the divinely ordained law each type of creature must follow if it is to realize its full identity.

Shi'a: Literally, "party," referring to those at the Prophet's death who followed Ali, the Prophet Muhammad's son-in-law. According to Shi'a belief, Ali inherited the Prophet's spiritual purity and passed that gift to the males of his lineage, who thereby are the Prophet Muhammad's rightful successors as leaders of the Muslim community.

Shirk: Literally, "association." More broadly, idolatry. Treating any created thing or idea, even religion itself, as if it had equal status with God. Shirk is the worst of Islam's sins since it directly denies Islam's assertion of God's *tauhid* (unicity), expressed in the Qur'an's frequently repeated line, "There is no god but God."

Shura council: The gathering where specific applications of Shari'ah are debated and rules established through ijtihad (individual reasoning) and ijma (consensus).

Shura: Literally,"consultation." The Prophet Muhammad's own preferred model for Muslim governance.

Sufi: Literally, "brown wool," used of the ascetic robes early Sufis are said to have worn. Sufis are Islam's mystics, gaining strength in Islam's early centuries in reaction to the domination of worldly princes (sultans) and jurists (mullas).

Sunnah: Literally, "custom, norm." The most reliable accounts of the Prophet's sayings and behavior. These accounts are used as detailed reference points for the ideal behavior of all Muslims, whether Shi'a or Sunni, of both genders and of all times.

Sunni: Literally, "majority," those at the Prophet's death who followed political criteria in choosing the Prophet's successors. Today, Sunnis comprise about 85% of the world's Muslims.

Sura: Word used of each of the Qur'an's 114 separate utterances. (The translation of sura as "chapter" is confusing, since the Qur'an is not organized systematically, as the word "chapter" implies.) The 114 suras are arranged roughly according to length, from longest to shortest, much as Saint Paul's letters are. Each sura has a name identifying it, though the names are usually not relevant thematically. The Qur'an is composed of two broad categories of suras, the Meccan suras revealed before the hijra (see definition), and the Medinan suras revealed after. The Meccan suras tend to be hymnic and prophetic; the Medinan discursive and legislative. Sura citations are indicated as in the following example: "*Sura al Baqarah* 2:17" refers to the sura named "al Baqarah," the second of the Qur'an's suras, and to verse 17 of that sura.

Tajwid: Literally, "making better." Elaborated pronunciation of the Qur'an's verses, marked by melodic flourishes, meditative pauses, emotional colorings. Distinguished from *tartil*: the plain, steady, unadorned style.

Zakat (alms): One of the Five Pillars of Islam. The giving of a fixed percentage of net income to the poor and marginalized. Enjoined on all Muslims during the month of Ramadan.

Permissions Acknowledgements

Al Faisal, Reem, mosque interior, *Diwan Al Noor* (Manama, Bahrain: Miracle Publishing, 1994) 92. Black and white photograph. Used by permission of the photographer.

Ali, Kazim, "Afternoon Prayer" from *The Fortieth Day*. Copyright 2008 by Kazim Ali. Reprinted with the permission of the poet and BOA Editions, Ltd., www.boaeditions.org

Ali, Mohammed, Photograph of Ali helping a family member of the Mali children apply spray paint to *To God We Belong*. Reprinted by permission of the Arts Council England, http://www.artsandislam.com

Ali, Mohammed, Photograph of *To God We Belong* [mural alone]. Reprinted by permission of the photographer, Daniel Richardson.

Arastu, Salma, *Tribal Joy*. Reprinted by permission of the artist. www.salmaarastu.com.

Cairns, Scott, text taken from "Nativity" and "The Leper's Return" from *Compass of Affection* ©2006 Scott Cairns. Used by permission of the poet and Paraclete Press, www.paracletepress.com

Fujimura, Makoto, *Countenance Three*. Created by Makoto Fujimura, 2008. Macro Photography by Makoto Fujimura. This work is licensed under a Creative Commons Attribution 3.0 United States License.

Geyer, Ginger Henry, *Fighting Fire with Fire*, 1999. Reprinted by permission of the artist. Photo by Rice R. Jackson, III.

Hafez, "Beneath the Veil," translated by John Slater and Jeffrey Einboden. © John Slater and Jeffrey Einboden. Reprinted by permission of John Slater and Jeffrey Einboden.

Jarman, Mark, "Today is fresh" from *Unholy Sonnets* (Ashland, Oregon: Story Line Press, 2000), reprinted by permission of the poet. "On the island of the pure in heart" from *Epistles*, (Louiseville, KY, Sarabande Books, 2007). Reprinted by permission of the poet and Sarabande Books.

Kahf, Mohja, "Most Wanted." First published at MuslimWakeUp.com. Unpublished revision reprinted by permission of the poet.

McCleary, Mary, *Ash Wednesday, Waller County*. Reprinted by permission of the artist.

Michelangelo, Buonarroti, *Pietà*. Published by permission of Scala/ Art Resource, 536 Broadway, NY, NY, 10012.

Mir, Shabana, "To Everyone I Disagree With." Published online by The American Muslim, http://www.theamericanmuslim.org. Reprinted by permission of the poet.

Mirza, Uzma, *Green Notes: A Goodly Tree* © 1997-2010 by Uzma Mirza, Pen and Inkpot: a Spiritual Art www.thepenandtheinkpot.org. Reprinted by permission of the artist.

Moustafa, Ahmad, *Landscape in Perfect Order and Proportion*. Reprinted by permission of the artist.

Rumi, "When I press my hand to my chest" and "I called through your door" translated by Coleman Barks, from *The Essential Rumi* (HarperSanFrancisco), 1995. © by Coleman Barks. Reprinted by permission of the translator.

Sanders, Peter, *Tic Toc to the Rhythm of Life*. ©Peter Sanders Photography, www.petersanders.com. Reprinted by permission of the artist.

Shikoh, Asma Ahmed, *The Activist*. Reprinted by permission of the artist.

Totonji, Huda, from "Calligraphy Projections Prayer Series". Color photograph. Used by permission of the artist.

Walker, Jeanne Murray, "To Mr. Auden in a time of war," *The Christian Century*, Feb. 6, 2007; "Poetry," *The Christian Century*, Dec. 26, 2006; "Sister Storm," *Image* journal #53 (Spring, 2007). All used by permission of the poet.

Zakariya, Mohamed, *Ardently Anxious*. Reprinted by permission of the artist.